Caro-Kann: Classical 4 ... ♗f5

Caro-Kann:
Classical 4 ... ♗f5

GARY KASPAROV
2740
ALEKSANDER SHAKAROV

Translated by John Sugden

Collier Books
Macmillan Publishing Company
New York

Macmillan Publishing Company
866 Third Avenue, New York, N.Y. 10022
Collier Macmillan Canada, Inc.

Library of Congress Cataloging in Publication Data

Kasparov, G. K. (Garri Kimovich)
  Caro-Kann: classical 4—Bf5.

  (Collier books)
  Includes index.
  1. Chess—Openings.   I. Shakarov, Aleksander.
II. Title.
GV1450.2.K36 1984   794.1′22   84-15429
ISBN 0-02-011490-7 (pbk.)

Macmillan books are available at special discounts for bulk purchases for sales promotions, premiums, fund-raising, or educational use. Special editions or book excerpts can also be created to specification. For details, contact:
  Special Sales Director
  Macmillan Publishing Company
  866 Third Avenue
  New York, New York 10022

10 9 8 7 6 5 4 3 2

Printed in the United Kingdom

Contents

Acknowledgments

The Publishers would like to thank John Sugden for an excellent translation, R.G.Wade for locating game references and inserting some recent material, Richard Sams for typesetting and Peter Large for proofreading.

Symbols

+	Check
± ∓	Slight advantage
± ∓	Clear advantage
±± ∓∓	Winning advantage
=	Level position
∞	Unclear position
!	Good move
!!	Outstanding move
!?	Interesting move
?!	Dubious move
?	Weak move
??	Blunder
corres	Correspondence
Ol	Olympiad
IZ	Interzonal
L	League
Ch	Championship
½f	Semi-final

Introduction

The Classical System is an old and yet still topical branch of the Caro-Kann. At one time it was considered a 'levelling' opening (Botvinnik's phrase) with a decidedly drawish tendency. It owed this reputation 'particularly to Capablanca, who attained supreme mastery in the art of drawing with Black' (Botvinnik).

Attempts by White to secure a lasting initiative just by relying on 'the advantage of the move' (5 ♗d3; 5 ♕f3; 5 ♘g3 ♗g6 6 ♗c4; etc.) or on the two bishops (5 ♘g3 ♗g6 6 ♘1e2 with ♘f4xg6 to follow) have never produced convincing results. The same goes for the freer game and greater space which White acquires in the variations 5 ♘g3 ♗g6 6 ♘f3 ♘d7 7 ♗d3, and 7 h4 h6 8 ♗d3.

An idea of Spassky's – 8 h5, followed by ♕e2 and ♘e5, as in the thirteenth game of his 1966 World Championship Match with Petrosian – enriched White's play by giving him new prospects in the endgame thanks to the advanced h-pawn. For a while, 'the Classical Caro-Kann' and 'the worse ending' became synonymous . . . .

A counter-strategy for the Black side took shape gradually. At first, interest focused on the position after 13 ♕e2 0-0-0 14 ♘e5 ♘b6!. Then Black grew bolder with 13 ... c5!, going over to the idea of kingside castling. Basically similar variations were devised to meet other varieties of White's plan – 13 c4, 13 ♔b1 and 13 ♘e4.

But in present-day tournament practice, following Larsen's example, the good old Caro-Kann is treated in a way that is nothing short of revolutionary: 10 ... e6, 11 ... ♘gf6 and 12 ... ♗e7. Castling on opposite wings is now taken for granted!

The Classical Caro-Kann has thus become a good deal more interesting . . . .

In working on this book, we have drawn on the most varied sources: Volume B of the *Encyclopaedia of Chess Openings*;* Boleslavsky's *Caro-Kann bis Sizilianisch*; the recent handbook by Konstantinopolsky and Veits, *The Caro-Kann Defence*; an old booklet with the same title (in

---

* Quoted subsequently as *ECO*

German), by B.Ulrich (1952); *Informator*, Volumes 1-34; *The New Chess Player*, Volumes 1-9; anthologies of games by Lasker, Chigorin, Botvinnik, Fischer, Karpov, Geller, Simagin and others; *Tournament Chess*, Volumes 1-5; various tournament books and collections of miniature games; the magazines *Shakhmatny Bulletin*, *Shakhmaty v SSSR*, *Shakhmaty* (Riga), and others.

We believe that this book takes into account all significant developments in the Classical Caro-Kann up until 1983.

G.Kasparov
A.Shakarov

Baku, April 1983

1 5 ♗d3, 5 ♕f3 and 5 ♘c5

1	e4	c6
2	d4	d5
3	♘c3	de
4	♘xe4	♗f5 *(1)*

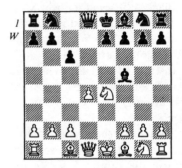

In this chapter, we examine:

A 5 ♗d3
B 5 ♕f3
C 5 ♘c5

In the final sections of this book, we shall be looking in detail at variations stretching into the middlegame (sometimes even the endgame), and analyses will end after thirty-odd or forty-odd moves. Here things are different; analysis cannot seriously extend so far when the point of departure is move five.

Does that mean that if White isn't fond of studying long opening variations, he has only to refrain from 5 ♘g3 – and scope for creativity (to coin a phrase) will be opened up before him? Perhaps.

However, Variation A gives 'scope' to Black too – not to mention an extra pawn! And underneath its attractive surface, Variation B is . . . hollow. Black easily solves his problems by playing virtually the most obvious moves.

Among those who have recommended 5 ♘c5 (Variation C) are Fischer and Bronstein. Perhaps for that reason, there is more here in the way of practical material. Still, on his fifth move Black has a wide choice – 5 ... e5, 5 ... b6, 5 ... ♕c7, 5 ... ♕b6 – and White has not managed to put any of these continuations out of action.

White's 'scope for creativity' is, then, procured at the cost of deliberately renouncing the best continuations in favour of second-rate ones.

A

5 ♗d3 *(2)*

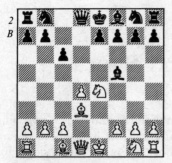

To sacrifice a pawn for a couple of tempi is a 'perennial' ploy in the fight for initiative in the opening.

Not everyone enjoys the role of defending against raids by an opponent who, though a pawn down, is ahead in development. Hence, against any gambit, Black would like to have not only the 'refutation' (in this case 5 ... ♕xd4), but also some alternative method of play, which, while renouncing material gains, avoids any positional concessions.

In the variation 5 ... e6 6 ♘f3 ♘d7 7 0-0 ♗xe4 8 ♗xe4 ♘gf6 9 ♗d3 ♗d6 Black has good development, yet since he has paid for it with an exchange of bishop for knight (which *is* a concession), he cannot be satisfied. On the other hand, after 7 ... ♘gf6 8 ♘xf6+ (8 ♗g5?! ♗xe4 9 ♗xe4 h6) 8 ... ♕xf6 9 ♗g5 ♕g6 10 ♗xf5 ♕xf5 11 c4, Black's backward development is disturbing.

A favourable version of the same idea is 5 ... ♘d7! 6 ♘f3 ♘gf

giving the following position *(3)*.

Black utilises a typical Caro-Kann motif: 7 ♘xf6+ ♘xf6 8 ♗xf5 ♕a5+, and White's chances of advantage are nil.

Instead of 6 ♘f3, White may play 6 ♕f3, which tranposes into Variation B after 6 ... e6 or 6 ... ♗g6.

Though perhaps 'unthematic', the move 5 ... ♘d7 seems to disarm the gambit 5 ♗d3 simply enough.

| 5 | ... | ♕xd4 |
| 6 | ♘f3 | ♕d8 |

Here the queen won't be attacked again in a hurry. However, the worse reputation of 6 ... ♕d5 is undeserved. After 7 ♕e2 ♘f6 (7 ... e6 8 ♘h4!? ♗g6 9 ♘xg6 hg 10 ♗f4) 8 c4 ♕d8 (again the familiar motif: 9 ♘xf6+ gf 10 ♗xf5 ♕a5+) 9 0-0, the same position arises as after 6 ... ♕d8, except for the unimportant difference in the placing of White's c-pawn.

7 ♕e2

In a game Badalov-Shakarov,

1982, White struck out at once with 7 ♘fg5, threatening 8 ♘xf7!

There followed: 7 ... ♘f6 (7 ... ♗xe4, 7 ... e6 and 7 ... ♗g6 are also playable) 8 ♘xf6+ ef (8 ... gf? 9 ♘xf7! ♔xf7 10 ♕h5+ is in White's favour; a weaker continuation is 10 ♗c4+ e6! 11 ♕xd8 ♗b4+) 9 ♕e2+ ♗e7 10 ♗xf5 ♕a5+ 11 ♗d2 ♕xf5 12 0-0-0! (Black hadn't foreseen that the piece sacrifice would be so strong. Two lines that are unpleasant, though in differing degrees, are 12 ... fg 13 ♖he1 ♕e6 14 ♕d3 ♕xa2 15 ♖xe7+, and 13 ... 0-0 14 ♕xe7) 12 ... ♘d7! 13 ♖he1 ♘e5 14 f4! (on 14 ♘f3 0-0-0, White regains his pawn, but that is all) 14 ... 0-0?! (after 14 ... 0-0-0 15 ♘xf7, White would retain his initiative, but an improvement was 14 ... fg 15 ♕xe5 ♕xe5 16 ♖xe5 f6 17 ♖e4 ♔f7 18 ♗b4 ♗xb4 19 ♖d7+ ♔g6 20 ♖xb4 b6 21 fg ♖hd8, with a draw) 15 g4! ♘xg4? (as on moves 7 and 14, Black's optimism gets the better of him. After 15 ... ♕xg4 16 ♕xg4 ♘xg4 17 ♖xe7, he would still have had drawing chances. However, to be more exact, we should not call it optimism but underestimation of the attacking possibilities afforded to White by this gambit variation as a whole) 16 ♕xe7 fg 17 fg ♖ad8? (the position was already difficult, but now Black loses by force) 18 ♗b4 ♕c8 19 ♖xd8 ♖xd8

20 h3!, and since on 20 ... ♘f2 White decides the game with 21 ♗c3 followed by 22 ♕e5, Black can resign.

7 ... ♘f6

We would not recommend 7 ... ♘d7. But 7 ... ♗xe4 8 ♗xe4 ♘f6 9 0-0 leads to the same position as 7 ... ♘f6.

To players of the Black side, we give the following variation as a warning: 7 ... e6?! 8 ♗f4 ♘d7 9 0-0-0 ♘gf6? 10 ♘xf6+ ♕xf6 11 ♗g5 ♕g6 12 ♗xf5 ♕xf5 13 ♕d2 ♕d5 14 ♕f4 and wins.

8 0-0

8 ♘xf6+ gf 9 ♗xf5 ♕a5+ 10 ♗d2 ♕xf5 11 0-0-0 is of interest only because of the trap 11 ... ♕e6 12 ♕d3 ♕xa2? 13 ♕d8+! – as occurred in a game of Koltanowski's in 1931. After 11 ... ♘d7 instead, Black completes his development while keeping his extra pawn.

A further possibility for White – 8 ♗d2, with 0-0-0 to follow – has not been tested in tournament games (nor, for that matter, has 8 0-0). To be more precise, no such games are known to us.

8 ... ♗xe4

9 ♗xe4 (4)

Not much is known about this position. *ECO* gives 9 ... ♘xe4 10 ♕xe4 e6 11 ♗g5 ♗e7 12 ♖ad1 ♕c7 13 ♖fe1 0-0 14 ♗f4 ♕a5 15 ♗e5, and concludes that White has 'compensation for the material'.

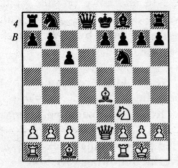

This is probably right. Finishing Black's development is an involved task, and White's threats may quickly become dangerous. The following are illustrations:

a) 15 ... ♖d8 16 ♕g4 g6 17 ♗c3 ♕c7 (17 ... ♕f5? 18 ♖xd8+ ♗xd8 19 ♕d4) 18 ♖xd8+ ♕xd8 19 ♘e5. Now 19 ... ♘d7 is unplayable, and Black needs to defend against ♕f4 followed by ♘g4.

b) 15 ... ♖d8 16 ♕g4 ♗f8 17 ♗f6 ♖xd1 18 ♖xd1 ♕f5 (if 18 ... ♘a6, then 19 ♘e5 is unpleasant) 19 ♕xf5 ef 20 ♖d8! gf 21 ♘d4, and it emerges that after 21 ... ♔g7 22 ♘xf5+ ♔g6 23 g4! h5 24 ♖xf8 hg 25 ♘d6 Black loses at once (the threat is 26 ♖c8, followed by ♘e8 and ♘c7; Black cannot bring his king across without losses, e.g. 25 ... f5 26 ♘xb7 ♔f6 27 ♘a5 ♔e7 28 ♖xb8, or 26 ... a5 27 ♘c5 a4 28 ♘d7); while after 21 ... h5 22 ♘xf5, he runs out of moves.

14 ... ♕c8, to prepare ... ♘d7, might appear safer than 14 ...

♕a5. But White's reply is obvious: 15 ♘e5 ♗f6 16 ♖e3 (or 16 ♖d3), and after 16 ... ♗xe5 17 ♗xe5 Black is again unable to play 17 ... ♘d7 on account of 18 ♗xg7.

Of course, mere analysis is inadequate to exhaust the mutual possibilities in the position after the ninth (!) move. If you ask what our 'feeling' is, it would seem that White's position after 10 ♕xe4 is worth the pawn.

However, one move earlier, the situation was less favourable for White. In Diagram 4, Black shouldn't be in a hurry to exchange. Of course, after 9 ... ♘xe4 the attacking pieces are fewer – yet those that remain can be more easily positioned for the assault. Besides, don't you think that the knight on f6 is more use to the defender than the bishop on e4 is to the attacker? We advise Black to play moves like 9 ... ♕c7, 9 ... ♘bd7 or 9 ... g6.

B

5   ♕f3 *(5)*

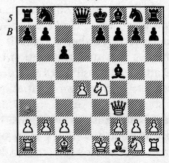

The moves 5 ♗d3 and 5 ♕f3 have an idea in common – the aim of seizing the initiative by fairly simple methods. Also, as we shall see, the methods echo each other in the two cases.

Strictly speaking, White's queen sortie involves holding up the development of his minor pieces. White should, however, be happy with variations like 5 ... ♗xe4?! 6 ♕xe4 ♘f6 7 ♕d3 (also 7 ♕h4); or 5 ... ♕d5?! 6 ♗d3 ♗xe4 7 ♕xe4 (also 7 ♗xe4!? ♕xd4 8 ♘e2) 7 ... ♕xe4 8 ♗xe4. The two bishops!

The most natural reply is:

5 ... e6

This ensures Black comfortable development of his pieces, for example:

a) **6 c3 ♘d7** (or 6 ... ♗e7 7 ♗d3 ♗g6 8 ♘e2 ♘f6 9 ♘f4 ♗xe4, etc) 7 ♗f4 ♘df6! 8 ♘d2 ♘e7 9 h3 ♘ed5.

b) **6 ♗e3 ♕a5+!?** (here too 6 ... ♘d7 is good; so is the immediate 6 ... ♘f6 7 ♘xf6+ ♕xf6) and now:

b1) **7 ♗d2 ♕d5 8 ♗d3 ♕xd4 9 0-0-0 ♘d7**, and Black has an extra pawn with a solid position, Velderhof-Euwe, The Hague 1931.

b2) *ECO* gives **7 c3 ♗a3 8 b4 ♕d5 9 ♗d3 ♗b2 10 ♖b1 ♗xe4 11 ♗xe4 ♗xc3+ 12 ♔f1 ♕xa2 13 ♘e2**, 'with compensation . . .'. This verdict should not be accepted: **13 ... ♗d2 14 ♕g3** (or 14 b5 ♘e7) **14 ... ♘f6! 15 ♕xg7 ♘xe4 16** ♕xh8+ ♔e7 17 ♖d1 ♕b3, with a won position for Black. Therefore, instead of 8 b4? we recommend the more modest 8 ♖b1 or 8 ♗c1.

There remains a gambit idea:

6 ♗d3!?

This may not be a bad chance for White, e.g. 6 ... ♕xd4 7 ♘e2 ♕d8 8 ♘g5 ♘f6 9 ♗xf5 ♕a5+ 10 ♗d2 ♕xf5 11 ♕xf5! ef 12 0-0-0 *(6)*.

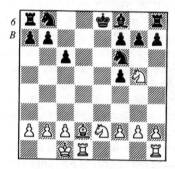

Despite the exchange of queens, White is able to create unpleasant threats. For example, 12 ... h6 13 ♖he1!? hg 14 ♘g3+ ♔d7 15 ♗a5+ ♘d5 16 c4.

Is it not, then, simpler (just as in Section A) to decline the gambit? A game Tal-Balashov, USSR Ch 1971, continued:

6 ... ♘d7
7 ♘e2 ♗g6

Neither 7 ... ♗xe4 8 ♕xe4, nor 7 ... ♘gf6 8 ♘xf6+ ♘xf6 9 ♗xf5 ♕a5+ 10 ♗d2 ♕xf5 11 ♕xf5 should satisfy Black if he is seeking the optimum, since in both cases White's chances are slightly better.

8	&f4	♘df6
9	♘g5	♘d5

Or 9 ... ♕d5!?

10	&xg6	hg
11	&d2	♘h6
12	0-0-0	&b4
13	c3	&e7
14	h4	

And White has the more active position.

Although not all Balashov's moves are above criticism, one of them – 7 ... &g6 – suggests the idea of refining Black's play earlier, with 5 ... &g6!? 6 &d3 ♘d7 7 ♘e2 ♘gf6, when it is not clear how he can be stopped from obtaining a comfortable position.

There is no doubt that 5 ... e6 is (objectively) the best answer to 5 ♕f3, yet if Black is especially worried about security, 5 ... &g6 will suit him as an alternative.

C

    5   ♘c5 *(7)*

'On tour (1964) I experimented with the weird 5 ♘c5!? Most of my opponents countered with 5 ... e5 6 ♘xb7 ♕xd4 (if 6 ... ♕b6 7 ♘c5 &xc5 8 dc ♕xc5 9 c3 White's better, Fischer-Petrosian, five-minute game, Bled 1961) 7 ♕xd4 ed 8 &d3 with the better ending. Some replied with 5 ... b6 6 ♘a6 ♘xa6 7 &xa6 ♕d5! Still others played 5 ... ♕c7 6 &d3 &xd3 7 ♘xd3 e6. White has more space, but only experience can tell whether he has the edge; however, the knight on d3 discourages the normal freeing manoeuvre ... c5 and/or ... e5. At least it's something to break the monotony!' (Fischer).

These lines by the former World Champion were written nearly fifteen years ago. At that time, 5 ♘c5 made a few appearances in tournaments, but did not become really popular. We are now going to examine the reasons.

Black has these choices:

C1 5 ... e5
C2 5 ... b6
C3 5 ... ♕c7
C4 5 ... ♕b6

C1

5	...	e5
6	♘xb7 *(8)*	
6	...	♕e7

This idea was tried out in a game Klovan-Machulsky, Riga 1978. The Bulgarian master Kaikam-dzozov has suggested instead 6 ... ♕b6 7 ♘c5 ed 8 ♕e2+ &e7 9 ♘e4

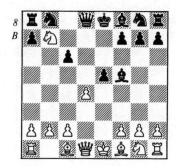

♘f6 15 ♕e2+ ♕e7 16 ♘d6+ ♔f8
17 ♕xe7+ ♔xe7 18 ♘f5+.

The point of the ingenious 10 ...
&b4 (in place of 10 ... &xd3) is
that after 11 ♘f3 &xd2+ 12 ♘xd2
♘e7 13 ♘ac4 ♕b4 14 ♖b1 ♕c5,
White can't play 15 ♘e4. But a
good enough line is (for example)
15 &xf5 ♘xf5 16 ♕e2+ ♕e7 17
♕xe7+ ♔xe7 18 ♖b7+.

By combining the two recom-
mendations, we arrive at 10 ...
&b4 11 ♘f3 &xd2+ 12 ♘xd2 ♕b4.
As a counter to this, we suggest
trying 13 &xf5 ♕xa5 14 &c8, for
example: 14 ... ♕c7 (14 ... ♕e5+ 15
♕e2 ♕xe2+ 16 ♔xe2 a5 is not as
risky) 15 ♘c4 (threatening 16
&b7!) 15 ... ♔f8 16 ♕xd4! ♕xc8
17 0-0-0 ♘a6 18 ♕d6+ ♘e7 19
♖he1 ♕c7 20 ♕a3.

C2

	5	...	b6
	6	♘b3	

The alternative is 6 ♘a6 (9).

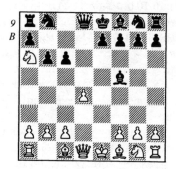

And now:

a) **6 ... ♘xa6 7 &xa6 ♕d5!**, as

♕b4+, or 8 ♘b3 &b4+ 9 &d2
♘f6 10 ♘f3 ♘e4. There is usually
some snag to this kind of play. In
the second variation, for example,
after 11 &d3 ♘xd2 12 ♘fxd2
&xd3 13 cd 0-0 14 0-0, there are
noticeable weaknesses in the black
camp.

7	♘a5	ed+
8	&e2	♕b4+
9	&d2	♕xb2

Klovan went on to win: 10 &d3
&xd3 11 cd &b4 12 ♘f3 &xd2+
13 ♘xd2 ♘e7 14 ♘ac4 ♕b4 15
♖b1 ♕c5 16 ♘e4 ♕d5 17 ♘ed6+
♔f8 18 0-0 c5 19 ♘b5 ♕d8 20 ♕f3
♘bc6 21 ♘bd6 f6 22 ♕e4 etc.
However, annotators of this game
have maintained that Machulsky's
idea is basically sound and would
have worked if he had played
more accurately with 13 ... ♕b4 or
10 ... &b4.

We are sceptical about this.
After 13 ... ♕b4 14 ♘c4, Black
cannot be satisfied either with
14 ... ♕e7+ 15 ♘e4!, or with 14 ...

indicated by Fischer. In view of the threats of 8 ... ♕xg2 and 8 ... ♕a5+, White has to retreat with 8 ♗f1. The loss of time is considerable, even though after 8 ... ♘f6 9 ♘f3 e6 10 ♗e2 ♗e7 11 0-0 0-0 all Black has done is come very close to equalising.

b) In Timman-Pomar, Orense 1976, Black played **6 ... e6** (if 6 ... ♘d7, then 7 d5! ♗e4 8 d6!). Taking the c6 point as an object of attack, Timman seized the initiative after 7 ♕f3 ♘e7 8 ♘xb8 ♕xb8 9 ♗f4 ♕b7 10 c3 ♘d5 11 g4! (11 ♗e5 f6 12 ♗g3 ♘b4!?) 11 ... ♘xf4 12 ♕xf4 ♗g6 13 ♗g2 ♗e7 14 h4 h5 15 ♘f3.

It appears that players tacitly consider the line in note (a) to be adequate for Black, since 6 ♘b3 is White's normal choice.

6 ... e6
7 ♘f3 (10)

Or 7 g3 ♘d7 8 ♗g2 ♖c8 9 ♘e2 ♘gf6 10 0-0 ♗d6 11 c4 0-0 12 ♗e3 ♕e7 13 ♖c1 c5 14 ♘c3 ♗g4 15 f3 ♗h5 16 g4 ♗g6 17 g5 ♘e8 18 f4 cd 19 ♘xd4 ♘c5 20 f5 ♗xf5 21 ♘d5 ♕d7 22 ♖xf5 ef 23 ♗h3 ♘e6 24 ♘xf5 ♔h8 and White's attack is unconvincing, Vitolins-Kivlan, Riga Cup 1979.

The games we shall now quote (as well as the last one) suggest that, as yet, both White and Black are merely feeling their way towards the correct plans in this variation.

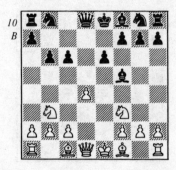

a) **7 ... ♘d7** 8 g3 ♘gf6 9 ♗g2 ♖c8 10 0-0 ♗d6 11 ♕e2 ♕c7 12 ♘h4! ♗g4 13 f3 ♗h5 14 ♘f5 0-0 15 ♘xd6 ♕xd6 16 ♗f4 ♕e7 17 c4, with the better chances for White, Birbrager-Shmit, USSR 1967.

b) **7 ... ♗d6** 8 g3 ♘e7 9 ♗g2 h6 (9 ... 0-0 10 ♘h4) 10 0-0 0-0 11 ♕e2 ♘d7 12 c3 ♖c8 13 ♘bd2 ♗g4 14 h3 ♗h5 15 ♘c4 ♗b8 16 b4 b5 17 ♘a5 (17 g4!? ♗g6 18 ♘ce5 ♗h7 19 a4) 17 ... ♘d5 18 ♗d2 ♖e8 19 c4 bc 20 ♘xc4 e5 21 de ♘xe5 22 ♘cxe5 ♗xe5 23 ♖ae1 ½-½ Bronstein-Petrosian, USSR Ch 1966.

c) **7 ... ♘f6** 8 ♗e2 h6 9 ♗d3!? (evidently Larsen didn't like to play 8 ♗d3 last move, because of 8 ... ♗g4 9 h3 ♗h5) 9 ... ♗xd3 10 ♕xd3 ♕c7 11 0-0 ♘bd7 12 ♖e1 ♗d6 13 ♘bd2 0-0 14 ♘c4 ♗e7 15 b3 c5, and Black has no worries, Larsen-Hübner, Tilburg 1979.

The general impression is that 5 ... b6 is a solid continuation. The same goes for the next variation too.

C3

5	...	♕c7
6	♗d3	♗xd3

Or 6 ... ♗g6!?

| 7 | ♘xd3 | e6 *(11)* |

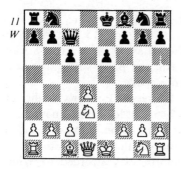

In practice, the spatial plus that Fischer wrote about has brought White no tangible gains:

a) **8 ♗f4 ♕a5+** 9 c3 ♘d7 10 ♘f3 ♘gf6 11 0-0 ♗e7 12 ♖e1 0-0 13 ♗g5 ♕d8 14 ♕b3 ♕b6 15 ♖ad1 ♕xb3 16 ab a5 17 ♖a1 ♖fd8 18 c4 ♔f8 19 ♗d2 ½-½ Bronstein-Barcza, Tallinn 1971.

b) **8 ♘f3 ♘d7** 9 0-0 ♘gf6 10 c4 (or 10 ♖e1 ♗e7 11 c4 0-0 12 ♗f4 ♗d6 13 ♘fe5 ♖fd8 14 ♕f3 ♘f8 15 ♖ad1 ♘g6 16 ♗g3 ♕a5 17 a3 ♗xe5 18 de ♘h5 19 ♕xh5 ♖xd3 20 ♕e2 ♖ad8 ½-½ Sigurjonsson-Burger, Brighton 1981), and now: **b1) 10 ... ♖d8** 11 ♕a4 a6 12 ♖e1 ♗e7 (12 ... b5!?) 13 ♗f4 ♗d6 14 ♗d2 ♕b8 15 ♗a5 ♖c8 16 ♘fe5 0-0 17 h3?! (17 ♗c3) 17 ... b5 18 ♕c2 c5 19 ♘xd7 ♘xd7 20 dc ♘xc5, and Black already has the more active

position, Jansson-Pomar, Göteborg 1971.

b2) 10 ... b6 11 ♖e1 ♗d6 12 b4 a5 13 c5 ♗e7 14 ♗f4 ♕b7 15 a3 0-0 16 ♖c1 ♘d5 17 ♗g3 ab 18 ab ♖a3, and again Black has come off well, Paoli-Timman, 1967.

C4

5	...	♕b6 *(12)*

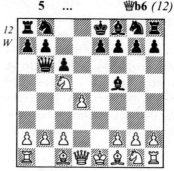

We feel that this obvious-looking move ought to have become the standard reply to 5 ♘c5. (White is deprived of the possibility of 6 ♗d3 ♗xd3 7 ♘xd3; after 6 ♘f3 e6, the knight on c5 has to retreat, and the whole operation turns out to have been a waste of time.) But it has not. Why?

The reason must probably be sought in a game won by Bronstein against Belyavsky in the USSR Ch, 1975. Bronstein's original idea in the opening was very highly esteemed by commentators, and yet originality is just about the only thing it has in its favour. The game went: 6 g4?! ♗g6 7 f4 e6 8 ♕e2 ♗e7 9 h4 h5 10 f5 ef 11 g5 (at the cost of a pawn, White has blocked up the bishop on g6, but we would still prefer to play the Black side here; the reason why Belyavsky lost was that he went on playing for a win when the position demanded caution after some mistakes he had made) 11 ... ♘d7! 12 ♘b3 (after 12 ♘xd7 ♔xd7 13 ♘f3 ♗d6, White's position would be worsened) 12 ... ♕c7 13 ♘h3 0-0-0 14 ♗f4 ♗d6 15 ♕h2 ♘f8 16 0-0-0 ♘e6 17 ♗xd6 ♖xd6?! (Black's 20th move speaks against his 17th) 18 ♗c4 ♘e7 19 ♘f4 ♘xf4 20 ♕xf4 ♖dd8 21 ♕xc7+ ♔xc7. Belyavsky was justified in playing for a win in this ending.

In the game Sigurjonnson-Santos from the Olympiad in Lucerne, 1982, White's play was more restrained: 6 ♘f3 e6 7 ♘d3 ♘d7 8 ♗e2 ♘gf6 9 0-0 ♗e7 10 c3 0-0 11 ♗g5 c5 12 ♕b3 cd 13 ♘xd4 ♗e4 14 ♕xb6 ♘xb6 15 ♖ad1 ♖fd8 16 ♖fe1 ♘a4 17 ♗c1 ♗d5 18 ♘b3 ♖ac8, and Black's game is a little more active.

We repeat Fischer's verdict on 5 ♘c5 – 'at least it's something to break the monotony'. Yet in the positions that arise from it, the opportunities afforded to White are very meagre.

Summary

5 ♗d3	e6		±
	♘d7		=
	♕xd4		∞
5 ♕f3	♗xe4		±
	♕d5		±
	♗g6		=
	e6		=
5 ♘c5	e5		±
	b6	6 ♘a6	=
		6 ♘b3	±/=
	♕c7		±/=
	♕b6	6 g4	∓
		6 ♘f3	=

2 5 ♘g3 ♗g6 6 ♘1e2

1	e4	c6
2	d4	d5
3	♘c3	de
4	♘xe4	♗f5
5	♘g3	♗g6
6	♘1e2 *(13)*	

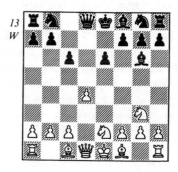

On the face of it, the idea of this continuation is simple: ♘f4, followed by ♘xg6. However, in eliminating the important bishop, White opens up the h-file for Black, and allows him to become active with ... e5. Isn't this operation rather pointless for White? That is the main question in this line, but it is not the only one.

Thus, in Variation A (below), it it turns out that after 6 ... e6 7 ♘f4, White's threat is not so much to exchange on g6 as to push

with h2-h4-h5 (since ... h6 is no longer playable).

In Variation B, the accepted view is that after 6 ... ♘d7 7 ♘f4 e5 Black has an easy game; therefore White doesn't usually hurry with 7 ♘f4, but seeks new chances in the position after 7 h4 h6 8 ♘f4 ♗h7 9 ♗c4.

Also, after 6 ... ♘f6 (Variation C), White has the same choice between 7 ♘f4 and 7 h4.

Positions that are analysed in this chapter sometimes arise after 6 h4 h6 7 ♘h3, or 6 ♘h3. A word about these possibilities:
a) **6 h4** h6 7 ♘h3 *(14)*.

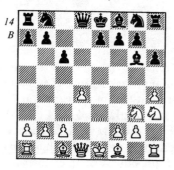

The most practical reply is 7 ... ♘f6 8 ♘f4 ♗h7, leading to Variation C. We advise the reader to refrain from 7 ... e5 8 de ♕a5+. After 9 c3 ♕xe5+ 10 ♗e2 ♘f6 11 ♗f4 ♕d5, or 11 ♕b3 ♕c7, Black would have a solid position. But 11 0-0 followed by 12 ♖e1 could turn out unpleasantly for him.

In a game Espig-Bönsch, East German Ch 1979, White sacrificed a couple of pawns with 9 ♗d2 ♕xe5+ 10 ♗e2 ♕xb2 11 0-0 ♕xc2 12 ♕e1, and won crushingly after 12 ... ♗e7 13 ♖c1 ♕a4 14 ♘f4 ♘d7 15 ♗c4 ♘f8 16 ♘xg6 ♘xg6 17 ♘f5 ♔f8 18 ♗c3 ♘f6 19 h5! ♘xh5 20 ♕e2 ♘f6 21 ♖fe1 ♗a3 22 ♘xg7! etc.

b) 6 ♘h3 (15).

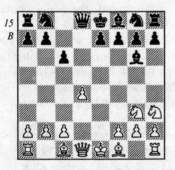

After 6 ... e5, does the same gambit work again? If it should turn out that in the variation 7 de ♕a5+ 8 ♗d2 ♕xe5+ 9 ♗e2 ♕xb2 10 0-0 ♕xc2 11 ♕e1 ♗e7 Black's position is more defensible than in the previous example, the alternative 8 c3 ♕xe5+ 9 ♗e2 ♘f6 10 0-0! (10 ♗f4 ♕d5) 10 ... ♘bd7 11 ♖e1 0-0-0 12 ♕a4 isn't at all

bad for White. Black has difficulty fending off the assaults of his opponent's pieces.

In answer to 6 ... e6 or 6 ... ♘f6, White brings his knight from h3 to f4, so for this see Variations A and C. On the other hand, after 6 ... ♘d7 (and here we see the one real point of 6 ♘h3), White avoids 7 ♘f4 e5, and first develops his bishop with 7 ♗c4. With White now ready to castle, the opening of the centre with 7 ... e5 looks risky, while the variation 7 ... ♘gf6 8 0-0 (8 ♘f4 e5 again leads to C below) 8 ... e6 9 ♘f4 ♘b6 (not 9 ... ♗d6 on account of 10 ♗xe6!) 10 ♗b3 (here 10 ♗xe6 is unconvincing: 10 ... fe 11 ♘xe6 ♕d7 12 ♖e1 ♔f7) 10 ... ♗d6 gives Black a position that is solid in appearance (11 ♖e1 0-0 12 h4 ♕c7 13 ♕f3 ♘bd5) but nonetheless arouses misgivings (due to the knight on b6).

But these niceties don't count for much, since in any case after 6 ♘1e2 the continuation 6 ... ♘d7 merely leads Black into trouble.

From Diagram 13, Black has:

A 6 ... e6
B 6 ... ♘d7
C 6 ... ♘f6
and also:

a) 6 ... e5, which was shown to be ineffective long ago, in a game Prins-Szabo, Venice 1949: 7 de ♕xd1+ (or 7 ... ♕a5+ 8 ♗d2 ♕xe5

9 ♗c3) 8 ♔xd1 ♗c5 9 ♘f4! ♗xf2
10 ♘xg6 hg 11 ♘e4 ♗d4 12 ♘d6+
♔e7 13 ♗c4 f6 14 ♘f7 ♖h5 15 c3
♗b6 16 ♗f4, and White's pieces
are dangerously active.

b) **6 ... h6** 7 ♘f4 ♗h7. Is it worth
Black's while to preserve his bishop
like this? Of course not. In comparison with regular lines (see 6 ...
♘f6 7 h4 h6 8 ♘f4 ♗h7 under
Variation C), White has saved
himself a tempo (the move h4),
and after 8 ♗c4 it will be hard for
Black to find his way out of a
tricky situation. For example,
ECO gives 8 ... e5 9 de ♕a5+ 10 c3
♕xe5+ 11 ♘fe2 ♘f6 12 ♗f4 ♕c5
13 ♕b3, or 8 ... ♘f6 9 0-0 e6 10
♖e1 ♗e7 11 ♗xe6! g5 12 ♗b3! gf
13 ♗xf4 ♗g6 14 ♕d2, with a
strong initiative for White in both
cases.

A

6   ...   e6
7   ♘f4 *(16)*

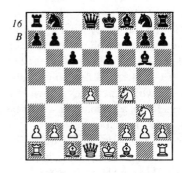

7   ...   ♗d6

Alternatively:

a) After **7 ... ♘f6**, the exchange
8 ♘xg6 hg would suit Black.
Comparing this situation with the
one in Variation A, Chapter 1
(5 ♗d3 e6?! 6 ♘f3 ♘d7 7 0-0 ♗xe4
8 ♗xe4 ♘gf6 9 ♗d3), we can see
that here White has paid a higher
price for the bishop, in terms of
both the h-file and the placing of
his own knight (which would like
to be on f3).

But the whole point is that the
transfer of the knight to the f4
square contains the dangerous
threat of 8 h4! After 7 ... ♘f6 8 h4
♗d6 9 h5 ♗f5 10 ♘xf5, White
obtained a clear plus in Tompa-
Urzica, Uljma 1981.

8 ... e5 (instead of 8 ... ♗d6) is
critical. The position is similar to
one that will be examined under C
(after 6 ... ♘f6 7 ♘f4 e5), and it
remains for us to decide whether
and how the assessment of the line
is altered by having the pawn on
h4 instead of h2.

Tompa sees a difference in the
fact that after 9 de ♕xd1+ 10
♔xd1 ♘g4, White can play 11
♗e3 (instead of 11 ♘xg6 as in the
variation with 6 ... ♘f6), keeping
up the threat of h5. This does in
fact radically alter matters: 11 ...
♘xe3+ 12 fe h6 13 ♘xg6 fg 14
♗d3, with appreciable winning
chances.

Things are less clear after 9 ...

♕a5+ 10 ♗d2 ♕xe5+ 11 ♗e2 ♕xb2. In the 6 ... ♘f6 line, this idea would be strongly answered by ♘xg6 with ♖b1 to follow, but here the pawn on h4 darkens the picture – it isn't clear where White's king is going. As to 12 0-0 ♗xc2 (or 12 ... ♕xc2) 13 ♕e1 – this would be splendid for White, only Black needn't hurry to take the c-pawn; 12 ... ♘bd7!?

In any event, we feel that Black is on dangerous ground here, and that something will be found for White somewhere (perhaps after 10 c3 ♕xe5+ 11 ♗e2) . . .

b) We are now in a better position to understand Flohr's move **7 ... ♕h4** – Black gets rid of the threat of h4-h5. The move has, however, nothing else to recommend it, and if in the first example (below) Black obtained a good game, in the other two the return trip with the queen permitted White to seize the initiative:

b1) **8 ♘xg6** hg 9 ♕d3 ♘d7 10 ♘e4 ♕d8 11 ♗e2 ♘df6 12 ♘xf6+?! gf, Bogatirchuk-Flohr, 1935.

b2) **8 ♕e2** ♘d7 9 c3 0-0-0 10 ♘xg6 hg 11 ♘e4 ♕e7 12 ♗g5, Ragozin-Flohr, Moscow 1935.

b3) **8 ♗e2** ♘d7 9 ♗e3 ♗d6 10 ♕d2 ♕e7 11 ♘xg6 hg 12 ♘e4 ♗c7 13 c4, Novopashin-Furman, 1963.

7 ... ♗d6 was played in a game Boleslavsky-Petrosian, Zurich C 1953. Black is ready to fight against h4-h5, but compared with 7 ... ♕h4 his method here is more subtle – on 8 h4 ♕c7, the knight's position on f4 turns out to be insecure. Play continued:

8 c3

White would like to meet 8 ... ♕c7 with 9 ♕f3, and therefore removes his c-pawn from danger. 8 h4 ♕c7 9 ♘gh5 fails against 9 ... ♗xh5 10 ♘xh5 g6.

But what if White attacks the g-pawn at once with 8 ♘gh5 . . .? Black could play something like 8 ... ♔f8 9 ♗e3 ♘f6, though this should rather be to White's liking. An interesting and strong line is 8 ... ♘f6! 9 ♘xg7+ ♔e7 (not 9 ... ♔f8?). In view of ... ♕a5+, the knight can't return from g7 to h5, and it's difficult to bring help to it, for example: 10 h4 ♗xf4 11 ♗xf4 h5, but not 10 ... h5? 11 ♘gxe6.

8 ... ♘f6
9 h4 ♕c7

'Now White has the choice between 10 ♕f3, giving rise to interesting complications, for instance 10 ... ♘bd7 11 h5 ♗c2 12 h6 g6 13 ♗c4 e5 14 ♕e2 0-0-0; and 10 h5, which sacrifices a pawn but gives Black a permanent weakness on e6. Boleslavsky chose the second, and better, line.' (Bronstein).

10 h5 ♗xf4
11 ♗xf4 ♕xf4
12 hg fg (17)

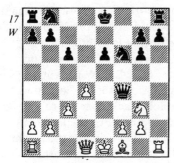

13 ♕d2

'White takes the interesting decision to offer a queen exchange though a pawn down! Perhaps Petrosian had been fondly hoping that Boleslavsky would fall for 13 ♕b3. The move played dispels his illusions of 13 ♕b3 ♘g4 14 ♕xe6+ ♔d8' (Bronstein).

13	...	♕xd2+
14	♔xd2	♘bd7
15	♖e1	♔f7
16	♗c4	♖ae8
17	♗b3	c5
18	♘e4	♘xe4+
19	♖xe4	♘f6
20	♖e5	cd
21	cd	♖e7

'Black's pieces are fettered to the point e6; on the other hand, White cannot improve his position either . . .' (Bronstein).

22	♖he1	♖he8
23	♔d3	h6
24	f4	

½-½

An instructive game. But one question has occurred to us: doesn't

7 ... ♗d6 make it more attractive for White to exchange with 8 ♘xg6 hg and follow with the blow 9 ♘e4 *(18)* . . .?

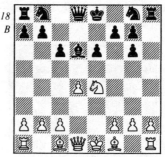

To sum up the results of this section: after 6 ... e6 7 ♘f4, both 7 ... ♘f6 (8 h4!) and 7 ... ♕h4 are dubious. To some extent, the same can be said of 7 ... ♗d6 (8 ♘xg6!?).

Black definitely ought to adopt the plan of ... e5, but since the immediate 6 ... e5 is weak, it must be postponed for one move (6 ... ♘d7 7 ♘f4 e5, or 6 ... ♘f6 7 ♘f4 e5) or for two moves (6 ... ♘f6 7 ♘f4 ♘bd7 8 ♗c4 e5).

B

| 6 | ... | ♘d7 *(19)* |

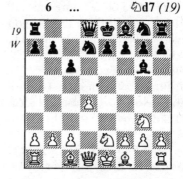

7 h4

It's generally held that 7 ♘f4 e5 8 ♘xg6 hg gives Black a comfortable position. However, let us try to set out the possibilities for both sides after 9 de ♘xe5 *(20)*.

a) **10 ♕xd8+ ♖xd8**. The exchange of queens leads to an ending where White has the bishop pair in an open position. On the other hand the black pieces are excellently placed, as becomes evident in the variations 11 f4 ♗b4+!? 12 c3 ♘d3+ 13 ♗xd3 ♖xd3 14 ♘e4 (14 cb ♖xg3) 14 ... f5, or 11 ♗d2 ♘g4 12 f3 ♘f2. However, if White starts off a little more carefully with 11 ♗e2!, there may be good prospects ahead for him after 11 ... ♗b4+ 12 c3 ♗c5 13 ♘e4, or 11 ... ♘f6 12 0-0 ♗c5 13 ♗f4.

b) Another method is **10 ♕e2!?** ♕a5+ (or 10 ... ♕e7 11 ♗d2) 11 ♗d2 ♗b4 12 0-0-0! (12 c3 ♗e7; or 12 ♗xb4 ♕xb4+ 13 c3 ♕e7 14 0-0-0 ♘f6 15 ♖e1? ♘d3+) 12... ♗xd2+ 13 ♖xd2 ♘e7 14 a3 (and if

14 ... 0-0?; then 15 f4). Here again, it would seem, proof of Black's well-being is wanting.

However that may be, in practice after 6 ... ♘d7 White's strategy is usually based on attempts to exploit Black's backward kingside development. In the last analysis, the point of bringing the knight to f4 was not solely to eat the bishop on g6 or make it suffer after h4. Another plan – sacrificing a piece on e6 – is also possible, and with his next few moves White sets about accomplishing it.

7 ... h6
8 ♘f4 ♗h7
9 ♗c4 *(21)*

9 ♗d3 ♗xd3 10 ♕xd3 is weaker. Black should not, of course, reply 10 ... ♘gf6? 11 ♘g6!, or 10 ... e5 11 ♘g6!; but 10 ... e6 gives him a promising position.

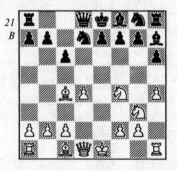

There can follow:

a) **9 ... e5** and now:

a1) Tal-Botvinnik, 7th World Championship Match game, 1960,

in which a level endgame arose, is well known: **10 ♕e2 ♕e7 11 de ♕xe5 12 ♗e3 ♗c5 13 ♗xc5 ♕xe2+ 14 ♔xe2 ♘xc5** etc.

a2) Tal's recommendation is also well known: **10 ♘d3!** ed (10 ... ♘gf6 11 de ♗xd3! 12 ♕xd3 ♕a5+ 13 c3 ♘xe5, or 13 ♗d2 ♕xe5+, is quite acceptable, but 11 ♕e2! favours White) **11 0-0**, with an attack. Indeed, while Black does manage to prepare for castling in the line 11 ... ♘gf6 12 ♖e1+ ♗e7 13 ♕e2 ♘b6 14 ♗b3 (14 ♗xf7+? ♔xf7 15 ♕e6+ ♔f8 16 ♘e5 ♕d5) 14 ... ♘bd5, it isn't easy for him to do so after 12 ♘h5! For example: 12 ... ♘xh5 13 ♕xh5 ♕f6 (or 13 ... ♗g6 14 ♖e1+ ♗e7 15 ♕e2) 14 ♖e1+ ♗e7 15 ♕e2 ♘b6 16 ♗b3 ♗xd3 17 cd ♖d8 18 ♗f4! So Tal's opinion twenty years back was probably right!

b) **9 ... e6** and now:

b1) **10 0-0 ♕xh4 11 ♗xe6 fe 12 ♘xe6 ♔f7** is not dangerous for Black.

b2) Nor is the situation clear after **10 h5 ♘gf6 11 0-0 ♗d6 12 ♗xe6 fe 13 ♘xe6 ♕e7 14 ♖e1 ♔f7**, or 12 ♖e1 0-0 13 ♘xe6 fe 14 ♖xe6 ♔h8 15 ♖xd6 ♘e8 16 ♖e6 ♗g8.

b3) The most unpleasant reply is **10 ♕e2!**, and if 10 ... ♘gf6 then 11 ♗xe6. In a different setting, the bishop sacrifice is not so dangerous: 10 ... ♗d6 11 ♗xe6 fe 12 ♘xe6 ♕e7 13 ♘f5 ♗xf5 14 ♘xg7+ ♔f7

15 ♘xf5 ♕xe2+ 16 ♔xe2 ♗c7 (compare the Keres-Olafsson game in Variation A, Chapter 3). However, 10 ... ♗d6 can be strongly answered by 11 ♘gh5!

c) Fears of the sacrifice on e6 gave rise to the continuation **9 ... ♘gf6 10 0-0 ♘b6 11 ♗b3** (22).

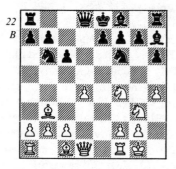

And now:

c1) **11 ... ♘bd5**. A game Ravinsky-Panov, Moscow 1947, now continued: 12 ♖e1 ♘xf4 (if 12 ... ♕c7, then 13 ♕f3 0-0-0 14 ♘xd5 cd 15 ♗f4) 13 ♗xf4 e6 14 ♘h5! (Black begins to have worries about his king; he will have them for the rest of the game . . .) 14 ... ♗g6 15 ♘xf6+ ♕xf6 16 ♕g4 ♗f5 (16 ... 0-0-0 17 ♖xe6!) 17 ♕g3 0-0-0 18 ♗b8 ♖d7 19 d5 ♗c5 20 dc bc 21 ♗e5 ♕d8 22 ♕f3 ♕b6 23 ♖ad1 ♖hd8 24 ♖xd7 ♖xd7 25 ♗xg7, with a won position. Thirty years later, in Kremenetsky-Gutop, 1978, White achieved the same reult by a different method: 11 ... ♘bd5 12 c4 ♘xf4 13 ♗xf4 e6 14 d5! ♗d6 15

♗xd6 ♕xd6 16 c5! ♕xc5 17 de.

c2) Petrosian, in a game with Black against Ravinsky (1950), unearthed an intersting possibility: **11 ... ♕c7 12 ♖e1 0-0-0!? 13 ♗xf7** e5 14 ♗e6+ (probably the position after 14 ♘e6 ♕xf7 15 ♘xd8 ♔xd8 16 de+ ♘fd5 offers White more chances) 14 ... ♔b8 15 ♘d3 ♖xd4 16 ♗e3 ♖d8 17 ♕e2 e4 18 ♘c5 ♗xc5 19 ♗xc5 ♕e5 20 ♗xb6 ab 21 ♗b3 ♕f4, with double-edged play.

c3) In Malchikov-Guseinov, USSR 1978, White answered 11 ... ♕c7 with **12 ♕e2**. If we recall the note to Black's 12th move in the Ravinsky-Panov game, it becomes clear that 12 ♕e2 is less energetic than 12 ♖e1. Subsequently too, White's play was inferior to his opponent's: 12 ... ♘bd5 13 ♘d3 ♗xd3 14 ♕xd3 e6 15 c4 ♘f4 16 ♕f3 g5 17 ♘e4 ♘xe4 18 ♕xe4 0-0-0 19 ♗xf4 ♕xf4! 20 ♕xf4 gf 21 d5 ♗c5 22 ♖ad1 ♖dg8! with a substantial plus.

But, to sum up: the plan based on 7 h4 exposes the minus side of 6 ... ♘d7; Black's delay in evacuating his king to the flank gives his opponent considerable attacking chances.

C

      6   **...**   **♘f6** *(23)*

This move too prepares ... e5, since after 7 ♘f4 e5 8 de, the balance of pawns is re-established either by 8 ... ♕a5+ or by 8 ...

♕xd1+ 9 ♔xd1 ♘g4.

But then, 'after h4 Black will be forced to play ... h6, and White will be able to bring his knight to the good square f4 with tempo' (Holmov). This is a tempting idea, which leads White into the various paths branching from C1 (below). We shall examine:

C1 7 h4

C2 7 ♘f4!

C1

      7   **h4**   **h6**

      8   **♘f4**   **♗h7** *(24)*

      9   **♗c4**

This is seen more often than the

alternatives, although with the solid 9 ... e6 Black can now transpose into Chapter 3, Variation A. For the dubious 9 ... ♘bd7, see Variation B above (6 ... ♘d7 7 h4 h6 8 ♘f4 ♗h7 9 ♗c4 ♘gf6).

Other moves for White:

a) 9 c3 e6 10 ♗d3 is dull. This position arose by transposition in a game Keres-Petrosian, 1961, which was drawn without much fight: 10 ... ♗xd3 11 ♘xd3 ♗d6 12 ♕f3 ♘bd7 13 ♗f4 ♗xf4 14 ♕xf4 ♕b8 15 ♕f3 ♕d6 16 0-0 ♕d5 17 ♕xd5 cd 18 f4 ♘e4 19 ♘xe4 de 20 ♘e5 ♖d8 ½-½.

b) Livelier play was initiated by Holmov against Ebralidze, 1949: 9 ♗e3 e6 10 ♗d3 ♗xd3 11 ♕xd3 ♘d5? ('Black's desire to exchange as many pieces as possible and thus ease his defensive problems seems entirely natural', Holmov writes. We would prefer 11 ... ♗d6 or 11 ... ♘bd7, since it is just here that Ebralidze's 'defensive problems' arise – for the very reason that he loses time by exchanging) 12 0-0-0 ♘xf4 13 ♗xf4 ♘d7 (as Holmov rightly notes, 13 ... ♗d6 is strongly met by 14 ♗xd6 ♕xd6 15 ♘h5! 0-0 16 ♖h3 or 15 ... ♕d5 16 ♘xg7+ ♔f8 17 c4 ♕a5 18 ♘xe6+ fe 19 ♖h3) 14 ♔b1 ♘f6 15 ♗e5 ♕b6 (White retains the initiative after both 15 ... ♗d6 16 ♕b3 and 15 ... ♘g4 16 ♕e2) 16 ♖h3! (in connexion with a subsequent ♘e4,

interesting possibilities arise for the rook on the third rank) 16 ... 0-0-0 17 ♘e4 ♗e7 18 ♕f3 ♖d5? (in a position that was already difficult – for example, 18 ... ♘xe4 19 ♕xe4 ♗f6 20 ♖f3! – Black commits suicide) 19 c4 ♖a5 20 d5! and the front is broken through.

9   ...   e5

9 ... ♘a6!? is Bellon-Campora, Torremolinos 1983.

For a long time this was thought to favour White after 10 ♕e2 ♕xd4 11 0-0 or 10 ... e4 11 ♗e3 ♘bd7 12 0-0-0. But old judgements need reconsidering.

10   ♕e2   ♕xd4
11   0-0   ♘bd7

Or 11 ... b5 12 ♗b3 ♗c5 13 ♗e3 ♕d6 14 ♖ad1 ♕e7 15 ♗xc5 ♕xc5 16 ♘fh5!, and Black's king is in danger, Spassky-Foguelman, Mar del Plata 1960.

12   c3   ♕d6
13   ♗e3   ♕e7

13 ... ef is risky, because after 14 ♗xf4+ ♕e7 15 ♕f3 the black king doesn't manage to escape: 15 ... 0-0-0? 16 ♕xc6+!

14   ♘d3   e4
15   ♘f4   g5
16   hg   hg
17   ♘h3   g4
18   ♘g5   ♗g6

White has not achieved anything, Kallai-Foldi, Hungary 1979. It probably doesn't pay White to avoid Variation C2.

C2

7 ♘f4! *(25)*

Now, following the stock move ... e5 (either at once or after 7 ... ♘bd7 8 ♗c4), an endgame usually arises in which White's bishops are a powerful factor. Powerful, but not of course decisive – the ending is not unplayable for Black, and hence White by no means always attempts to reach it.

Black has:

C21 7 ... e5
C22 7 ... ♘bd7

C21

7 ... e5
8 ♘xg6

Is White being over-hasty in playing this move without exploiting the chances given to him by the threat of h4-h5 (compare Variation A) . . .? Let us see: 8 de ♕a5+ 9 ♗d2 ♕xe5+ 10 ♗e2 ♘bd7 (not 10 ... ♕xb2 11 ♘xg6 hg 12 ♖b1; also 11 0-0!? as recommended by Espig) 11 h4. Here Black has two possibilities – 11 ... ♕xb2, and

11 ... 0-0-0 – which will presumably be evaluated by practical tests. Nor are things clearer after 9 c3 (when offering a queen exchange without having played ♘xg6, White has to remove his c-pawn from attack) 9 ... ♕xe5+ 10 ♕e2 ♘bd7 11 h4 0-0-0. For example: 12 h5 ♗c2 13 ♗e3 ♗c5!?

After 8 de, a game Kremenetsky-Bagirov, Yaroslav Otborochnii 1982, continued instead **8 ... ♕xd1+ 9 ♔xd1 ♘g4 10 ♘xg6 hg** *(26)*.

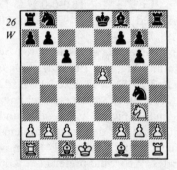

There followed: 11 ♗e3 (an unusual decision. If the books – and your own eyes! – are to be believed, the endgame after 11 ♘e4 ♘xe5 is attractive for White. For example, 12 ♗e2 f6 13 c3 ♘bd7 14 ♗e3 0-0-0 15 ♔c2, Fischer-Foguelman, Buenos Aires 1960; or 12 ♗f4 ♘bd7 13 c3 f6 14 ♔c2, Stein-Holmov, 1964) 11 ... ♘xe3+ 12 fe ♔e7 13 ♗c4 ♘d7 14 e6 ♘b6 15 ♗b3 c5 16 a4 c4 17 ♗a2 fe 18 ♔e2 ♖c8, and the game was drawn. More often it is Black who takes steps to avoid the endgame which would arise after 11 ♘e4.

8	...	hg
9	de	♕a5+
10	♗d2	♕xe5+
11	♕e2 (27)	

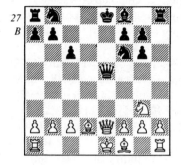

And now:

a) **11 ...** ♘bd7 12 ♕xe5+ ♘xe5 13 ♗c3 ♘ed7! 14 ♗c4 ♖h4! 15 ♗b3 ♘c5 16 0-0-0 ♘xb3+ 17 ab ♖d8. White has no ambitions here (except to draw), Abashalumov-Kasparov, USSR 1977.

b) **11 ...** ♕xe2+ 12 ♗xe2 ♘bd7 13 0-0-0 ♗c5 14 f4 0-0 15 f5 gf 16 ♘xf5 ♖fe8 17 ♗f3 g6 18 ♘h6+ ♔g7 19 ♘g4 ♘xg4 20 ♗xg4 ♘e5 21 ♗e2 f6 22 h4 ♘f7 23 ♗d3 ♗e3 etc, Tsheshkovsky-Bagirov, USSR 1978. Again a draw!

What is it that stops White from gaining a minimal advantage in this two-bishop ending? Probably, it's just that Black's pieces are finely placed and co-operating very well (incidentally, Bagirov once said that instead of 14 ... 0-0

in his game against Tseshkovksy, 14 ... ♔f8!? was more promising; the e-file is kept for the queen's rook, while the king's rook is active on the h-file anyway). It is possible, though, that White's powerlessness is the result of not arranging his own forces in the best way (for example, we feel he ought to castle short, firmly protecting the pawn on f2).

If White keeps the queens on with 11 ♗e2 (instead of 11 ♕e2), there are chances for both sides: 11 ... ♘bd7 (11 ... ♕xb2 12 ♖b1 is dangerous) 12 0-0 ♕c7 (with the idea of meeting 13 ♗c4 with 13 ... ♘e5).

C22

| 7 | ... | ♘bd7 |
| 8 | ♗c4 | e5 (28) |

The postponement of ... e5 by one move introduces nothing fundamentally new into the play. The only point is that White's bishop has already committed itself.

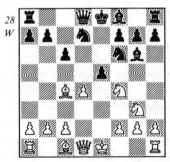

Some examples from practice:

a) **9 de ♕a5+**, and now:

a1) Keres-Kasparian, USSR Ch 1952, took a curious course: **10 ♗d2 ♕xe5+ 11 ♘ge2 ♗c5 12 0-0 0-0-0 13 ♘g3 ♕d4 14 ♗d3 ♖he8 15 b4 ♗xb4 16 c3 ♗xc3 17 ♘ge2 ♗xa1 18 ♘xd4 ♗xd4 19 ♕c2**. To quote the tournament book: 'An exceptionally interesting position has arisen. Strangely enough, Kasparian offered a draw here, and Keres accepted.' Indicating that 14 ... ♘e5! would have given Black the advantage, the same book recommends White to play line (b) below.

a2) In Panchenko-Guseinov, USSR 1979, White played **10 c3 ♕xe5+ 11 ♕e2 ♕xe2+ 12 ♔xe2**, and – for once! – achieved success: 12 ... ♘e5 13 ♘xg6 hg 14 ♗b3 ♗c5 15 ♗f4 ♘ed7 16 ♔f3 ♔f8 17 h3 a5 18 a4 ♗e7 19 ♖ad1 ♘c5 20 ♗c2 ♘d5 21 ♗c1 ♘b6 22 ♖he1 ♘bxa4 23 ♗xa4 ♘xa4 24 ♖d7, and Black's position is very difficult. The failure of 16 ... ♔f8?! is obvious. But even before that, Black's operations lacked precision. A line more in keeping with 12 ... ♘e5 would be 14 ... ♖d8, but because this is dubious (15 ♗e3), Black ought to have developed his bishop on move twelve – 12 ... ♗c5. Now 13 h4 is ineffective (for instance 13 ... ♘e5 14 ♗b3 ♖d8 15 ♖d1 ♖xd1 16 ♗xd1 ♘e4), while after 13 ♘xg6 hg White would

have two tempi less than in the actual game (♗b3 and ♗f4).

b) **9 ♘xg6** hg 10 de ♕a5+ 11 ♗d2 ♕xe5+ 12 ♕e2 gives another position of the familiar type. After 12 ... ♕xe2+ 13 ♗xe2, Black is simply a tempo up on Tseshkovsky-Bagirov; if 13 ♔xe2, an interesting reply is 13 ... ♖h4!? (14 ♗b3 ♘c5, or 14 f4 ♗d6).

c) Against Portisch (Tilburg 1978), Ljubojević chose a plan that might seem wholly innocuous: **9 ♕e2 ♕e7 10 de ♕xe5 11 ♗e3 ♗b4+ 12 c3 ♗c5 13 ♗xc5 ♕xe2+ 14 ♗xe2 ♘xc5 15 0-0-0** *(29)*. But the position didn't prove so simple.

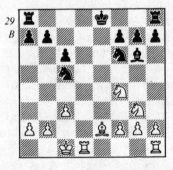

After **15 ... ♖d8 16 f3!** (this move, depriving the black knights of the e4 square, would also be the answer to 15 ... 0-0) 16 ... ♖xd1+ 17 ♖xd1 ♔e7 18 ♖e1 ♔d7 19 h4 h6 20 ♘xg6, White obtained the better ending.

Couldn't Black have utilised e4 sooner? 15 ... ♘ce4 16 ♘xg6 hg 17 ♘xe4 ♘xe4 18 ♗f3 ♘g5 (18 ...

♘xf2? 19 ♖he1+ ♔f8 20 ♖d2), or 18 ♖he1 ♔f8 19 ♗c4 ♘f6, doesn't seem to give White anything tangible.

Virtually the whole question about the 6 ♘1e2 line boils down

to whether White has a plus in the ending (see Tseshkovsky-Bagirov, Panchenko-Guseinov and Ljubojević-Portisch). Still, let us not forget one other problematic position from Variation A: 6 ... e6 7 ♘f4 ♗d6 8 ♘xg6 hg 9 ♘e4.

Summary

6 h4	h6	7 ♘h3	e5				±
			(♘f6! — cf. 6 ♘1e2)				
6 ♘h3	e5						±
	♘d7						±
	(♘f6! — cf. 6 ♘1e2)						
6 ♘1e2	h6						±
	e5						±
	e6	7 ♘f4	♘f6				±
			♕h4				±
			♗d6				±/∞
	♘d7	7 ♘f4	e5				±/∞
		7 h4	h6	8 ♘f4	♗h7	9 ♗c4 e5	±
						e6	±
						♘gf6	±
	♘f6	7 h4	.h6	8 ♘f4	♗h7	9 c3	=
						9 ♗e3	=
						9 ♗c4 e5	∞
						(♘bd7 — cf. 6 ... ♘d7)	
						(e6! — cf 6 ♗c4)	
		7 ♘f4	e5	8 de	♕xd1+		±
					♕a5+		=/∞
				8 ♘xg6			=/∞
				♘bd7 8 ♗c4	e5	9 de	=
						9 ♘xg6	=
						9 ♕e2	±/=

3 6 ♗c4

1	e4	c6
2	d4	d5
3	♘c3	de
4	♘xe4	♗f5
5	♘g3	♗g6
6	♗c4	e6
7	♘1e2	♘f6 (30)

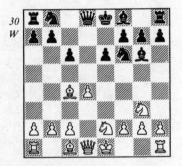

Chapters 2 and 3 have a common factor – the white king's knight takes the same route. Indeed, in the previous chapter the white bishop also frequently arrived on c4.

By developing his bishop first, White has forestalled play based on ... e5 (6 ... ♘d7 7 ♘1e2 e5 8 0-0 is risky for Black). His own plans have remained essentially the same – he has sacrifices on e6 in Variation A (8 h4 h6 9 ♘f4), as

well as hopes of the two bishops (supplemented by the threat of h4-h5) in Variation B with 8 ♘f4.

A new element is introduced by 8 0-0 ♗d6 9 f4 (Variation C), with the intention of storming Black's kingside after f5.

7 ... ♗d6 a move earlier, as played by Petrosian against Simagin, USSR 1956, is intended as an antidote to the last-mentioned plan. There can follow:
a) **8 0-0 ♘d7** (31).

And now:
a1) Against **9 f4** Petrosian had prepared 9 ... ♘e7, and, since f5 is impossible, White is left in a strategically suspect position with weak squares and little mobility for his pieces.

a2) Simagin played **9 &b3**, which was met by 9 ... ♘e7 all the same (though 9 ... ♘gf6 10 f4, leading to positions in Variation C, should be to Black's liking with the moves ... ♘d7 and &b3 interposed). The game deserves to be quoted more fully: 10 ♘f4 ♕c7 11 ♕f3 ♘f6 12 ♖e1 0-0-0!? 13 c3 ♔b8 14 a4 h5! 15 ♘xg6 ♘xg6 16 &c2 ♘f4?! (better 16 ... h4 17 ♘f1 ♘f4, with good chances on the kingside) 17 h4! ♘4d5 18 ♘e4 ♘xe4 19 &xe4 ♘f6 20 &c2 ♘g4 21 g3 ♖he8 22 a5 e5?! (22 ... a6!) 23 &g5! f6 24 &d2 ed 25 cd ♖xe1+ 26 ♖xe1 c5 27 a6! and Black's king position became insecure. However, despite White's eventual success, the move 9 &b3 is clearly of no great strength.

a3) **9 ♘f4** is more active, and stronger – seeing that on 9 ... ♕c7 the piece sacrifice 10 &xe6! fe (or 10 ... &xf4 11 &xd7+ ♔xd7 12 ♕g4+) 11 ♘xe6 ♕c8 12 ♘f5! &xf5 13 ♘xg7+ ♔d8 14 ♘xf5 gave White a palpable advantage in Simagin-Goldberg, USSR 1961. The sacrifice 10 &xe6 is also powerful against 9 ... ♘gf6. Still, 9 ... ♘b6 10 &b3 (not 10 &xe6? &xf4) 11 ... ♘f6 is less clear.

b) The principal rejoinder is **8 h4!** h6 9 ♘f4 &xf4 (since 9 ... &h7 10 ♘gh5 is unfavourable for Black, he has to give up a bishop for a knight and put his trust in the solidity of his position) 10 &xf4

♘f6 *(32)*.

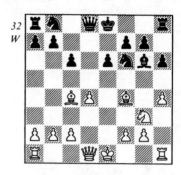

There can follow:

b1) **11 ♕d2** ♘bd7 12 0-0-0 ♘d5 (Black succeeds in eliminating one of the white bishops) 13 ♖de1 ♘7b6 14 &b3 ♘xf4 15 ♕xf4 ♘d5 16 ♕e5 0-0 17 ♘e4 ♕b8 18 ♘d6 ♖d8 19 ♘c4 ♘b6 20 ♕xb8 ♖axb8, and Black secured a draw in Tal-Botvinnik, 15th match game 1960.

b2) **11 c3** ♘bd7 12 ♕e2 ♘b6 13 &b3 a5 14 h5 &h7 15 0-0 0-0 16 ♖fe1 a4 17 &d1 ♘bd5 18 &d2 b5 19 ♖c1 ♕b6 20 b3 ab 21 &xb3 ♖fc8 22 c4 bc 23 ♖xc4 ♘e8 ½-½ Matanović-Darga, Bled 1961. In this game White's advantage was not in evidence.

b3) In *ECO*, Geller-Bagirov, 27th USSR Ch 1960, is quoted as a model: **11 h5** &h7 12 ♕e2 ♘bd7 (accepting the pawn sacrifice is dangerous) 13 0-0-0 ♘d5 14 &d2 ♘7f6 15 &d3 &xd3 16 ♕xd3 ♕c7 17 ♔b1 0-0-0 18 ♖h4 ♕e7 19 c4. This position is evaluated with a

'±' sign, yet Bagirov's comment is worth putting on record: 'I got the draw easily . . .'

An inferior but solid position is a doubtful achievement – hence, 7 ... ♘f6! From Diagram 30, White has:

A 8 h4
B 8 ♘f4
C 8 0-0

A

    8   h4 (33)

    8 ...   h6

In Spassky-Foguelman, Amsterdam IZ 1964, Black's play was original: 8 ... ♘h5 9 ♘xh5 ♗xh5 10 f3 h6 11 ♘f4 ♗d6, but White's was powerful: 12 ♕e2! ♗xf4 13 ♗xf4 ♘d7 14 g4 ♗g6 15 0-0-0 ♕f6 16 ♗d6 0-0-0 17 ♗b3 h5 18 ♕e3! ♖hg8 20 d5!

    9 ♘f4   ♗h7 (34)

The only difference between this position and one that we examined in Chapter 2 (Variation B) is in the placing of Black's

knights – before, he had a knight on d7, now there is one on f6. But this difference is very important, since in the first place it is easier for Black to prepare castling, and secondly White's chances of a successful sacrifice on e6 are reduced (the tactical motif of playing ♗xe6 and answering ... ♗xf4 with ♗xd7+ is not available).

    10 0-0

Kingside castling seems out of keeping with the move h4; yet it prepares for sharp play following a piece sacrifice on e6, and in that kind of game the position of the h-pawn is an insignificant detail.

Alternatively:

a) Ciocaltea-Botvinnik, Tel Aviv 1964, went **10 ♗b3 ♗d6 11 ♘fh5 ♖g8!** (after 11 ... 0-0 it isn't clear how serious White's attacking chances are; compare Santurian-Makogonov, under b2 below. The line chosen by Botvinnik demonstrates that castling long is more reliable) 12 &f4 &xf4 13 ♘xf4 ♘bd7 14 ♕d2 ♕c7 15 0-0-0 0-0-0 16 ♘d3 c5 17 ♕f4 cd 18 ♕xd4 ♘b6 19 ♕f4 (19 ♕e3 ♘g4 20 ♕e2 ♘xf2!) 19 ... &xd3 20 ♕xc7+ ♔xc7 21 ♖xd3 ♖xd3 22 cd ♖d8, with positional plus for Black in the endgame. The move 10 ... &d6 is natural and best, whether White plays 10 0-0, 10 &b3, 10 c3 or 10 ♕e2. However, in the next example Black plays differently.

b) **10 c3**, and now:

b1) Aronin-Kasparian, Sochi 1952, saw **10 ... ♘bd7**. This recalls a position from Variation B, Chapter 2, but of course the time wasted by White on the move 10 c3, which doesn't help his attack, eases Black's task. The game is noteworthy for the way in which this task was mastered by Kasparian: 11 ♕e2 ♕e7!? (11 ... &d6 is also possible, transposing into c2 below) 12 0-0?! (12 &e3, with queenside castling to follow, was correct) 12 ... g5! 13 hg hg 14 ♘h3 g4 15 ♘g5 &g6 16 f4 gf 17 ♕xf3 &h6 18 &f4 ♘d5 (Black has gained firm possession of the initiative, and now safely avoids the trap 18 ... 0-0-0 19 ♕xc6+) 19 &xd5 &xg5 20 &e4 ♖h4! 21 &xg5 ♕xg5 22 &xg6 ♕xg6 23 ♖ae1 0-0-0, and the attack against the white king ended successfully.

b2) A game Santurian-Makogonov, USSR 1948, in which **10 ... &d6** was played, ended in defeat for Black, but is not convincing: 11 ♘fh5 0-0 12 &g5 &e7 13 &xf6 &xf6 14 ♕g4 ♔h8 15 ♘e4 &xe4 16 ♕xe4 ♘d7 17 &d3 g6 18 g4 ♕a5 19 ♘f4 ♖fe8 20 ♘xg6+ fg 21 ♕xg6 ♖e7 22 0-0-0 ♕c7 23 g5 ♕f4+ 24 ♔b1 ♖f8 25 ♕xh6+ ♔g8 26 ♖hg1 ♖g7 27 &h7+.

c) The continuation **10 ♕e2** was described by Keres as 'strong and elastic'. Is it? 10 ... &d6, and now:

c1) In Tal-Botvinnik, 5th match game 1960, where 10 ♕e2 appears to have been played for the first time, the game soon developed in Black's favour: **11 &e3** (11 &xe6? 0-0!) 11 ... ♘bd7 12 ♘gh5 ♘xh5 13 ♘xh5 ♖g8! ('after this game, defending the g7 pawn by such means became the norm in the present situation. Black is not afraid to castle long, since White too can only castle on that side' – Botvinnik) 14 g4 ♕c7 15 g5 &g6! 16 0-0-0 (16 gh? ♕a5+) 16 ... 0-0-0 17 ♘g3 hg 18 &xg5 &f4+ 19 &xf4 ('after 19 ♔b1 &xg5 20 hg, the pawn on g5 would be weak' – Botvinnik) 19 ... &xf4+ 20 ♕e3 ♕h6! 21 &d3 &xd3 22 ♖xd3 ♘b6 23 ♕xh6 gh, and White will have to struggle to draw.

c2) A game Keres-Olafsson, Bled 1961, saw what Keres called 'a new and successful experiment': **11 c3** *(35)*:

35
B

11 ... ♘bd7 12 ♗xe6! (this
sacrifice is 'undoubtedly correct,
and leads virtually by force to an
endgame with bishop and three
pawns against two knights. This
distribution of forces is most
unusual, but the better prospects
are on White's side' – Keres) 12 ...
fe 13 ♘xe6 ♕e7 14 ♘f5! ♗xf5 15
♘xg7+ ♔f7 16 ♘xf5 ♕xe2+ 17
♔xe2 ♔e6? ('Black would have a
perfectly acceptable position if he
succeeded in playing ... h5, to
prevent White from fixing the
weakness on h6. To this end, he
should have played 17 ... ♗f8! On
18 h5, Black would considerably
relieve his position by 18 ... ♔e6
19 ♘h4 ♖g8 20 ♘g6 ♗d6! 21
♗xh6 ♘xh5 22 ♖xh5 ♖xg6' –
Keres) 18 ♘xd6 ♔xd6 19 ♗f4+
♔e6 20 h5! Now White's advantage
is evident, and after some more
mistakes by his opponent, Keres
achieved the win.

So the experiment *was* successful.
However, as Keres himself wrote,

'after White had opened the h7-b1
diagonal with 11 c3, queenside
castling became risky for him.
Therefore Black could have played
11 ... 0-0!, after which I doubt if
White would have had the slightest
chance of organising a successful
attack.'

Twenty years later, in Hébert-
Vranesić, Montreal Z 1981, Black
acted on this advice: **11 ... 0-0!** 12
♘d3 ♘bd7 13 ♘e5 ♕c7 14 ♘xd7
♕xd7 15 ♖h3 e5 16 de ♗xe5 17
♗e3 ♖fe8, with the initiative.

10 ... ♗d6

10 ... ♘d5 is no good because of
11 ♗xd5 (another strong reply is
11 ♕g4 ♘f6 12 ♕e2, or 11 ... ♘d7
12 ♗xd5 cd 3 ♘xd5 ed 14 ♖e1+
♗e7 15 ♕xg7) 11 ... cd 12 ♕h5,
with the threat of ♘xe6 which is
hard to parry. For example: 12 ...
♕f6 13 ♖e1 ♔d8 14 ♘xd5! ed 15
♕xd5+ ♘d7 (or 15 ... ♔c7 16
♘h5) 16 ♗d2 ♖b8 17 ♘h5 ♕c6?
18 ♗a5+ 1-0 Hjorth-Tempone,
Junior World Ch 1982.

11 ♘xe6

If Black safely castles, he has an
obvious advantage owing to the
pawn on h4. Yet in Bellon-
Seirawan, Las Palmas 1981, White
unaccountably allowed this to
happen: 11 ♘gh5 0-0 12 ♖e1 ♖e8
13 c3 ♘bd7 14 ♗d2 e5 15 ♕b3
♖f8 16 de ♘xe5 17 ♖ad1 ♘xh5 18
♘xh5 ♕xh4 19 ♗f4 ♘xc4 20
♕xc4 ♗b8 21 ♕b4 c5 (21 ...

♕xh5? 22 ♕xf8+) 22 ♕xc5 ♗xf4 23 g3 ♗xg3, with an extra pawn.

11 ... **fe**

12 ♗xe6 *(36)*

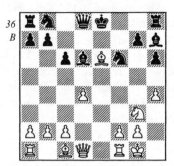

36
B

This position, which occurred for the first time in Tal-Botvinnik, 9th match game 1960, has remained controversial ever since. In particular, Black has been quite unable to decide on the best move to be played now.

a) Barczay-Schneider, Hungarian Ch 1977, went: **12** ... ♔e7 13 ♖e1 ♖e8 14 ♗xh6 ♔f8 15 ♘h5 gh 16 ♕f3, and . . . Black resigned! This miniature gives rise to a whole host of questions. Why not 14 ... gh . . .? Then neither 15 ♕d2, nor 15 ♕f3, nor 15 ♘h5 gives sufficient attack. Why not 14 ♘h5 (with the same intentions as in the game)? And the chief question is, why not the obvious 14 ♗c8+ ♔f8 15 ♗xb7 . . .? In the variation 15 ... ♗xg3 16 fg ♗xc2 17 ♖xe8+ ♕xe8 18 ♕xc2 ♕e1+ Black gives mate; but White obtains the advantage

after 18 ♕d2, as he does in the case of the transposition 15 ... ♗xc2 16 ♖xe8+ ♕xe8 17 ♕xc2 ♗xg3 18 ♗e3!

b) A more solid line is **12** ... ♗xg3 13 fg ♕e7 14 ♖e1 ♗e4, as in Biriescu-Rooze, 1980. There followed: 15 ♗f5 ♗xf5 (15 ... ♘bd7 is dubious because of 16 g4, but 15 ... 0-0 is perfectly playable. For example, 16 ♗xh6 gh 17 ♗xe4 ♘xe4 18 ♕g4+ ♕g7 19 ♖xe4 ♘d7 with the better chances for Black; also 16 g4! ♕f7! 17 ♗xe4 ♘xe4 18 ♖xe4 ♕f2+ 19 ♔h2 ♕xh4+ 20 ♔g1 ♕f2+ with a draw, or – if Black wants it – unclear play after 21 ♔h2 ♘d7!? 22 ♗e3) 16 ♖xe7+ ♔xe7. Although Rooze lost this position (17 ♕e1+ ♔f7 18 ♕b4 b6 19 ♗d2 ♘bd7 20 ♖f1 ♗e6 21 g4 a5 22 ♕d6 ♗xg4 23 ♕xc6 ♖ac8 24 ♕b5 ♖he8 25 ♕b3+ ♔f8 26 ♖f4 ♖e4 27 c4 ♖ce8 28 c5 bc 29 ♖xe4 ♖xe4 30 dc a4 31 ♕d3 ♔f7 32 c6 ♘e5 33 ♕b5 ♖e2 34 ♗c3 ♘g6 35 ♕c4+ ♔f8 36 ♗xf6), it is clear that either of the other results would also have been possible.

c) In Tal-Botvinnik, Black prepared for queenside castling without worrying about the discovered check: **12** ... ♕c7 13 ♖e1 ♘bd7. This forced White to play 14 ♗g8+ ♔f8 15 ♗xh7 ♖xh7 16 ♘f5. There followed: 16 ... g6!? (Black acquiesces in material equality – a piece for three pawns

– but quickly completes his mobilisation. His pieces will now be operating in harmony' – Botvinnik) 17 ♗xh6+ ♚g8 18 ♘xd6 ♛xd6 19 ♗g5 (in Tal's opinion, 19 ♛d2 ♖e7 20 ♗f4 was stronger) 19 ... ♖e7 ('the rook exchange reduces the attacking potential of White's pieces. An essenatial feature of the position is that White doesn't yet have a single pased pawn. If he tries to obtain some with 20 ♖xe7 ♛xe7 21 h5, then Black will have attractive possibilities either in the endgame after 21 ... gh 22 ♛xh5 ♘xh5 23 ♗xe7 ♘f4, or in the attacking line 21 ... ♚g7 22 hg ♖h8' – Botvinnik) 20 ♛d3 ♚g7 21 ♛g3? ♖xe1+ 22 ♖xe1 ♛xg3 23 fg ♖f8!, and Botvinnik won the endgame. Eighteen years later, the position in Diagram 36 occurred once more in a game by Tal. This time his opponent was Vukić (Bugojno 1978). On 12 ... ♛c7, White played 13 ♘h5 ♖f8 14 c4 (M.Kondratiev gives 14 f4 ♗g6 15 ♘xf6+ ♖xf6 16 f5 ♗f7 17 ♗g5 hg 18 hg ♖xe6 19 fe ♗xe6 20 ♛h5+ ♚d7 21 ♖ae1, or 19 ... ♗g6 20 ♛f3 ♛e7 21 ♛h3 ♚d8 22 c4, and assesses White's chances optimistically; this analysis is probably open to doubt) 14 ... ♗g6 15 ♘g3 ♘bd7 16 c5 ♗xg3 17 fg ♘d5 18 ♖e1 0-0-0 19 ♛g4 ♗f7 20 ♗xd5 ♗xd5 21 ♗f4 (this bishop is White's last hope) 21 ...

h5 22 ♛g5 (22 ♛xh5 would be met by 22 ... ♖xf4) 22 ... ♛a5, and White's chances are of a purely practical nature.

d) **12 ... ♘bd7** 13 ♖e1 ♛c7. Botvinnik went so far as to recommend this as a way of avoiding 12 ... ♛c7 13 ♘h5 ♖f8 14 f4, which used to be considered strong for White – although against Vukić, as we saw, Tal took a different course.

Chances of a practical nature – this is probably the truest appraisal of the possibilities given to White by the 8 h4 variation. Objectively, Black's chances are at least no worse.

B

8 ♘f4 (37)

37
W

We have here a position from Chapter 2 (Variation A), with the difference that instead of the very powerful h4 (after 6 ♘1e2 e6 7 ♘f4 ♘f6), White has played ♗c4. The threat of 9 h4 is still there, but Black has gained an important tempo.

8 ... ♗d6

The following line looked good in practice: 8 ... ♘d5 9 ♘xg6 hg 10 ♗b3 ♘d7 11 ♗d2 ♕h4 12 c3 ♗d6 13 ♕f3 ♘7f6 14 ♘e2 (or 14 0-0-0 ♗f4) 14 ... ♕e4 15 ♕xe4 ♘xe4 16 ♗c1 0-0-0 17 ♗c2 ♘ef6 18 h3 e5 19 de ♗xe5, Polugayevsky-Osnos, USSR 1965.

Criticising the slowness of White's play (10 ♗b3, 11 ♗d2), Boleslavsky reommended an aggressive set-up with **10 ♘e4! ♕h4 11 ♕e2 ♗e7** (11 ... ♘f6 12 ♘g5 ♕xd4? 13 ♘xf7) 12 ♗d2 ♘d7 13 0-0-0 ♘7f6 14 ♘g5, when White has the better chances.

9 ♗b3

All this is familiar from the previous chapter; in case of 9 h4 Black is ready to attack the knight on f4 (9 ... ♕c7), while White defends his c-pawn so as to answer 9 ... ♕c7 with 10 ♕f3.

Alternatives:

a) In Tal- Botvinnik, 17th match game 1960, White played **9 ♘xg6** hg 10 ♗g5 ♘bd7 11 0-0 ♕a5. As Tal has written, 'White hasn't a scrap of opening advantage. But he could still have steered towards the haven of a draw with 12 ♕d2. He has not much choice; any retreat of the bishop on g5 is inconsistent, the exchange on f6 is wholly devoid of positional sense, defending with 12 ♕c1 is passive,

and the move 12 f4 is simply bad ...' Yet 12 f4 was just what he played, and after 12 ... 0-0-0 13 a3 ♕c7 14 b4 ♘b6 15 ♗e2 ♗e7 (with threats of 16 ... c5 17 bc ♖xd4, or 16 ... ♘fd5), a position was reached which bears out his judgement of White's 12th move.

b) In the second game of the return match in 1961, Tal played **9 0-0** *(38)*.

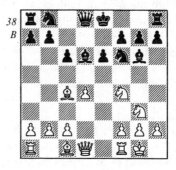

38 B

– and Botvinnik found a strong reply: 9 ... ♘d5! (after 9 ... ♕c7 10 ♕f3 ♗xc2, Black is dangerously behind in development; White can play, for example, 11 ♘fh5 ♘xh5 12 ♘xh5 0-0 13 ♗h6). This challenges White to exchange on g6, after which Black would have chances of exploiting the h-file. After 10 ♘gh5 0-0 11 ♗b3 ♘d7 12 ♘xg6 hg 13 ♘g3 ♕h4 14 ♕d3 ♖ad8, Black obtained a comfortable game.

9 ... ♕c7

Or:

a) At this point, **9 ... ♘d5** is

ineffective, as a game Korchnoi-Petrosian, Stockholm 1962, showed: 10 &xg6 hg 11 &e4! &e7 12 0-0 &d7 13 c4 &5f6 14 &g5! &h7 15 &f3 ₩c7 16 g3 c5 (on 16 ... 0-0-0, Boleslavsky advised 17 ₩e2 ℤhe8 18 &f4 &d6 19 &e3!, threatening 20 c5 or 20 d5) 17 d5 e5 18 &a4, with a substantial plus for White. This game brings out some subtle points connected with the exchange on g6; the h-file is important, yet Black needs to be fully equipped to meet &g3-e4 – when White's worst piece is activated.

b) It's interesting to compare the above game with Jansa-Bagirov, 1966: **9 ... &bd7** 10 ₩f3 (on 10 0-0 Black would play 10 ... &d5! all the same, while 10 h4 ₩c7 11 ₩f3 transposes into a line given below, in Note (a) to White's 11th) 10 ... a5 11 a4 &d5 12 &xg6 hg 13 &e4 &7f6! Bagirov doesn't waste time retreating his bishop, since on 14 &xd6+ ₩xd6 he wins a pawn (one threat being 15 ... ₩b4+). Jansa sacrificed the pawn, obtaining some compensation after 15 &d2 ℤxh2 16 0-0-0 ℤxh1 17 ℤxh1 &e7.

10   ₩f3   &bd7
11   0-0 *(39)*

11 h4, which was the main threat, is now rejected because of 11 ... e5, with the following variations:

a) **12 de** &xe5 13 ₩e2 0-0-0 14 h5

&eg4 15 hg hg 16 ℤxh8 ℤxh8, and it's difficult for White to defend (17 ₩f3 &h2, or 17 ₩c4 ₩b6 18 &d3 &xf2 19 &xf2 &xg3).

b) **12 &xg6** hg 13 &e3 0-0-0 14 0-0-0 (14 &xf7? ed 15 &xd4 &e5) 14 ... ed 15 &xd4 &c5 with a good game.

After 11 &e3, Black had no problems in Kupreichik-Chandler, Hastings 1981-2: 11 ... 0-0-0 12 0-0-0 c5 13 &xg6 hg 14 dc &xc5 15 &b1 &e5 16 h3 a5 17 &xc5 ₩xc5 18 &e4 &xe4 19 ₩xe4 ℤd4 etc.

The move 11 0-0 was preferred by Simagin, who won two correspondence games with it.

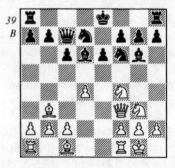

Both his opponents continued:
11   ...   e5
12   &xg6   hg
And now:

a) Simagin-Holetschek, corres 1964, went **13 h3!?** (after 13 ℤe1 0-0-0 14 &xf7 ed 15 &xg6 &e5 16 &f5+ &b8 16 &f5+ &b8 17 ₩d1 g6 18 &h3 &d5 White is in a dangerous situation, Kotkov-Antoshin, 1963) 13 ... 0-0-0 (if 13 ... ed, then 14 ♕e2+ is unpleasant) 14 c3 ♖df8 15 ♗e3 ♖h4 16 ♗g5 e4 17 ♕e2 ♖hh8 18 ♖ae1 (Black has a strong initiative after 18 ♘xe4 ♗h2+ 19 ♔h1 ♖e8 20 f3 ♘h5) 18 ... ♘h7 (Holetschek's conception will be refuted, but 18 ... ♗xg3 19 fg is bad too. Evidently the chief mistake occurred earlier) 19 ♘xe4! ♗h2+ 20 ♔h1 f5 21 ♗e7 ♖e8? (21 ... fe 22 ♗xf8 ♘hxf8 23 ♕xe4 favours White, but Black would not yet be doomed) 22 ♘c5 ♘g5 23 ♗xg5!? (after 23 ♗e6 ♘xe6 24 ♕xe6, or 23 ... ♖xe7 24 ♗xd7+ ♖xd7 25 ♘xd7 ♕xd7 26 ♔xh2 f4 27 ♔g1!, White wins fairly simply. However, one annotator has maintained that on 23 ♗e6 Holetschek had prepared 'winning variations starting with 23 ... ♘xh3'. We have managed to ascertain that after 24 ♗xd7+ ♕xd7 25 ♘xd7 ♘f4! White has no defence against . . . perpetual check! But 25 gh ♕d5+ 26 ♔xh2 ♖xe7 27 ♕d3!, or at once 24 gh, would not even give Black that chance) 23 ... ♖xe2 24 ♖xe2 ♘xc5 25 dc ♗e5 26 g3! (the point of Simagin's original idea; ♖fe1 next move will force the bishop on e5 to retreat. After that, the white bishops will create irresistible threats from e6 and f4. The situation is so grave that on

the last move Black ought to have returned the queen – 25 ... ♗f4 26 ♖e7 ♗xg5 – with some slight drawing chances) 26 ... b6 (26 ... ♗xg3 27 fg ♖xh3+ 28 ♖h2 does not alter matters) 27 ♖fe1 ♗f6 28 ♗f4 ♕d8 29 ♖e6, and White won. In our view, instead of 15 ... ♖h4 followed by 16 ... e4, Black should have played 15 ... ed 16 ♗xd4 ♘e5, or 16 cd ♘b6. With this plan in view, it is better if he also places his king on the other wing – 13 ... 0-0.

b) In a game against Dubinin, corres 1966, Simagin chose **13 c3**, and after 13 ... c5?! (13 ... 0-0) 14 ♗g5 0-0 15 dc ♗xc5 16 ♖ad1 ♕c6 17 ♕xc6 bc 18 ♖fe1 a5 19 ♘e4 ♗a7 20 ♗xf6 ♘xf6 21 ♘xf6+ gf 22 ♖d7, he obtained a clearly superior endgame (the bishop on b3 is very powerful!).

The white king's bishop played a major role in both these games, and one can't help wondering why it was necessary (in the position on Diagram 39) to lengthen this bishop's diagonal with 11 ... e5. While the counter-stroke 11 ... e5 was natural as a reply to 11 h4, it seems more appropriate to meet 11 0-0 with 11 ... 0-0 (12 h4 e5!), or 11 ... 0-0-0 (perhaps followed by ... c5).

And finally, before we finish with 8 ♘f4, let us recall Jansa-Bagirov. It may be that the order of moves in that game (9 ... ♘bd7) was the most accurate.

C

8   0-0   ♗d6

A few words about 8 ... ♘bd7, the chief aim of which is to counter 9 f4 with an immediate 9 ... ♘b6 10 ♗b3 c5. Instead of 9 f4, there is more point in 9 ♘f4, forcing 9 ... ♘b6 (9 ... ♗d6 10 ♗xe6!) 10 ♗b3 ♗d6. We have examined this position before (6 ♘h3 ♘d7 in Chapter 2), and repeat that we doubt the soundness of bringing the knight to b6.

9   f4 (40)

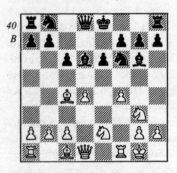

Black can choose between:
C1 9 ... ♕c7
C2 9 ... ♗f5
C3 9 ... ♕d7
and also 9 ... ♘e4 10 f5! ♗xg3 11 ♘xg3 ♘xg3 12 fg ♘xf1 13 gf+ ♔xf7 14 ♕g4 ♖e8 15 ♗h6! (Keres) – compare C1 below.

C1

9   ...   ♕c7
10   f5!   ef

11   ♘xf5 (41)

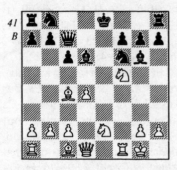

11   ...   ♗xh2+

It's easier for Black to organise his defences if he doesn't waste time taking this pawn – 11 ... ♗xf5 12 ♖xf5 ♘bd7. An example is Zaitsev-Pavlov, 1967: 13 ♔h1 0-0 14 ♕f1 ♖ae8 15 ♗g5 b5 16 ♗d3 ♘d5 17 ♕f3 f6 18 ♗d2 g6 19 ♖xd5 cd 20 ♗h6 ♖f7 21 ♕xd5 a6, with chances for both sides.

12   ♔h1   0-0

Or 12 ... ♗xf5 13 ♖xf5 ♗d6 14 ♗h6! ♖g8 15 ♘f4 ♕e7 16 ♘h5 ♘bd7 17 ♘xg7+ ♔d8 18 ♕e1 ♘g4 29 ♗g5 ♘df6 20 ♘h5 etc, Sejkora-Groszpeter, 1979.

13   g3

We are following the game Keres-Golombek, Moscow 1956; the way Black's position now collapsed was a good start for the opening line. A game Shianovsky-Spiridonov, played ten years later, is a variation on the same theme: 13 ♕e1 ♗d6?! 14 ♘xg7! ♔xg7 15

&xf6 &d7 16 ♕h4 ♖fe8 17 &h6+
&h8 19 &g5 &e7 20 ♖xg6 etc.

13	...	&xf5
14	♖xf5	&xg3
15	♖xf6!	♕e7

There followed: 16 ♕f1 ♕e4+
17 ♕f3 ♕h4+ 18 &g2 ♕h2+ 19
&f1 ♕h3+ 20 ♕g2 etc.

C2

| 9 | ... | &f5 |

The general opinion (notwith-
standing the Zaitsev-Pavlov game
under C1) is that Black ought not
to allow f5. The reason is not
merely that this advance is dangerous for him. The pawn on f4
has curtailed the mobility of the
white queen's bishop and king's
knight; and if Black succeeded in
turning this short-term factor into
a long-term one, he could contend
for the opening advantage.

This idea is so attractive that it
gave rise to such an unusual recipe
(suggested by Furman).

| 10 | &xf5 | ef (42) |

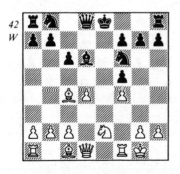

The f4 pawn is blocked, and
weak points in the White camp
(on e3 and e4) have been exposed.
But no small price has been paid
for this. Black's pawn structure
has been spoilt, and his king
position is not entirely secure.
(The move ... g6 is not to be
avoided, but after that White's
bishop on the a1-h8 diagonal may
prove dangerous, especially in
conjunction with an eventual
piece sacrifice on f5.) What has
practice revealed?

| 11 | &g3 |

The advantages of bringing the
knight to e5, by 11 &h1 ♕c7
12 &g1 etc, are doubtful. In
Westerinen-Kagan, Ybbs 1968,
White surrendered the e3 square
for the sake of the a1-h8 diagonal:
12 b3!? &bd7 13 &b2 0-0 14 &d3
g6 15 ♕e1 ♖fe8 16 ♕h4 &d5 17 a3
♕d8 18 ♕h6 &e3?! 19 ♖f3 &f8 20
♕h3 &xc2? (a mistake which
Kagan had been preparing with
his 18th move; he should have
played 20 ... &g4, or, earlier, 18 ...
&f8. After the capture on c2,
Black comes under a heavy
attack) 21 ♖c1 &xa3 22 &g3 &b5
23 &xf5! &f6 24 d5! &a3? 25 ♕h6
&f8 26 ♕h4, with a won position.

11	...	g6
12	♖e1+	&f8
13	♕f3

A tense, unclear position resulted
after 13 b3 &bd7 14 ♕f3 h5! 15
&b2 h4 16 &f1 &e4 17 d5 ♕b6+

18 ♘e3 ♘df6 19 dc bc 20 h3 ♖h7
21 ♖ad1 ♗b4 22 ♖e2 ♗c3
23 ♗a3+ ♔g8 24 ♔h2 ♖e8,
Panchenko-Bagirov, Burevestnik
Ch, 1975.

13 ... ♕c7

Not 13 ... ♘bd7? 14 ♕b3.

14 ♗d3 c5

15 d5!

In the correspondence game,
Altshuler-M.Zagorovsky, 1964, the
weaker 15 c3 was played. While
White, with this move, prevented
his own bishop from coming out
onto the aggressive diagonal,
Black made full use of his chances
to seize the initiative: 15 ... ♘bd7
16 ♔h1 h5! 17 ♗e3 ♘g4 18 dc
♗xc5 19 ♗xc5 ♘xc5 20 ♗c2 ♘e6
21 ♖f1 h4 22 ♘e2 ♘g5! 23 ♕d3 h3
0-1.

15 ... c4

16 ♗xf5! gf

17 ♘xf5 ♘bd7

18 ♗d2 ♖g8

19 ♗c3 ♖g6

The knight on f5 and bishop on
c3 ensure Black continual worries
about the defence of his king.
Here 19 ... ♗xf4? fails against
20 ♗b4+ ♘e5 21 ♕xf4!

20 ♔h1 ♖d8

21 ♖ad1 ♘b6

22 ♘h4! ♘bxd5

Or 22 ... ♖h6 23 ♕g3.

23 ♘xg6+ hg

24 ♖xd5 ♘xd5

25 ♕xd5 ♗xf4

26 ♕f3! ♖e8

By now there is no defence:

a) 26 ... ♗g5 27 ♕h3.

b) 26 ... ♗d2 27 ♗xd2 ♖xd2
28 ♕f6.

c) 26 ... ♔g8, and now not 27
♕h3? ♗e5!, but 27 ♗f6!

d) 26 ... ♖d7 27 ♕h3 ♗e5 28 ♖xe5
♕xe5 29 ♕xd7.

27 ♗g7+

and Black resigned, Yefimov-
Shakarov, corres 1981.

In the position after 17 ♘xf5,
there is probably no necessity for
Black to lose. Still less would we
take it upon ourselves to condemn
9 ... ♗f5 outright on the basis of
this game (together with Westerinen-
Kagan). The conclusion that
suggests itself, though, is that the
drawbacks to this continuation
(insecure king position) outweigh
its advantages.

Long ago, Boleslavsky suggested
a different way of preventing f5.
We shall now turn to this.

C3

9 ... ♕d7

10   ♗d3

Also:

a) At this point, the pawn sacrifice **10 f5?!** ef 11 ♗d3 ♘e4 is dubious.

b) An idea that looks logical is **10 ♗b3**, followed by c4 and d5, so as to remove the pawn from e6 and renew the threat of f5. But this is hardly practicable after 10 ... ♘a6 11 c4 ♘c7.

c) In Eolian-Kasparov, USSR Junior Ch 1977, the pointless **10 ♔h1?!** allowed Black to seize the initiative at once with 10 ... h5! (the knight on g3 is short of room) 11 f5 ef 12 ♘f4 ♗xf4 13 ♖xf4 h4 14 ♕e1+ ♔f8 15 ♘e2 h3.

10	**...**	**♗xd3**
11	**♕xd3**	**g6** *(44)*

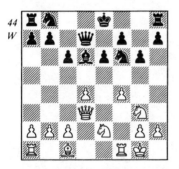

As Boleslavsky wrote, 'although the black queen is depriving the knight on b8 of its natural square,

the white pieces are not well enough placed to exploit this'. It only remains for us to give a game which confirmed Boleslavsky's opinion and drew attention to the strategic risk that White has incurred by playing f4.

Van der Wiel-Seirawan, Baden bei Wien 1980: 12 b3 ♘a6 13 ♗b2 ♗e7 14 c4 ♘c7 15 ♕f3 0-0 16 ♘c1 ♘ce8! 17 ♘d3 ♘g7 18 ♘e5 ♕c7 19 h3 ♖ad8 20 ♖ad1 (the annotators were right to advise a more energetic course of action: 20 ♘e2, with g4 to follow) 20 ... h5! 21 ♘e2 h4! 22 ♘g4 ♘fh5 23 ♕c3 ♔h7 24 ♖f3 ♘f5 25 ♘e3 ♗f6 26 ♘g4 ♗h8 27 ♘e5? (after 27 ♕c1 White would 'merely' have a bad position) 27 ... ♘xf4!, and Black won.

To conclude: efforts by White to create sharp play (8 h4, or 8 0-0 ♗d6 9 f4) should be welcome to Black. The line 8 ♘f4 is more solid, but there again the choices at Black's disposal are not bad, and are at any rate more interesting than in Chapter 2, where the knight is transferred to f4 without a preliminary 6 ♗c4.

Summary

7 ...	♗d6						±
	♘f6	8 h4	♘h5				±
			h6	9 ♘f4	♗h7	10 ♗b3	=
						10 ♕e2	=
						10 0-0 ♘d5	±
						♗d6	11 ♘gh5	∓
						11 ♘xe6	∞/=
		8 ♘f4	♘d5				±
			♗d6	9 ♘xg6			=
				9 0-0			=
				9 ♗b3	♘d5		±
					♘bd7		=
					♕c7	10 ♕f3 ♘bd7	11 h4	=
						11 ♗e3	=
						11 0-0	∞/=
		8 0-0	♘bd7	9 f4			∞
				9 ♘f4			±
			♗d6	9 f4	♕c7		±
					♗f5		±
					♕d7		=

4 6 ♘f3

1	e4	c6
2	d4	d5
3	♘c3	de
4	♘xe4	♗f5
5	♘g3	♗g6
6	♘f3 (47)	

The plans for White that we examined in the preceding sections were not lacking in aggressiveness. In the present chapter, we shall be analysing variations and positions of a different nature, in which White sets his hopes of advantage merely on his slightly more active pieces and slightly greater manoeuvring space.

Another move to have been played with the aim of consolidating White's spatial gains is 6 f4 (45).

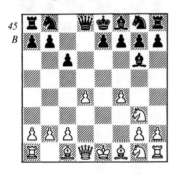

45
B

However – just as in Variation

C, Chapter 3 – practice has shown that in the subsequent play the weaknesses formed in the white camp by the advance of the f-pawn make themselves felt. Thus:

a) The game Marshall-Capablanca, New York 1927, is characteristic: 6 ... e6 7 ♘f3 ♗d6 8 ♗d3 (or 8 ♗c4 ♘e7 9 0-0 ♘d7 10 ♘e5 ♘f6 11 c3 ♕c7 12 ♕e2 0-0 13 ♗e3 c5 14 dc ♗xc5 15 ♗xc5 ♕xc5+ 16 ♔h1 ♖ad8 with a fine position for Black, Stolz-Flohr 1931) 8 ... ♘e7 9 0-0 ♘d7 10 ♔h1 ♕c7 11 ♘e5 ♖d8 12 ♕e2 ♗xd3 13 ♘xd3 0-0 14 ♗d2 c5 15 ♘e4 ♘f5 16 dc ♘xc5. If White could now move his pawn back to f2, he would equalise . . .
b) *ECO* gives some interesting lines: **6 ... h5!?** 7 ♘f3 (7 f5? ♗xf5) 7 ... h4 8 ♘e2 ♘d7 9 ♘e5 ♘xe5 10 fe e6 11 ♘f4 ♗f5, with the better chances for Black; or 7 h4 e6 8 ♘f3 ♘d7 9 ♗c4 ♗e7 10 0-0 ♕c7 (10 ... ♗xh4? 11 f5! with an attack) 11 ♘e2 0-0-0.

In practice, the trouble with Black's idea in (b) above is its lack of adaptability. By a change of move order – 6 h4 h6 (6 ... h5 7

♘h3!) 7 f4 – White eliminates the possiblility of ... h5. Then, after 7 ... e6 8 ♘f3 ♘d7 9 h5 ♗h7 10 ♗d3 ♗xd3 11 ♕xd3 ♕c7 12 ♗d2 *(46)*, we reach positions of a modern kind, only with a white pawn on f4.

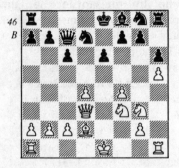

There can follow:

a) **12 ...** ♘gf6, and now:

a1) 13 ♘e5 ♗d6 14 0-0-0 0-0 15 ♘e2 (or 15 ♕f3 ♖fd8 16 ♔b1 c5 17 ♘xd7 ♖xd7 18 dc ♗xc5 19 ♗c3 ♘d5 20 ♗e5 ♗d6 21 ♗xd6 ♖xd6 22 ♖d4 ♖c6 23 c3 ♖c8, with an active position for Black, Shamkovich-Dely, 1981) 15 ... c5 16 ♘xd7 ♘xd7 17 ♔b1 ♖fd8 18 g4 cd 19 g5 ♘c5 20 ♕xd4 ♗f8 21 ♕e3 hg 22 fg ♖d5 23 ♗c3 ♖xd1+ 24 ♖xd1 ♖d8 25 ♖f1 ♖d5, with chances for both sides, Dückstein-Hort, 1968. Dückstein's handling of the position was good if only because it stopped the defects of the move f4 from showing. Hort's play needs refining – this purpose seems to be served by 15 ... ♖fd8,

threatening to capture twice on e5 (if 16 ♘xd7, then 16 ... ♖xd7).

a2) 13 0-0-0 c5 14 ♕e2 0-0-0 15 ♘e5 ♘b6 16 dc ♗xc5, and Black obtained a fully satisfactory position in Kavalek-Saidy, Las Palmas 1973. However, the modern treatment of the Caro-Kann demands a different decision: 14 ... ♗d6, with kingside castling to follow. *ECO*'s recommendation must be viewed as an oddity: 15 ♘f5 ♗xf4 16 dc, with the evaluation '±'. After the natural 16 ... 0-0 Black has a winning position!

b) **12 ... 0-0-0** 13 0-0-0 ♗d6 appears more subtle. In Ciocaltea-Golombek, Moscow 1956, White was forced to renounce ♘e5 and play 14 ♘e2 ♘gf6 etc. Of course, 13 ♕e2 is more accurate.

But, to return to 6 ♘f3:

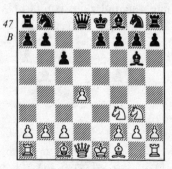

Here Black has:

A 6 ... ♘f6
B 6 ... ♘d7

Variation A is played now and again when Black is sceptical

about White's possible ♘e5. Variation B occurs considerably more often. In this chapter we shall look at some insipid plans by White, beginning with 7 ♗c4 (B1) or 7 ♗d3 (B2). The remaining two thirds of the book will be devoted to the continuation 7 h4.

A

6 ... ♘f6 *(48)*

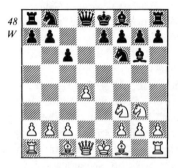

We have often happened to read that '6 ... ♘d7 is essential here, in view of the threatened 7 h4 h6 8 ♘e5'. However, there do exist other opinions.

7 h4

7 ♘e5 ♘bd7 8 ♘xg6 hg is to Black's liking, just as it was in similar positions in Chapters 2 and 3. In exchange for the bishop, White has given not only a knight (his better one, incidentally) but also the h-file and a certain amount of time.

7 ... h6

Or:

a) If Black plays 7 ... e6,

disregarding the advance of the h-pawn, White obtains a highly favourable position after 8 h5 ♗e4 9 ♘xe4 ♘xe4 10 ♗d3 ♘f6 11 ♕e2.

b) In Suetin-Ratner, USSR 1951, Black halted the h-pawn with 7 ... ♘h5. Suetin's further conduct of the game has been very highly praised in opening handbooks: 8 ♘e2 *(49)*.

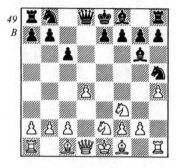

8 ... ♘d7 9 g4 ♘hf6 10 h5 ♗e4 11 ♘g3 ♕a5+ 12 ♗d2 ♕d5 13 ♗g2 ♗xf3 14 ♕xf3 ♕xd4 15 g5 ♘d5 16 0-0-0 ♘e5 17 ♕b3 0-0-0 18 ♗a5 ♕f4+ 19 ♔b1, and in view of his very backward development Black is unable to organise a defence.

However, a full two decades ago Suetin himself asserted that after 8 ... e6! 9 g4 ♘f6 10 h5 ♗e4 11 ♘g3 ♗xf3 12 ♕xf3 ♕xd4 13 g5 ♘d5 14 g6, the position is 'not easy to assess'. This is the first reason for questioning whether 6 ... ♘d7 is 'essential'.

8 ♘e5

Gaining a tempo . . .

It could be maintained that a more practical choice is 8 h5 (or 8 ♗d3) 8 ... ♗h7 9 ♗d3, taking the game into familiar variations. Yet there is no certainty that after 9 ... ♗xd3 10 ♕xd3 e6 Black will not achieve a scheme of development which is original (without ... ♘d7) and good.

8 ... ♗h7
9 ♗c4 e6 (50)

So White has utilised the defect of 7 ... ♘f6, and his pieces have taken up active posts. But what now? Fischer, for example, has written that after 10 ♕e2 ♘d5 (10 ... ♕xd4? 11 ♘xf7), with ... ♘d7 to follow, Black equalises. The following game shows that the forward position of the knight on e5 may actually prove a hindrance to White, facilitating his opponent's counterplay.

10 ♕e2 ♘d5 11 0-0 (White probably does better to castle long: 11 ♗d3 ♘d7 12 ♗d2 and 13 0-0-0) 11 ... ♘d7 (11 ... ♕xh4?

12 ♗xd5) 12 h5 ♗d6 13 ♖e1 0-0 14 a3 ♕c7 15 ♗a2 ♖ad8 16 c4 ♘5f6 17 b4 b6 18 ♗b2 c5 19 ♖ac1 cd 20 ♗xd4 ♘xe5 21 ♗xe5 ♗xe5 22 ♕xe5 ♕xe5 23 ♖xe5 ♖d2 with a favourable endgame, Liao-Campora 1982.

So we see there is more to 6 ... ♘f6 than just its shortcomings.

B

6 ... ♘d7

We now examine these continuations:
B1 7 ♗c4
B2 7 ♗d3
and also 7 ♗e2 (51). It isn't entirely clear why White should want his bishop on the a2-g8 diagonal if it isn't supported by a knight on f4. Therefore even 7 ♗e2 looks no worse than 7 ♗c4, although here too, as the following games show, the position offers few chances to White:

7 ... e6 8 0-0 (would the reader like some entertainment? Geissert-Stark, 1973, went 8 c3 ♕c7 9 ♘h4

♘gf6 10 ♗f3 ♗e7 11 ♕b3 0-0 12 ♘xg6 hg 13 h4 e5 14 h5 ♘xh5 15 ♗xh5 gh 16 ♖xh5 ♘f6 17 ♖h4 ed 18 ♕c2 ♖fe8 19 ♔f1 ♕a5 20 ♘f5 ♖ad8 21 ♘xd4 ♖xd4 22 cd – an inaccuracy – 22 ... ♕e1+) 8 ... ♘gf6, and now:

a) **9 c4** ♗e7 10 b3 0-0 11 ♘h4 ♕c7 12 ♗b2 ♖fd8 13 ♘xg6 hg 14 ♕c2 e5! 15 ♖ad1 ed 16 ♗xd4 ♗c5 17 ♗c3 ♗d6 18 b4 c5 19 b5 ♗e5 20 ♗f3 ♗xc3 21 ♕xc3 ♘f8 22 ♘e4 ♘xe4 23 ♗xe4, and a draw was agreed, Dizdarević-Kelečević, Sarajevo 1982.

b) **9 ♖e1** ♗d6 10 ♗f1 ♕c7 11 c4 0-0 12 ♗d2 c5 13 ♗c3 ♖fd8 14 ♕e2 cd 15 ♘xd4 a6 16 ♖ed1 ♘c5 (already Black's game is more active) 17 ♘f3 ♘ce4 18 ♗e1 ♘xg3 19 hg e5 20 c5 ♗xc5 21 ♕xe5 ♕b6 with initiative for Black, Spassky-Seirawan, 1982.

B1

7 ♗c4 *(52)*

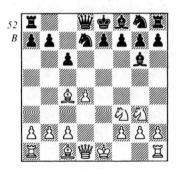

7 ... e6
8 0-0 ♘gf6

In Holmov-Kasparov, Daugavpils Otborochnii 1978, the desire for a livelier game prompted Black to choose queenside castling: 8 ... ♕c7 9 ♕e2 0-0-0 10 c3 ♘gf6 11 ♖e1 *(53)*.

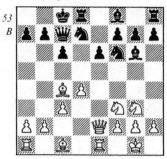

11 ... ♗e7 (one could advise Black to be more enterprising here: 11 ... ♘d5 12 a4 ♔b8 13 a5 ♗d6, or 12 ... a5 13 ♗d2 ♗d6 14 ♘e4 ♗f4, or 11 ... c5) 12 a4 ♘d5 13 a5 a6 14 ♗d2 ♖he8?! (14 ... h5 is more logical) 15 b4 f6 16 ♗d3! ♗f8 (or 16 ... ♘f8 17 ♖ab1, with c4 to follow. All Black's chances to improve have already gone) 17 ♗xg6 hg 18 ♘h4! g5 19 ♘g6 ♗d6 20 ♕g4, and Black is hard pressed.

We feel that experiments with queenside castling could be continued.

9 ♕e2

Or 9 ♘g5 – a move played by Tal. White is not averse to sacrificing a bishop with 10 ♗xe6. Tal-Petrosian, Bled 1961, went 9 ... h6 10 ♘h3 ♗d6 11 ♘f4 ♗xf4 (was there danger in 11 ... ♗h7 12 ♗xe6 fe 13 ♘xe6 ♕e7 14 ♖e1 ♔f7 ...?) 12 ♗xf4 ♘d5 13 ♗c1 (if 13 ♗d2, then 13 ... ♕b6! is good) 13 ... ♕h4 14 ♗d3 (this isn't a pawn sacrifice – 14 ... ♕xd4 15 ♗xg6 ♕xd1 16 ♗xf7+ – but nor does it 'fight for the advantage'; to that end, 14 c3 would be more to the point) 14 ... ♗xd3, with equal chances.

9	**...**	**♗e7**

Whether to develop the bishop on e7 or d6 is a matter of taste. The first edition of *ECO* has a low opinion of 9 ... ♗d6, pointing out that on 10 ♘e5 the move 10 ... 0-0 is weak on account of 11 ♗xe6 fe 12 ♘xg6 hg 13 ♕xe6+. This is true, but if castling is delayed with 10 ... ♕c7 *(54)*, the unpleasant consequences can be avoided.

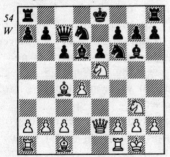

54
W

11 ♖e1 0-0, and now:
a) **12 ♗g5** ♘d5 13 ♖ad1 b5 14 ♗b3 a5 15 h4 ♗xe5 16 de h6 17 h5 ♗h7 18 ♗d2 a4 19 ♗xd5 cd 20 ♗b4 ♖fc8 21 c3 ♕c4 and Black has nothing to fear, Klovan-Suleimanov, 1979.

b) **12 ♗b3** c5 13 ♘xg6 hg 14 ♗e3 leads to transposition of moves to a situation from the game Torre-Bukić, Biel 1977. Black manoeuvred ineffectively – 14 ... ♖ad8 15 ♖ad1 ♘b6 16 dc ♗xc5 17 ♗xc5 ♕xc5 18 ♘e4 – and the position changed from harmless to unpleasant; Black will soon have an inferior endgame to defend. We would prefer 14 ... ♖ac8! (15 dc ♘xc5), and we think this position promises White nothing.

10	**♖e1**

Here 10 ♘e5 is wholly lacking in strength because of 10 ... ♘xe5 (this is just the difference between ... ♗d6 and ... ♗e7) 11 de ♘d5 12 ♖d1 ♕c7, and Black castles long.

10	**...**	**0-0**
11	**♗b3**	

Preparation for c4. After the modest 11 c3 *(55)*, White's game is active only in appearance; there is no clear plan for strengthening his position.

55
B

For example:

a) **11** ... **♕c7**, and now:

a1) **12 ♗g5** h6 13 ♗h4 ♖ad8 14 ♖ad1 ♖fe8 15 ♖d2 ♗h7 16 ♘f1 ♘e4! 17 ♗xe7 ♘xd2 18 ♗xd8 ♘xf3+ 19 ♕xf3 ♖xd8 20 ♘e3 ♘f6 21 ♗b3 c5 22 dc ♗e4 23 ♕e2 ♗d3 24 ♕f3 ♗e4 etc, Hübner-Portisch, Montreal 1979.

a2) **12 a4** c5 13 a5 (this position arose in the game by a different move order) 13 ... ♖fe8 (13 ... a6 was rather more 'solid'. Hübner aims for a sharp struggle and gets one, but his hands will be tied by his weak queenside pawns) 14 a6 ♗f8 15 ♗b5 ♖eb8 16 ♗g5 ♘d5 17 ♘e5 ♘xe5 18 de ♕b6 19 ♗c1 ba 20 ♗xa6 ♖d8 21 h4 h6 22 h5 ♗h7 23 ♘e4 ♕c7 24 f4 ♘b6 25 ♗d3 c4 26 ♗c2, and subsequently Black was on the defensive (the pawns on a7 and c4 need guarding); Kagan-Hübner, Lucerne 1979.

b) **11** ... **♘d5** 12 ♗d2 a5 13 ♖ad1 ♖e8 14 a3 ♕c7 15 ♗c1 ♘7b6 16 ♗a2 ♘f4 17 ♕f1 ♘d7 18 ♘e5 ♘xe5 19 ♖xe5 ♘d5 20 ♖ee1 ♗d6 21 ♕e2 ♗f4 22 ♗xd5 cd 23 ♕g4 ♗d6! 24 ♕e2 ♖eb8 25 ♗d2 b5, and Black outplayed his experienced opponent, Klovan-Kivlan, Riga Cup 1980.

11 ... **♘d5!**

The best move. The knight aims towards b4 (in the case of 12 c4) or f4 (after, say, 12 a3 ♕c7 13 c4 – although in this line 12 ... b5 is not

at all bad either).

| 12 | c4 | ♘b4 |
| 13 | a3 | |

13 ♖d1 would be met by 13 ... a5 14 a3 a4!

13	...	♘d3
14	♖d1	♘xc1
15	♖axc1	(56)

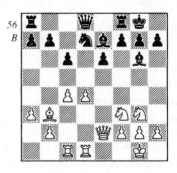

There was a time when this position was thought to favour White. But good continuations for Black are readily to hand, for example:

a) **15** ... **♕b6** 16 ♗a2 ♖fe8 (16 ... a5 17 d5) 17 ♗b1 a5 18 ♗xg6 hg 19 ♘e4 ♖ad8 20 b4 ab 21 ab ♖a8 22 ♘c5 ♘xc5 3 bc ♕c7 24 ♖b1 ♗f6 25 ♕e4 ♖a4, as in Korolev-Akopov, corres 1981. A more thematic try is 17 b4, and if 17 ... a5, then 18 c5 ♕c7 19 b5. Even so, 19 ... cb 20 ♕xb5 ♕c6 21 a4 ♖ec8, with ... b6 to follow, gives Black a comfortable position.

b) An even simpler method is **15** ... **♖e8** 16 ♗c2 a5, or 16 ♘e5 ♘xe5 17 de ♕b6 18 ♗a2 ♖ad8.

B2

7   ♗d3 *(57)*

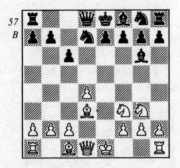

In opening manuals this move tends to be followed by a cluster of variations ending in the verdict '±'. In almost every case, the '±' sign could be exchanged for a '=' with a clear conscience, because, despite the seemingly greater freedom and activity of his pieces, White lacks efficient, concrete methods of breaching his opponent's position – even when Black handles it passively.

One of Black's slight problems in this variation is the question where the bishop exchange should take place – d3 or g6. Black exchanges on d3 when he plans to castle short and 'doesn't like having to consider whether his king will be safe if his h-pawn moves up to g6' (Gligorić). Although . . . ♗xd3 is a concession – it does, after all, lose time – practice shows that either way of exchanging bishops is acceptable.

We shall treat 7 ... e6 – followed by kingside castling – as the main line. Alternative plans for Black are as follows.

a) In Spassky-Larsen, Bugojno 1978, Black gave up a tempo with 7 ... ♕a5+ 8 ♗d2 ♕c7, so as to induce 9 ♗xg6 hg. The h-file gives chances to Black if his opponent should castle short. What are Black's prospects if White castles on the queenside? This game does not answer the question, since Larsen played it on an off day: 10 ♕e2 e6 11 ♘e4 0-0-0 12 g3 c5 13 ♗f4 ♕c6? 14 0-0-0 c4 15 ♘c3! ♘h6 16 d5 ed 17 ♖xd5 ♗c5 18 ♖hd1 f6? 19 ♖d6! ♗xd6 20 ♖xd6 ♕c5 21 ♖d5, and Black resigned.

b) In a similar situation, in the game V.Ivanov-Kuksov, Nikolayev 1978, Black coped better: 7 ... ♕c7 8 ♗xg6 hg 9 ♘e4 0-0-0 10 ♕e2 ♘h6 11 ♗g5?! f6 12 ♗d2 e5 13 0-0-0 ♘f5 14 de ♘xe5 15 g3 ♘xf3 16 ♕xf3 ♕f7 17 ♔b1 ♗e7 etc.

Games of particular interest are those where White exchanges on g6 and then castles kingside all the same, without fearing his opponent's possible threats on the h-file; and also games where Black castles long without even bringing about an opening of the h-file first. Basically, what is at issue is an attempt by Black to change a quiet (perhaps the quietest) variation of the Caro-Kann, by violent means,

into something unclear but interesting. For example:
c) Chistiakov-Furman, ½f 28th USSR Ch **7** ... ♕c7 8 0-0 ♘gf6 9 ♗xg6 (blatantly disregarding Black's chances on the rook's file! In Rovner-Zhilin, 1928, White succeeded with a *Blitzkrieg*: 9 ♖e1 e6 10 ♘g5 ♗xd3 11 ♕xd3 h6? 12 ♖xe6+ ♗e7 13 ♘f5 ♘d5 14 ♖xe7+ ♘xe7 15 ♘xg7+ 1-0. Of course, if Black had taken just a bit more care, with 11 ... ♗d6, he would have had no problems) 9 ... hg 10 ♕e2 e6 11 c4 ♗d6 12 ♗d2 ♗f4 13 ♗c3 0-0-0! 14 ♖fe1 *(58)*

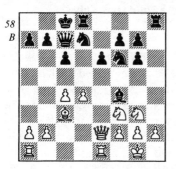

14 ... g5?! (Furman's fine opening play could have culminated effectively in 14 ... ♘g4!, with a highly promising position) 15 ♘f1! ♘h7 16 g3 ♗d6 17 d5! ed 18 cd c5 19 ♗xg7 ♖hg8 20 ♗c3 f5 21 ♖ac1 ♔b8 22 ♕e6 f4 23 ♘3d2 ♘b6 24 ♘e4! ♖ge8 25 ♘xd6! ♖xe6 26 de ♘d5 27 e7 ♘xe7 28 ♘b5 ♕d7 29 ♗e5+ ♔a8 30 ♘c7+ ♔b8 31 ♘e6+ ♔a8 32 ♘xd8 ♕xd8 33

♖xc5, and White won.

Observe that when Furman castled long, he already held both the h-file and the b8-h2 diagonal. In Dückstein-Petrosian (below), Black was bolder.
d) **7** ... **e6** 8 0-0 ♕c7 9 c4 0-0-0 10 ♗xg6 (what if White plays, say, 10 ♗e3 ♔b8 11 ♖b1 ...? Then 11 ... ♘h6 12 b4 ♘g4 13 b5 c5, or 13 c5 e5) 10 ... hg 11 ♕a4 ♔b8 12 b4 ♘h6 13 ♕b3 ♘f5 *(59)*

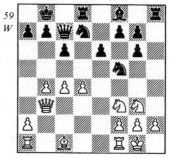

And now:
d1) **14 a4** e5! 15 de ♘xe5 16 ♘xe5 ♕xe5 17 ♗b2 ♕c7 18 c5 a5!! 19 ♖ad1 ♖xd1 20 ♖xd1 ♖h4! (Petrosian isn't playing for the 'kingside attack' – it's the weak pawns that attract him!) 21 ba ♗xc5 22 a6 b6 23 ♖e1 ♔a7 24 ♗e5 ♕d7 25 ♘e4 ♗d4 26 g3 ♗xe5! 27 gh ♘d4 28 ♕d1 ♕d5 29 ♖e3 ♘f5 30 ♖e1 ♘d4 (30 ... ♗d4!?) 31 ♕d3 f5 32 ♘g5 c5 33 ♖e3 c4 34 ♕d1 ♔xa6, and Black won, Dückstein-Petrosian, Varna 1962.
d2) **14 ♖e1** is more precise, as was shown by the game Neuronov-

Mandzhdaladze, USSR 1980. White forestalls ... e5; the game is now characterised by the players' attacks on each other's kings: 14 ... ♗e7 15 a4 ♘f8 16 ♗b2 f6 17 a5 g5 18 b5 cb 19 cb ♕d7 20 ♘xf5 ef 21 a6 g4 (21 ... b6 22 d5, and ♘d4) 22 ab! ♕xb7 (or 22 ... gf 23 b6!) 23 d5! gf 24 ♗d4 a5 25 ♖xa5! ♕c7 26 d6 ♕xa5 (26 ... ♗xd6 27 ♕a4) 27 ♗c3 ♕b6 28 dè ♖e8 29 ♗b4! ♕c7 30 g3 ♘d7 31 ♕a3!, and, finding no defence against the threats, Black resigned. A fine win by Neuronov – but couldn't Black have improved somewhere? 15 ... ♗f6 16 ♗b2 g5, for instance, is not a bad idea.

In the next two games, White refrained from exchanging on g6. e) 7 ... e6 8 0-0 ♕c7 9 b3 0-0-0 10 ♗b2 ♘gf6 11 c4 (or 11 ♘g5 ♗xd3 12 ♕xd3 ♘e5 13 ♕e2 ♘g6) 11 ... ♗d6 12 ♕e2 ♘h5! 13 ♘xh5 ♗xh5 14 h3 ♘f6?! 15 ♖ad1 ♖he8?! (surely he could have thought of something more suited to creating threats against the white king – or else tried to initiate play in the centre with 14 ... ♖he8 a move earlier, aiming for 15 ... e5) 16 ♗b1 ♗f4 17 ♖fe1 g5 18 g4 ♗g6 19 ♗xg6 hg 20 ♗c1 ♖h8 21 ♔g2 ♗xc1 22 ♖xc1 ♘xg4!? 23 hg ♖xd4 24 ♕e5! ♖xg4+ 25 ♔f1 ♖h1+ 26 ♔e2 ♖xe1+ 27 ♖xe1 ♕xe5+ 28 ♘xe5 ♖f4, and Black has no more than chances of a draw, Racine-Antom, 1977.

f) N.Zhuravlyov-Shakarov, corres 1977, went: 7 ... ♕c7 8 0-0 0-0-0 9 ♕e2 e6 10 ♖d1 ♘gf6 11 c4 ♘h5?! (imitating Antom; 11 ... e5 was probably better) 12 d5! ed 13 cd c5 14 b4 ♔b8 15 ♗xg6 hg 16 ♗g5 f6 17 ♗e3 ♘xg3 18 hg ♗d6 19 ♖ac1 ♖h5. In this position, in which White could have counted on an advantage (20 ♕c2!), the players agreed a draw.

It appears that games which would fully clarify the assessment of Black's risky plan of queenside castling have yet to be played.

The plan of castling short is more solid (but duller).

| 7 | ... | e6 |
| 8 | 0-0 | ♘gf6 |

The moves 8 ... ♗d6?! 9 ♕e2?! ♘e7?! were played in Kashdan-Taube, 1928, one of the best games in the 2nd Olympiad. The players wre not particular about accuracy in the opening, or Taube would have played 9 ... ♗xd3 10 ♕xd3 ♘gf6, and Kashdan would have preferred 9 ♖e1 (9 ... ♘gf6 10 ♘f5). We shall give the score of this game in full, since it illustrates one of the themes of the variation – the possibility, and the method, of attacking Black's king after an exchange on g6: 10 ♘g5 ♘f6 11 ♘3e4 ♘ed5 12 f4?! 0-0?! (12 ... ♗e7) 13 ♘xd6 ♕xd6?! (13 ... ♗xd3) 14 ♗xg6 hg 15 ♗d2 ♖ad8 16 ♖ad1 ♕c7 17 c4 ♘e7 18 ♗c3

♖d7 19 ♕e3 ♕b6 20 ♕h3 ♘f5 21 c5! ♕b5 22 d5! ♕xc5+ 23 ♔h1 ♘h5 24 g4 ♖xd5 25 gh gh 26 ♕xh5 ♘h6 27 ♗xg7 ♔xg7 28 ♖g1 1-0.

9 b3

It's difficult to tell whether this move is the very best or whether 9 ♖e1 or 9 c4 is more exact. In any event, White is playing without a clear notion of how to gain the advantage; for example:

a) **9 c4** ♗e7 10 ♗f4 0-0 11 ♗xg6 hg 12 ♕e2 ♕b6 13 ♖fd1 ♖fd8 14 b3 a5 15 ♘e4 ♘xe4 16 ♕xe4 a4 17 ♖ab1 ab 18 ab ♖a2, and a draw was agreed a few moves later, Spassky-Seirawan, Baden bei Wien 1980.

b) **9 ♖e1** ♗e7 10 c4 and now:

b1) **10 ... 0-0** 11 ♗xg6 hg 12 ♗f4 ♖e8 13 ♕c2 c5 14 ♖ad1 cd 15 ♘xd4 ♗b4 16 ♗d2 ♗xd2 17 ♕xd2 a6 18 b4 ♕c7 19 ♖c1 ♖ad8 20 ♕c3 ♘b6 was played in Najdorf-Kotov, Zurich C 1953. 'White has just one slight advantage – his queenside pawn majority. Black, on the other hand, has an extra pawn in the centre. This means that in an ending the chances will be on White's side, but in a complex struggle with queens on the board Black will have a perfectly viable game.' (Bronstein) b2) **10 ... ♗xd3** 11 ♕xd3 0-0 12 ♗d2 a5 (or 12 ... ♕c7 13 ♗c3 ♖ad8 14 ♕e2 ♖fe8 15 ♖ad1 c5 16 dc ♗xc5 17 b4 ♗e7 18 ♖c1 ♖c8 19

♘d2 ♗d6 with an easy game for Black, Unzicker-Golombek, 1952) 13 ♖ad1 ♗b4 14 ♘e4 ♕c7 15 ♘c3 ♖fd8 16 ♗g5 h6 17 ♗h4 ♕f4 18 a3 ♗xc3 19 ♕xc3 ♕f5 etc, Sznapik-Hort, 1980. It's plain that Hort wanted not so much to 'equalise' as to upset the stable positional balance.

9 ... ♗e7

Spassky-Karpov, match 1974, saw 9 ... ♗d6 10 ♗b2 0-0 11 ♗xg6 hg 12 c4 ♕c7 13 ♕e2 ♖fe8 14 ♘e4 (14 ♘e5 c5) 14 ... ♘xe4 15 ♕xe4 ♗e7 ('Black guards the g5 square. However, 15 ... e5 may have been better, aiming for simplification in the line 16 c5 ♗e7! – not 16 ... ♗f8 17 ♕h4 ♗e7 18 ♕g3 – 17 ♘xe5 ♘xe5 18 de ♗xc5' – Botvinnik; 'but it seems White could have kept some initiative after 15 ... e5 16 ♖ae1 ♘f6 17 ♕h4' – Karpov) 16 ♖ad1 ♖ad8 17 ♖fe1 ♕a5 18 a3 ♕f5 19 ♕e2 g5! 20 h3 ('20 d5 would have led to sharp play, for example 20 ... ed 21 cd – or 21 ♘d4 ♕e4 – 21 ... g4! 22 ♘d4 ♕xd5 23 ♕xg4 ♘f6, and Black's chances are no worse' – Karpov) 20 ... g4 21 hg ♕xg4 22 d5 ('White's position is freer, but the opening of the centre deprives him of this, his only advantage. It was worth considering 22 ♖d3' – Karpov) 22 ... cd 23 cd e5! 24 d6 ('it would have been more sensible to simplify with 24 ♕b5 ♗c5 25

♘xe5 ♘xe5 26 ♗xe5 ♗xf2+ 27 ♔xf2 ♖xe5 28 ♖xe5 ♕f4+ 29 ♔g1 ♕xe5, with approximate equality. On the other hand, playing for a draw in too straightforward a fashion, with 24 ♘xe5 ♕xe2 25 ♖xe2 ♗d6 26 ♖de1 ♘xe5 27 ♗xe5 ♗xa3, would have led to some advantage for Black' – Botvinnik) 24 ... ♗f6 25 ♘d2? ('in the endgame White will have nothing but worries, in view of the weak pawn on d6. Therefore the indicated line was 25 ♕b5 e4 26 ♘h2 ♕e6 27 ♗xf6 ♘xf6 28 ♕xb7 ♖d7 29 ♕c6 ♖ed8, with a probable draw' – Botvinnik) 25 ... ♕xe2 26 ♖xe2 ♖c8 27 ♘e4 ♗d8 28 g4 f6, and Karpov won the ending.

10	♗b2	0-0
11	♗xg6	hg
12	c4 *(60)*	

The picture is a usual one for the 7 ♗d3 variation; White's game combines outward harmony with a lack of constructive ideas, as the following examples confirm.

a) **12 ... ♕b6** 13 ♖e1 ♖fe8 14 ♕c2 c5 15 a3 a5 16 dc ♘xc5 17 ♖ab1 ♖ed8 18 ♗d4 ♕c6 19 ♕e2 ♘ce7 20 ♗b2 ♘c5 21 ♘e5 ♕e8 22 b4 ab 23 ab ♘cd7 24 ♘d3 ♖ac8 25 ♖ec1 ♘b8 26 h3 ♘c6 27 ♗a1 ♕d7 28 ♖d1 ♕c7 ½-½ Spassky-Portisch, Montreal 1979.

b) **12 ... ♕c7** 13 ♕e2 a5 14 ♖fd1 ♖fe8 15 ♘e4 a4 16 ♘xf6+ gf!? 17 h3?! (17 g3, followed by ♔g2 and h4, was more appropriate) 17 ... ♗f8 18 ♕c2 ♗g7 19 ♘d2 ab 20 ab f5 21 ♘f3 ♘f6 22 ♘e5 ♘e4 23 ♘f3 ♖ed8 24 ♖xa8 ♖xa8 25 ♘d2 ♕f4 26 ♘xe4 ♕xe4, and already White's position is difficult, Fedoruk-Kasparov, USSR 1978.

So we have seen how few problems Black faces in the variations 7 ♗c4 and 7 ♗d3 – so few that at times he is prepared to make some for himself (and for White too, of course) by castling queenside and thus intensifying the struggle.

Summary

6 f4								=/∓
6 h4	**h6**	**7 f4**						=
6 ♘f3	**♘f6**							∞
	♘d7	**7 ♗e2**						=
		7 ♗c4	**e6**	**8 0-0**	**♕c7**	**9 ♕e2**	**0-0-0**	±/∞
					♘gf6	**9 ♘g5**		=
						9 ♕e2	**♗d6**	=
							♗e7	=
		7 ♗d3	**♕c7**	**8 ♗xg6**				∞
				8 0-0	**0-0-0**			±/∞
			e6	**8 0-0**	**♘gf6**	**9 c4**		=
						9 ♖e1		=
						9 b3		=

5 6 ♘f3 ♘d7 7 h4

1	e4	c6
2	d4	d5
3	♘c3	ed
4	♘xe4	♗f5
5	♘g3	♗g6
6	♘f3	♘d7
7	h4 *(61)*	

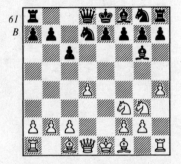

61
B

Obviously, White's purpose in advancing his rook's pawn is to unsettle the bishop on g6. After 7 ... h5 (Variation A) or 7 ... h6 8 ♗d3 (Variation B), Black is forced to exchange on d3, when White finishes his development a little more quickly. To judge from a number of games in Variation B of Chapter 4, this achievement is, in itself, insignificant.

A new factor is the weakening of the kingside, making it less of a safe haven for the kings. Whereas in Chapter 4 (Variation B2) castling long seemed virtually an act of daring, the opposite is now the case – it is now kingside castling that introduces sharpness into the position.

Nonetheless, plans involving kingside castling (for White or Black) became widespread when practice had demonstrated the solidity of Black's position after 7 ... h6 8 ♗d3 ♗xd3 9 ♕xd3 ♕c7 10 ♗d2 e6 11 0-0-0 ♘gf6 12 c4 (Variation B1), or 12 ♔b1 (B2) – and 8 ♗d3 had been supplanted by 8 h5 ♗h7 9 ♗d3. Incidentally, many positions in Variation B differ only in the placing of White's h-pawn from those we examine in later chapters. We therefore recommend to the reader a parallel study of such situations, bearing in mind that there are many ideas which are practicable whether the pawn is on h4 or h5.

From Diagram 61, Black has:
A 7 ... h5
B 7 ... h6

A

7	...	h5 *(62)*

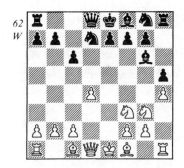

The only defect of Black's position is that the g5 square may be utilised by White to create threats.

8 ♗d3

In a game against Bikhovsky, USSR 1979, Kapengut played 8 ♗g5 *(63)*.

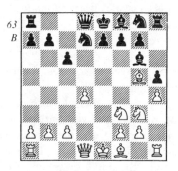

By move 17, Black already had a lost position: 8 ... ♕b6 9 ♗d3! ♗xd3 10 ♕xd3 ♘gf6 11 0-0-0 e6 12 ♘e5 ♗e7 13 ♖he1 ♘xe5 14 de ♖d8 15 ♕f3 ♖xd1+ 16 ♖xd1 ♘g4 17 ♘xh5! But this should chiefly be blamed on his inconsistency. If taking the b-pawn was dangerous

(10 ... ♕xb2 11 0-0 ♕b6 12 ♖ab1 ♕c7 13 ♖fe1), Black ought to have played 8 ... ♘gf6 at once. White would then perhaps have been unable to achieve much.

8 ... ♗xd3
9 ♕xd3 e6
10 ♗d2

Karpov-Larsen, Bugojno 1978, saw instead 10 ♘e4 ♕a5+ 11 ♗d2 ♕f5 12 0-0-0 0-0-0 13 ♗e3 ♘h6 14 ♘eg5 ♕xd3 15 ♖xd3 ♗e7 (a draw would be the rightful outcome of this situation, though the need to defend the f7 point ties Black down) 16 ♖e1 ♖hf8 17 ♘h3 ♘g4 18 ♗g5 ♖fe8 19 ♗xe7 ♖xe7 20 ♘fg5, etc. In the end Larsen lost this game, although it was a long time before the balance was seriously upset.

10 ... ♘gf6
11 0-0-0 ♕c7 *(64)*

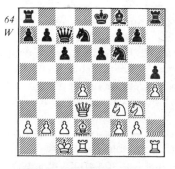

And now, in Matulović-Hort, Sombor 1968, White played 12 ♘e4, on the lines of Karpov-Larsen. There followed: 12 ...

♘xe4 13 ♕xe4 ♗e7 14 ♔b1 ♘f6?!
(Hort condemns the knight manoeuvre to g4, considering 14 ...
0-0-0 to be more accurate) 15 ♕e2
♘g4 16 ♘g5 ♗d6 17 c4 0-0-0 18
♗c3 ♖he8 19 ♖he1 ♕d7 20 g3.
Here too White's gains look
insignificant, yet the appearance is
deceptive; Black's game is cramped
and passive.

Boleslavsky considered 12 ♘g5
more aggressive, preventing castling.
'Then 12 ... ♗d6 is bad because of
13 ♖he1, with threats of 14 ♖xe6+
and 14 ♘f5. The only move Black
can play is 12 ... ♘b6, which is met
by 13 ♘e2 ♗d6 (if 13 ... 0-0-0, then
14 ♗f4 ♗d6 15 ♗xd6 ♖xd6 16
♕a3, with the double threat of
17 ♘xf7 and 17 ♕xa7) 14 c4 0-0-0
15 ♔b1 c5 16 b3, and Black's
position is unsatisfactory: 16 ... cd
17 ♘xd4 ♗c5 18 ♗c3, or 16 ...
♘g4 17 ♕f3'.

We don't entirely agree with the
final verdict (it's too severe), but
after 16 b3 White does, of course,
have the better chances.

To deprive his opponent of the
whole possibility of ... h5, White
need only alter the move order to 6
h4 h6 7 ♘f3, since 6 ... h5 7 ♘h3! is
unacceptable for Black. (7 ... e5
would lead to variations similar to
those examined in Chapter 2 after
6 h4 h6 7 ♘h3 e5.)

B

| 7 | ... | h6 |

| 8 | ♗d3 | ♗xd3 |
| 9 | ♕xd3 (65) | |

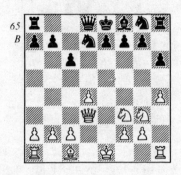

65
B

| 9 | ... | ♕c7 |

This queen move, preventing 10
♗f4, used to be thought essential.
The newest approach (see the
next chapter) dispenses with it.
That is understandable; if Black
plans to castle short (which *is* 'the
newest approach'), it makes little
difference to him whether White's
bishop is placed on f4 or d2; while
there are other squares for the
queen than c7.

In practice, this old-fashioned
line with 8 ♗d3 has hardly ever
come up against the currently
fashionable treatment. Here is
perhaps the only example: 9 ... e6
10 ♗d2 ♘gf6 11 0-0-0 ♗e7 12
♔b1 c5 13 ♖he1 0-0 14 ♘e4 ♖c8
15 dc ♘xc5 16 ♘xf6+ ♗xf6 17
♕xd8 ♖fxd8 18 ♗e3 ♖xd1+ 19
♖xd1 a6 20 c3 ♔f8 etc, Hort-
Larsen, Buenos Aires 1980.

Of course, a game in which
White was 'not trying' doesn't

mean much. We would again refer the reader to the next chapter, where analogous cases will help him to understand situations that could arise from the line now under discussion.

Let us now turn to some older games where White answered 9 ... e6 with 10 ♗f4 (*66*). From just such games it was formerly concluded that playing the queen to c7 is indispensable for Black.

10 ... ♘gf6 11 0-0-0, and now:

a) **11 ... ♘d5** (in our day, Black would choose either 11 ... ♗e7 here, or 10 ... ♕a5+ last move) 12 ♗d2 b5 (we may regard this as forced, since 12 ... ♕c7 13 c4 ♘f4 14 ♕e4 is bad for Black, while after 13 ... ♘gf6 he simply loses a tempo in comparision with normal lines) 13 ♔b1 ♗e7 (or 13 ... ♗d6 14 ♘e4 ♘7f6 15 ♖hg1 ♖b8 16 g4 b4 17 ♘xd6+ ♕xd6 18 g5 ♘d7 19 ♖de1, and Black's king is in danger, Matanović-Wade, Opatija 1953) 14 ♘h5 ♗f6 15 g4 g6 16 ♘xf6+ ♘5xf6 17 g5 hg 18 ♗xg5 ('a superficial move; 18 hg ♘h5 19

♕e4 was considerably better, giving White strong pressure' – Yudovich) 18 ... ♕c7 19 ♘e5 (he should have played 19 ♖he1, and when appropriate c4 – Yudovich) 19 ... ♘xe5 20 de ♘d5 21 ♖he1? (21 c4) 21 ... ♖b8 22 ♕f3 ♖h5 23 ♖e4 b4, Suetin-Kasparian, USSR 1952. Black stands quite well here, but the position he had a few moves ago is one which nobody will want to have again.

b) **11 ... ♕a5** 12 ♔b1 0-0-0 13 c4 ♗e7 14 ♕c2 ♖de8 15 ♖d3 a6 16 ♖hd1 ♗d8 17 d5! e5 18 dc bc 19 ♖a3 ♕c7 20 ♗e3 with a won position, Matanović-Germek, Yugoslavia 1961.

10 ♗d2 e6
11 0-0-0

Against Donner, Varna 1962, Fischer played 11 c4 ♘gf6 12 ♗c3 ('the whole idea is to prevent Black from swapping bishops' – Fischer. The ex-World Champion is referring to 12 0-0-0 ♗d6 13 ♘e4 ♗f4) 12 ... a5! 13 0-0!? ♗d6 ('the logical continuation was 13 ... ♗b4. If anyone's kingside is weak, it is White's, not Black's' – Mednis) 14 ♘e4 ('Tal suggested 14 d5!? mixing it up, but 14 ... ♗xg3! holds: 15 fg cd 16 cd ♘xd5 17 ♗xg7 ♖g8 18 ♕h7 ♘7f6 19 ♗xf6 ♘xf6 20 ♕xh6 ♕xg3 21 ♕d2 =' – Fischer) 14 ... ♘xe4 15 ♕xe4 0-0, and Fischer judges the position to be level.

11 ... ♘gf6

A position known long ago . . .
White's main choices are:
B1 12 c4
B2 12 ♔b1
and also the following:
a) **12 ♖he1 0-0-0** (67)

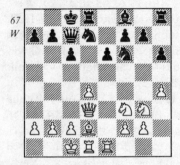

And now:
a1) Lasker-Lee, London 1899!,
continued **13 ♕b3 ♗d6 14 ♘e2
♘g4** (14 ... ♘e4!? 15 ♗e3 ♘df6)
15 ♖f1 ♘df6 16 ♕a4 ♔b8 17 c4
♕e7? 18 ♘c3 ♕c7 19 g3 ♕c8 20 b4
e5 21 de ♘xe5 22 ♗e3!, and
already Black is defenceless.
a2) **13 ♕e2 ♘d5!? 14 ♘e5 ♘xe5 15
de ♗e7 16 h5** (16 ♕g4 h5! 17 ♕xg7
♗xh4 – not 17 ... ♘c3? 18 ♕xf7! –
18 ♘e4 ♖dg8 19 ♘d6+ ♔b8 20
♕xf7 ♕xf7 21 ♘xf7 ♖h7 22 ♘d6
♖xg2, with the better chances for
Black – Botvinnik) 16 ... ♖he8 17
♕g4 ♗f8 18 f4 c5! 19 ♘e4 (as to 19
c4 ♘b4 20 ♗xb4 cb, see the game
Spassky-Botvinnik in Chapter 11,
Variation A – where a similar
position arose) 19 ... c4! 20 ♕f3
♔b8 21 g4 b5 22 a3 a5 23 c3 ♖d7!

24 ♗e3 b4 25 ab ab 26 ♗d4 ♕a5,
Grigoriev-Panov, Moscow Ch
1928. Grigoriev has handled the
game ineffectually, and as a result
we receive a vivid illustration of
what Black is dreaming of in such
positions.
a3) **13 ♔b1 c5** (13 ... ♗d6 14 ♘e4
♘xe4 15 ♕xe4 ♖he8 is also good)
14 c3?! (14 c4; 14 dc) 14 ... ♗d6 15
♘e4 ♘xe4 16 ♕xe4 ♘f6 17 ♕e2 c4
18 ♗e3 ♔b8 19 ♘d2 ♖c8,
Rabinovich-Makogonov, USSR
1939; here again Black's dreams
come true.
b) Chigorin-Popiel, Hanover 1902!,
saw **12 ♘e4 0-0-0 13 g3** (a similar
position, only with pawn on h5
improving White's possibilities,
is examined in detail in Chapter 9,
Variations A and B) 13 ... ♘xe4 14
♕xe4 ♗d6 15 ♖he1 ♖he8 16 ♔b1
♘f6 (16 ... c5!?) 17 ♕e2 ♕b6?!
(17 ... c5) 18 c4 c5 19 ♖c1! ♔b8 20
♘e5! ♖e7 21 ♘d3! ♔a8 22 ♔a1
(22 b4!) 22 ... ♕c7 23 b4! ♕d7,
and now, instead of 24 ♖ed1? cd
(as played), White could have won
with 24 ♘xc5 (24 ... ♗xc5 25 dc
♕xd2 26 ♖ed1).
c) **12 ♕e2 0-0-0** (nowadays 12 ... c5
is thought to be simplest; compare
Chapter 10) 13 ♘e5 ♘xe5 (and
here, ideas based on 13 ... ♘b6 or
even 13 ... ♘b8 might be suitable;
compare Chapters 11 and 12) 14
de ♘d7 15 f4 ♗e7 16 h5 ♘c5, and
the chances are probably level

(Black's extra tempo compared with Chapter 11, Variation A, must be worth something!), Rossolimo-Eliskases, 1949.

B1

12   c4

The set-up which White envisages with this move will prove unrealisable (Black will manage to turn the position of the king on c1 to his own account); White should, therefore, initiate the same plan with 12 ♔b1 as in Variation B2.

12   ...   b5!? *(68)*

The most resolute answer to 12 c4; Black attempts to seize the initiative. Alternatively:

a) '12 ... ♗d6! 13 ♘e4 (if 13 ♘e2 0-0-0 14 ♔b1 e5 =) 13 ... ♗f4! leads to immediate simplifications' (Fischer). But simplification isn't the same as equalisation. (Compare Chapter 8, Variation A, although it must be admitted that with the pawn on h4 White has less chance of keeping up the pressure.)

b) 12 ... 0-0-0 (This allows White to make good his 'mistake' of 12 c4, and transpose into Variation B2 with 12 ♔b1. But he persists in his error) 13 ♗c3, and now:

b1) Fischer-Steinmeyer, US Ch 1963-4, concluded: **13 ... ♕f4+?** 14 ♔b1 ♘c5? 15 ♕c2 ♘ce4 16 ♘e5! ♘xf2 17 ♖df1!, and Black resigned! 'On 17 ... ♕xg3 18 ♖xf2 ♕e3 19 ♖e2 ♕f4 20 ♘xf7 wins at

least the exchange' (Fischer).

b2) **13 ... ♗d6!** 14 ♘e4 ♗f4+ 15 ♔b1 ♘e5! 16 ♘xe5 ♗xe5. By this manoeuvre Black has achieved the favourable exchange of the knight on d7 for the one on f3. A game Szabo-Barcza, Leningrad 1967, continued: 17 ♕e3 ♘xe4 18 de (18 ♕xe4 is weaker; 18 ... ♗f6, followed by ... ♖d7 and ... ♖hd8, bombarding the pawn on d4) 18 ... ♖xd1+ 19 ♖xd1 ♖d8! (had White played 15 ♔c2, Black would not have this opportunity. But that would not matter; after 18 ... ♘xc3 19 ♕xc3 ♖d1 20 ♖xd1 ♖d8, it is hard to imagine the game ending in anything but a draw) 20 ♖d4?! ♘xc3+ 21 ♕xc3 c5! 22 ♖xd8+ ♕xd8 23 g3 ♕d1+ 24 ♕c1 ♕e2 25 ♕f4 ♕d1+ 26 ♕c1 ♕d3+! 27 ♔a1 ♕e2 28 f4 ♕f2 with winning chances, which Barcza did not let slip.

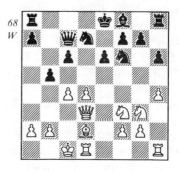

68
W

13   cb

In our view, White ought to play 13 c5 here. This possibility is discussed in detail in Chapter 8, Variation A.

13 ... cb+

14 ♔b1

Thanks to 12 ... b5, Black has gained control of the d5 point. This plan has, however, been condemned in all the books, on the basis of a game Smyslov-Kasparian, Parnu 1947: 14 ... ♕b7 15 ♖he1 ♗e7 16 ♖c1 a6 17 ♘e5 ♘xe5 18 de ♖d8 19 ♕e2 ♘d5 20 ♕g4! ♔f8 21 ♘e4 etc.

But wouldn't 17 ... 0-0 have given Black a solid position?

Besides, 14 ... ♗d6! as played in a correspondence game Meyer-Shakarov, USSR 1979, is highly promising: 15 ♘e4 ♘xe4 16 ♕xe4 0-0 17 ♘g5!? (trying to regain the lost initiative; instead 17 ♖c1 ♘f6! 18 ♕d3 ♕b7 favours Black) 17 ... hg!? (a similar reply was 17 ... ♘f6 18 ♕f3 ♖ac8, with the better chances) 18 hg ♖fc8 19 ♖c1 ♕d8 20 ♕h7+ ♔f8 21 ♖ce1 ♔e7! (Black would lose after 21 ... ♕b6? 22 d5 e5 23 ♕f5 ♔e7 24 g6, or 21 ... ♘b6? 22 ♖xe6! fe 23 ♕h8+ ♔f7 24 g6+) 22 d5 (or 22 ♕xg7 ♕g8 23 ♕h6 ♘b6) 22 ... ♕g8 23 de fe 24 ♕d3 ♘c5 25 ♕d4 ♕f7 26 ♖h3 ♖c6 27 f4 ♖h8! 28 ♖f3 (28 ♖xh8? ♕f5+ 29 ♔a1 ♘b3+ is only too obvious, but interposing an attack on the knight with 28 b4 would also be refuted: 28 ... ♖xh3 29 bc ♕g6+ 30 ♔b2 ♗xc5 31 ♗b4 ♖d3,

or 30 f5 ♕xf5+ 31 ♔b2 ♗e5! 32 ♖xe5 ♖d3) 28 ... ♕f5+ 29 ♔a1 ♔f7 30 ♖c3 ♖hc8 31 g4 ♕d5 32 g6+ ♔g8 (not 32 ... ♔xg6? 33 ♖xe6+!) 33 ♕xd5 ed, and Black won.

So 12 c4 allows Black good drawing chances with 12 ... ♗d6 13 ♘e4 ♗f4, a fully satisfactory game with 12 ... 0-0-0 13 ♗c3 ♗d6, or the hope of something more with 12 ... b5.

B2

12 ♔b1 (69)

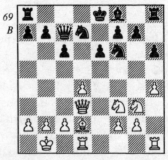

As we have said, White's plans involve 13 c4 and 14 ♗c3 – i.e. the build-up which he didn't manage to achieve with 12 c4.

12 ... 0-0-0

12 ... c5!? is also possible; compare Chapter 8, Variation C.

13 c4 c5

Also 13 ... ♗d6 14 ♘e4 ♘xe4 15 ♕xe4. Black has never yet managed to find anything after 15 ... ♖he8 16 ♗c3, so instead he usually plays 15 ... ♘f6 16 ♕e2 c5 (by playing ... c5 on his thirteenth,

Black sometimes gets this position with himself to move). A game Timoshenko-Bagirov, Lvov 1977, continued: 17 ♗c3 cd 18 ♗xd4!? (if 18 ♘xd4, then not 18 ... ♗c5? 19 ♘b5 ♕b6 20 b4!, but 18 ... a6, when 19 ♘b3?! ♕c6 20 g3 ♗c7 equalises, though 19 ♘f3!? gives prospects of initiative) 18 ... ♗c5 19 ♗xc5 ♕xc5 20 ♘e5 ♕c7 21 g4 ♖xd1+ 22 ♖xd1 ♖d8 23 ♖xd8+ ♔xd8 24 h5, and the endgame (though of a type that is generally drawn) is unpleasant for Black to defend.

14 ♗c3

14 ♕e2 looks illogical, but is not without its subtleties. The point is that on 14 ♗c3, Black normally replies 14 ... cd 15 ♘xd4 a6. In this position, White would like to have his queen on e2. His bishop, on the other hand, could go to a5 (its usual destination) from either c3 or d2.

So, 14 ♕e2 and now:

a) **14 ... cd** (14 ... a6? 15 ♘e5) 15 ♘xd4 a6 16 ♘b3! ♗d6 (if 16 ... ♘c5, then 17 ♗a5 ♖xd1+ 18 ♖xd1 b6 19 ♕f3 is disturbing) 17 c5 (or 17 ♗a5!? b6 18 ♗c3 ♗xg3 19 fg ♕xg3 20 c5) 17 ... ♗xg3 18 ♗a5 ♕e5 19 ♕c2 ♖de8 20 c6 ♘b8! 21 cb+ ♔xb7 22 fg ♖c8 23 ♕f2, and Black's king position is insecure, Parma-Vukić, Yugoslav Ch 1972.

b) Black should, of course, play **14 ... ♗d6** 15 ♘e4 ♘xe4 16 ♕xe4 ♘f6. If 17 ♕e2, Black has gained a tempo in comparison with Timoshenko-Bagirov, above. Further:

b1) **17 ... ♖he8** 18 ♗c3 ♘g4!? is interesting, e.g: 19 dc ♗xc5 20 ♘d4 h5 21 f3 (or 21 ♘b5 ♕b6 22 f3 ♘e3) 21 ... ♘f2! 22 ♕xf2 e5, etc.

b2) A dubious endgame results from **17 ... ♕c6?!** 18 ♘e5 ♗xe5 19 de ♕e4+ 20 ♕xe4 ♘xe4 21 ♗e3, when the knight is in danger from the threatened 22 g4, for example: 21 ... ♖xd1+ 22 ♖xd1 b6 23 g4, or 21 ... h5 22 ♔c2 b6 23 ♖xd8+ ♖xd8 24 ♖h3.

b3) **17 ... cd** 18 ♘xd4 a6 19 ♗c3 *(70)*.

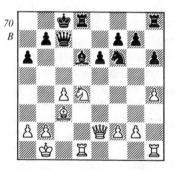

By a different move order, we have arrived at a position from Smyslov-Botvinnik, 3rd game of the return World Championship match, 1958. The continuation was 19 ... ♖d7! (Botvinnik has written that this move 'defuses the chief positional threat of ♘f3-e5', since 'in the event of 20 ♘f3 Black

completes his development, and
equalises, by 20 ... ♖hd8! The
move played has only one drawback:
the advance c5-c6 becomes unpleasant, since the rook will be
under attack') 20 ♖c1! ♕c5 21
♘b3 ♕f5+ 22 ♖c2 ♗c7 23 c5 ('the
threat of c5-c6 cannot now be
prevented, but the d5 square
comes under Black's control' –
Botvinnik) 23 ... ♖d5 24 c6 ♗b6
25 ♘d2! (now Black has to make
counter-measures against the threatened 26 ♘c4 ♗c7 27 ♘e3; the
continuation 25 ... ♕xf2 26 ♘c4
♖hd8 27 a4 is clearly no good for
him) 25 ... ♕d3 26 ♘c4 ♗c7 27
♕xd3 ♖xd3 28 ♘e5? (a blunder;
better 28 cb+ ♔xb7 29 ♗e5 ♗xe5
30 ♘xe5 ♖d5 31 f4 ♘d7! 32 ♖hc1
♘xe5 33 ♖c7+ ♔b6 34 fe, upon
which Botvinnik gives the following
sample variation: 34 ... ♖f8 35 b4
♔b5 36 ♖b7+ ♔a4 37 ♖c5 ♖xc5
38 bc ♖c8 39 ♖xf7 ♖xc5, with a
draw) 28 ... ♖xc3, and Black won.

So the essential choice for Black
is between (b1) and (b3).

14 ... cd

15 ♘xd4

On 15 ♗xd4, various writers
concur in giving 15 ... ♗c5 16 ♘e4
♗xd4 17 ♕xd4 ♔b8 =, but of
course Black could also vary –
16 ... ♘xe4 17 ♕xe4 ♘f6.

15 ... a6

15 ... ♘e5 16 ♕e2 ♘xc4? does
not work. On the other hand, 15 ...

♘c5 16 ♕e2 ♘a4! 17 ♘b5 ♘xc3+
18 ♘xc3 ♖xd1+ 19 ♖xd1 a6 20 h5
♗e7 21 ♘ge4 ♖d8 gave Black an
easy game in Padevsky-Barcza,
Kecskemet 1966. It's hard to
understand why Padevsky rejected
16 ♕c2! a6 17 ♘f3. For example,
after 17 ... ♗d6 18 b4 ♘cd7 (18 ...
♗xg3 19 bc) 19 ♘e4 ♘xe4 20
♕xe4 ♘f6 21 ♕e2, White has the
initiative.

16 ♘f3

16 ♕e2 could lead to a position
we have examined already: 16 ...
♗d6 17 ♘e4 ♘xe4 18 ♕xe4 ♘f6
19 ♕e2 (see Smyslov-Botvinnik,
above). But Black also has better
lines, for example 18 ... ♘c5 19
♕c2 ♗e5 20 ♖he1 ♗f6 21 g3 ♖d7!,
Unzicker-Porath, Munich 1958;
'and the game quickly ended in a
draw, seeing that 22 b4 would fail
to 22 ... ♖hd8' (Botvinnik). Also
17 ... ♗e5!? or 16 ... ♘c5!?.

In Spassky-Portisch, Budapest
1961, Black had a perfectly sound
position after 16 ♘b3 ♘c5 17 ♕f3
♗e7 18 ♗a5 ♖xd1+ 19 ♖xd1 ♕e5
20 ♗c3 ♕c7. However, in a game
between the same opponents two
decades later (1980), Portisch
rejected ... ♘c5 in favour of an
immediate ... ♗e7 (see Chapter 8,
Variation B).

16 ... ♗c5

Here 16 ... ♘c5 is bad: 17
♕xd8+ ♕xd8 18 ♖xd8+ ♔xd8
19 ♘e5!

17 ♕e2 ♗d6

According to *ECO*, in Sokolov-Sušić, Yugoslavia 1965, Black solved the problem differently: '17 ... ♘g4 18 ♘e4 ♘df6 19 ♘xf6 gf 20 ♘d4 ♖hg8 21 b4 ♕e5 ='. But even the simple 19 ♘xc5 ♕xc5 20 ♗d4 secures White the better chances.

18 ♘e4 *(71)*

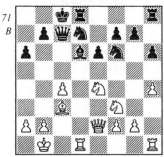

Spassky-Petrosian, 1st game, World Championship match (1966), now continued: 18 ... ♗e7 (on 18 ... ♘xe4 19 ♕xe4 ♘f6 20 ♕e2 ♕c6, *ECO* recommends 21 ♖de1 ♗c7 22 ♘d4 and judges the position to be in White's favour) 19 ♘xf6 (in an earlier game against Matulović, in 1964, Spassky obtained a plus after 19 ♖he1

♘xe4 20 ♕xe4 ♗f6 21 ♕e3 ♗xc3 22 ♕xc3 ♘f6 23 ♖xd8+ ♖xd8 24 ♘e5 ♘e8 25 c5!, achieving the win in a long endgame. Among a number of possibilities for improving Black's play, we would point to 24 ... h5!? or 19 ... ♕f4!? 20 ♘xf6 ♗xf6 21 ♗xf6 ♘xf6 22 ♘e5 ♘d7) 19 ... ♗xf6 20 ♗xf6 ♘xf6 (Boleslavsky considered 20 ... gf stronger, with ... ♘e5 to follow) 21 ♘e5 ♖xd1+ 22 ♖xd1 ♖d8 23 ♖xd8+ ♔xd8 24 ♕d3+ (or 24 h5 ♔e7 25 g4 ♘d7) 24 ... ♔e7 25 ♕d4 h5! 26 a3 ♘d7! 27 ♘xd7 ♕xd7, with a drawn endgame (28 ♕xg7? ♕d3+).

The material we have examined shows that, given the plan which White has chosen here, his slim chances of advantage would be substantially increased by having his pawn on h5. We have not analysed 12 ... c5 (probably the best reply to 12 ♔b1) – there are no practical examples. But the reader can learn a lot from the essentially similar Variation C in Chapter 8.

Summary

7 ...	h5					±
	h6	8 ♗d3 ♗xd3 9 ♕xd3 e6	10 ♗d2			=
			10 ♗f4 ♘gf6 11 0-0-0 ♘d5			±
			(11 ... ♗e7, 10 ... ♕a5+ – cf. 8 h5)			
		♕c7 10 ♗d2 e6	11 0-0-0 ♘gf6			

and now:

12 ♖he1					=
12 ♘e4					=
12 ♕e2					=
12 c4	♗d6				±/=
	0-0-0 13 ♗c3				=
	(13 ♔b1! – cf. 12 ♔b1)				
	b5 13 cb				=/+
	13 c5				∞
12 ♔b1	c5 (cf. 8 h5)				
	0-0-0 13 c4	♗d6			±
		c5 14 ♕e2 cd			±
			♗d6		=
		14 ♗c3 cd	15 ♗xd4		=
			15 ♘xd4 ♘c5		±
				a6 16 ♕e2	=
				16 ♘b3	=
				16 ♘f3 ♘c5	±
					♗c5	=

6   8 h5 with 10 ... e6

1	e4	c6
2	d4	d5
3	♘c3	de
4	♘xe4	♗f5
5	♘g3	♗g6
6	♘f3	♘d7
7	h4	h6
8	h5	♗h7
9	♗d3	♗xd3
10	♕xd3	e6 *(72)*

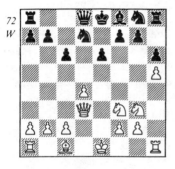

72
W

The present-day fashion. Instead of 10 ... ♕c7 followed by ... 0-0-0, which used to be thought essential, Black prepares to castle short. This livens up the play, although the cost is a less secure king position (g4-g5 is threatened).

Games played with this line fall into three categories. In Variation A, White continues just as if Black had played 10 ... ♕c7, that is with 11 ♗d2. In B1, White tries to profit from the active placing of his queen's bishop after 11 ♗f4 ♘gf6 12 0-0-0. In B2, Black answers 11 ♗f4 by checking with 11 ... ♕a5+, ready to transpose into the more usual lines after 12 ♗d2 ♕c7; but White rejects this with 12 c3. The choices, then, are:

A 11 ♗d2
B 11 ♗f4

In Spassky-Karpov, match 1974, White developed his bishop by 11 b3 ♘gf6 12 ♗b2. Considering Black's reaction – 12 ... ♕a5+! 13 ♗c3 (or 13 c3 ♗a3) 13 ... ♗b4. we may take it that the f nk development of White's queen's bishop makes more sense if Black has played 10 ... ♕c7.

A

11	♗d2	♘gf6
12	0-0-0 *(73)*	

12 ...   ♗e7

Also:

a) As a game between high-ranking International Grandmasters showed, opening up the position with one's king uncastled is bad. Kavalek-Hübner, Montreal 1979, went: **12 ... c5?** 13 ♖he1 ♗e7 (not 13 ... cd 14 ♖xe6+!) 14 d5! ♘xd5 15 ♖xe6? (succumbing to the temptation . . .) 15 ... fe 16 ♕g6+ ♔f8 17 ♕xe6 ♘c7 18 ♕f5+ ♘f6 19 ♘e5 ♕c8 20 ♘g6+ ♔f7 21 ♘xh8+ ♕xh8 22 ♖e1 ♖e8, and the position favours Black. However, 15 ♘f5! would have secured White a considerable plus; Hübner gives 15 ... 0-0 16 ♘xe7+ ♘xe7 17 ♗xh6, or 15 ... ♔f8 16 c4 ♘5f6 17 ♘xe7 ♕xe7 18 ♗f4 ♔g8 19 ♗d6.

b) **12 ... ♕b6** (in the working out of the whole system with 10 ... e6, Larsen, who is constantly introducing something new into Black's play, has earned special credit. He started by bringing the queen out to b6) 13 ♘e5 (in Tatai-Larsen,

1971, 13 c4 was played; see Chapter 7, Variation A) 13 ... ♗e7 14 f4 ♖d8 15 ♕c4 ♘xe5 16 de ♖d4! 17 ♕b3 ♕xb3 18 ab ♘g4, with equal chances, Andersson-Larsen, 1971. Improvements to have been suggested for White are 14 ♖he1 ♖d8 (14 ... 0-0 15 ♘f5) 15 ♕e2, threatening ♘xf7; and 13 ♕e2!? Perhaps it was thinking about this game that gave Larsen the idea of leaving the queen on d8, where it defends the king's bishop and thus ensures that Black can castle (the threat of ♘f5 is removed).

The 'idea' of castling kingside was, of course, of small value in itself. It was necessary to think up, and elaborate, a scheme of play in which Black's unsafe king position would not be the prime factor. In this connexion Larsen did a great deal.

13   ♘e4 *(76)*

Alternatively:

a) **13 ♖he1 a5!?** *(74)*

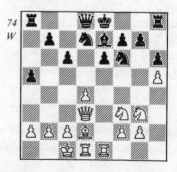

A recent idea of Larsen's. Everyone had somehow got used to thinking that in such positions Black 'must' play the 'freeing' move ... c5. Yet it turns out that another policy, relying on the firmness of Black's central outposts and the lack of concrete threats from the white side, is also possible. After 14 ♕e2 0-0, play can continue:

a1) **15 ♔b1 ♕b6** 16 ♘e5 a4 17 c4? a3 18 b3 ♕xd4 19 ♗b4 ♕xe5, and Black won a pawn; Hübner-Larsen, Tilburg 1980.

a2) In Glatt-Burger, Budapest 1982, White sacrificed a pawn with 15 ♘f5!?, reckoning on 15 ... ef 16 ♕xe7 ♘xh5 17 ♘h4. When Black replied instead 15 ... ♗b4, there followed: 16 ♘xh6+!? gh 17 c3. Burger declined to test the strength of White's attack (after 17 ... ♗e7 18 ♗xh6 ♖e8 19 ♘e5), played 17 ... ♖e8 (threatening ... ♗f8), which forced 18 cb ab. The position of both kings is now shaky, but it was Black who triumphed: 19 ♘e5 ♖xa2 20 ♗xh6?! (20 ♗xb4?!) 20 ... b3! 21 ♘xd7? (counting on 21 ... ♕xd7? 22 ♕e5. On 21 ♕d3 ♖a1+ 22 ♔d2 ♕a5+ 23 ♔e2 ♘xe5 24 ♕g3+ ♘eg4 25 ♖xa1 ♕b5+, as indicated by Byrne and Mednis, the situation would remain unclear) 21 ... ♕a5!! 22 ♘xf6+ ♔h8, with unanswerable threats.

b) Grünfeld-Lobron, Lugano 1981, saw **13 ♕e2 a5!?** 14 ♘e5 a4 15 f4 a3 16 b3 0-0 *(75)*

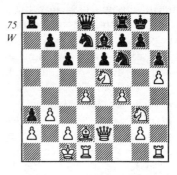

17 f5 ♘xe5! 18 de ♘d5 19 ♔b1 (19 f6 ♗xf6!) 19 ... ♕b6 20 c4 ♕d4 21 ♗e1 ♘c3+ 22 ♗xc3 ♕xc3 23 ♖d3 ♕a5 24 f6?! gf 25 ef ♗xf6 26 ♘e4 ♗g7 27 c5 f5 28 ♘d6 ♕xc5 29 ♖c1 ♕a7 30 ♕xe6+ ♔h8, and White's king is in greater danger.

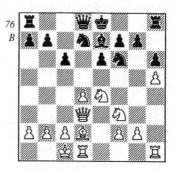

13   ...   ♘xe4

It's evident that the main idea of 13 ♘e4 consisted in 14 ♘xf6+ ♘xf6 15 ♘e5, with ♕g3 to follow, aiming at the point g7. For that reason, ... a5-a4 looks out of place

here. The alternatives are:
a) **13 ... ♕b6?!** 14 ♘xf6+ ♘xf6 15
♘e5 ♖d8 16 ♕g3, Hübner-
Larsen, Bugojno 1982; now Black
could find nothing better than
16 ... ♔f8.
b) **13 ... a5?!** 14 ♔b1 (avoiding the
attack on the a-pawn after 14
♘xf6+ ♘xf6 15 ♘e5 ♕d5) 14 ...
♘xe4 (better late than never?
That isn't always true. In the
subsequent play, the queen sortie
to d5 will no longer gain a tempo.
Of course, 14 ... a4 is met by
15 ♘xf6+ ♘xf6 16 ♘e5) 15 ♕xe4
♘f6 16 ♕d3 ♕d5 17 ♖de1!
(directed against 17 ... ♕e4) 17 ...
b5 18 ♘e5 0-0 19 g4 c5 20 g5 c4
(Hort gives question marks to
17 ... b5 and 20 ... c4, but we won't
do likewise, since after 17 ♖de1
we already don't like Black's
position) 21 ♕g3! hg (or 21 ...
♘e4 22 ♖xe4 ♕xe4 23 ♖g1) 22
♗xg5 ♘e4 23 ♖xe4 ♗xg5 24
♕xg5 f6 25 h6! 1-0 Hort-
Chandler, Wijk aan Zee 1982.
c) With Black against Kavalek
(1980), Hort himself simply castled;
after **13 ... 0-0** 14 ♘xf6+ ♘xf6 15
♔b1, he solved his problems by
means of the old-fashioned 15 ...
c5. There followed: 16 ♕e2 cd 17
♗e3 ♗c5 18 ♗xd4 ♗xd4 19 ♖xd4
♕b6 20 g4 ♖fd8 21 c3 ♖d5 22
♖xd5 ♘xd5 23 ♔a1 ♖d8 24 ♘d4
♕c7, with a good game for Black.

14 ♕xe4 ♘f6

15 ♕e2
In Kavalek's opinion, 15 ♕d3
♕d5 16 c4 ♕e4 17 ♕b3 is worth
trying for White.

15 ... ♕d5
16 c4 (77)

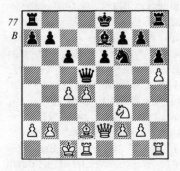

Play can continue:
a) **16 ... ♕f5** 17 ♘e5 c5 18 g4 ♕e4
19 ♕xe4 ♘xe4 20 ♗e3 ♖c8 21
♔b1 (21 d5!?) 21 ... 0-0 22 f3 ♘f6,
Karpov-Larsen, Linares 1981;
Larsen drew this somewhat inferior
ending.
b) **16 ... ♕e4!** 17 ♖de1 (Kavalek
recommends answering 17 ♕f1
with 17 ... ♘g4, and 17 ♗e3 with
17 ... ♘g4 18 ♘d2 ♕f5) 17 ... ♕xe2
18 ♖xe2 0-0 19 ♘e5 ♖fd8 (we
agree with Kavalek that the need
to defend the pawns on d4 and h5
means that White's position is
worse) 20 ♗c3 ♖ac8! (intending
21 ... b5), and Black holds the
initiative; Ivanović-Kavalek, 1982.
B
11 ♗f4
Now Black can choose between:

B1 11 ... ♘gf6
B2 11 ... ♕a5+

In Karpov-Larsen, Tilburg 1982, the Danish Grandmaster played 11 ... ♗b4+ 12 c3 ♗e7, and answered 13 ♘e4 with 13 ... ♘gf6!? (you would rather have expected 13 ... ♘df6) 14 ♘d6+ ♗xd6 15 ♗xd6 ♕a5! The queen attacks the pawns on h5 and a2, giving White problems about castling, yet Black's important bishop has been 'sacrificed' . . . The surprise, clearly, had such an effect on the World Champion that seven moves later his position was not a pleasant sight: 16 ♗b4 ♕c7 17 ♗a3 b5 18 ♕e2? (18 ♕d2 a5 19 ♖c1) 18 ... ♘d5 19 ♕d2 a5 20 ♖c1 ♕b8 21 c4 b4! 22 cd cd. Still, Karpov did win this game!

It isn't easy to determine what benefit Larsen thought he would have had from the position of the pawn on c3 if White had played the normal 13 0-0-0 ♘gf6 14 ♘e5.

B1

11 ... ♘gf6

12 0-0-0 ♗e7 *(78)*

12 ... ♘d5 13 ♗d2 b5 14 ♖de1 ♗e7 15 ♘e4 b4 16 g4 a5 17 g5 was Tisdall-Hartein, Lugano 1983.

13 ♘e5

Practice has brought this move to the forefront. Alternatively:

a) Just as in positions with the bishop on d2, **13 ♘e4** here can be met by 13 ... ♘xe4 14 ♕xe4 ♘f6 15

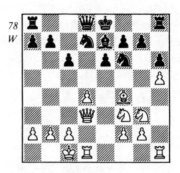

78
W

♕d3 (15 ♕e2 ♕d5 16 ♔b1 ± – Karpov) 15 ... ♕d5 (but not 15 ... ♕a5 16 ♔b1 ♘xh5? 17 ♗d2) 16 c4 ♕e4.

b) In Torre-Karpov, Moscow 1981, White took the precaution of **13 ♔b1**. There followed: 13 ... a5!? (13 ... ♕a5 14 ♘e5 ♖d8 is inferior: 15 ♘c4! ♕b5 16 ♗c7 ♖c8 17 ♘d6+ ♗xd6 18 ♗xd6 ♕xd3 19 ♖xd3 with a plus, Timman-Larsen, 1980) 14 ♘e4 ♘xe4 15 ♕xe4 ♘f6 (15 ... a4!? 16 ♘e5 a3, Karpov-Larsen, Linares 1983) 16 ♕e2 (the queen is probably better placed on d3, with the prospect of going to g3) 16 ... a4 17 ♘e5 ♕d5 18 g4 (it seems he should first have taken control of e4 with 18 f3, but then 18 ... b5 19 g4 b4, followed by ... ♕b5, isn't bad for Black) 18 ... a3 19 b3 ♕e4 20 ♗e3 0-0 21 ♕d3?! (after the queen exchange, Black seizes the initiative. The situation arising after 21 f3 ♕d5 22 ♖d3 ♘h7 23 ♗d2 is less clear) 21 ... ♕xd3 22 ♖xd3 ♗d6 23 f3 ♖fd8 24

Xhd1 ♘d5 25 c4 ♘b4 26 X3d2 b5 27 f4 bc 28 bc Xab8 etc.

c) On **13 c4**, Black can again play 13 ... a5 *(79)*.

Tal-Larsen, Tilburg 1980, continued 14 Xhe1 (Karpov-Larsen, Amsterdam 1980, saw 14 ♔b1 a4 15 ♘e5 ♘xe5 16 ♗xe5. These days, Black castles kingside in such positions without giving it a thought – 16 ... 0-0, or 15 ... 0-0. Three years ago, however, Larsen was attracted by 16 ... ♕a5?! 17 ♘e4 0-0-0. After 18 c5! ♘xe4 19 ♕xe4 ♗f6 – 19 ... Xhg8 20 Xh3 – 20 ♗xf6 gf 21 ♕f4 f5 22 Xd3, his pawn weaknesses and unsafe king position made Black's game difficult) 14 ... b5!? (this idea is quite a good reaction to c4, and was playable last move too) 15 c5 ♘d5 16 ♗e5 0-0 17 ♘e4 ♘7f6 18 ♘xf6+ ♘xf6 19 ♗xf6 ♗xf6 20 g4 ♕d5 21 ♔b1 Xfd8, and Black's game is more active.

  13 **...** **0-0** *(81)*
Or:

a) **13 ... a5** 14 Xhe1 *(80)*.

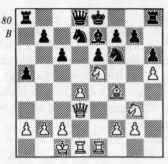

And now:

a1) Belyavsky-Larsen, Tilburg 1981, continued **14 ... a4?** 15 ♘g6!! ♘d5 (Belyavsky's analysis demonstrates that Black already has no satisfactory continuations: 15 ... fg 16 ♕xg6+ ♔f8 17 Xxe6 ♕e8 18 Xde1 ♕xg6 19 hg ♗b4 (19 ... ♘d5 20 Xxe7) 20 c3 ♘d5 (20 ... ♗a5 21 ♗d6+ ♔g8 22 ♘f5) 21 ♗d2 ♗a5 22 c4 ♗xd2+ 23 ♔xd2 ♘5f6 24 Xe7 with a won position; or 15 ... a3! 16 b3! fg 17 ♕xg6+ ♔f8 18 Xxe6 ♕e8 19 ♘f5! ♕xg6 20 hg ♗b4 21 c3 ♘d5 22 cb ♘xf4 23 Xe7) 16 ♘f5! ♗f8 17 ♗d6! Xg8 18 c4 ♘b4 19 ♕h3! fg 20 Xxe6+ ♔f7 21 hg+ ♔xe6 22 Xe1+ ♘e5 23 ♗xe5, and Black resigned. The 15 ♘e5 line received good publicity from this game.

a2) Consequently, against Suradiradja, Indonesia 1982, Chandler played **14 ... 0-0**, and after 15 ♔b1 a4 16 c4 a3 17 b3 ♗b4 18 Xh1 ♕e7 19 ♘e4 Xad8 obtained a comfortable position. If he had been facing Belyavsky, the issue would have been more complex. Instead of 15 ♔b1?!, White should probably have played 15 ♕e2, aiming for 16 ♘g6.

b) **13 ...** ♘d5 14 ♗d2 ♗g5 is strongly met by 15 ♘e4 ♗xd2+ 16 ♕xd2 0-0 17 g4, as indicated by Belyavsky.

c) Psakhis-Larsen, Las Palmas IZ 1982, went **13 ...** ♘xe5 14 ♗xe5 b5?! 15 ♘e4 ♖c8 16 ♔b1 a5 17 ♗xf6 gf (17 ... ♗xf6 18 g4 0-0 19 f4, or 18 ♕g3 0-0 19 ♘xf6+ ♕xf6 20 ♖h4) 18 g4 ♕d5 19 f4, with a clear edge.

To return to 13 ... 0-0:

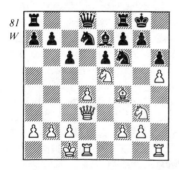

If White fails to demonstrate his advantage after developing his forces so actively, this will strongly influence our appraisal of the stability of Black's set-up with 10 ... e6. Some examples:

a) **14 ♕e2** ♕a5 (14 ... a5 15 c4 a4 16 ♔b1 a3 17 b3 ♖a6 18 ♕f3 ♕c8 19 ♖he1 ♖d8 20 ♕e3 c5 21 ♘xd7 ♖xd7 ½-½ Timman-Lobron, Plov-div 1983) 15 ♔b1 ♖ad8 16 c4 (analysing 16 ♘g6!?, Tal concludes that there are chances for both sides after 16 ... fg 17 ♕xe6+ ♔h8 18 ♕xe7 – 18 hg ♘g8 – 18 ... ♘d5 19 ♗d2 ♕xa2+ 20 ♔xa2 ♘xe7 21 ♗b4 c5) 16 ... ♘xe5 17 de ♘d7 18 ♖d2 (Tal recommends 18 a3 ♘c5 19 ♕c2) 18 ... ♗g5! 19 ♗xg5 hg 20 h6 (20 ♖hd1? or 20 ♖e1? would fail against 20 ... ♘xe5!) 20 ... ♘xe5! (20 ... ♕xe5? loses to 21 h7+ ♔h8 22 ♖xd7 ♕xe2 23 ♖xd8; while if 20 ... g6, then 21 h7+ ♔h8 22 ♖hd1 is strong) 21 ♖d5! (21 hg? ♖xd2, or 21 ♖xd8? ♖xd8 22 hg ♔xg7 favours Black) 21 ... ♖xd5 22 cd ♕xd5 23 hg ♔xg7, and a draw was agreed (24 ♘h5+ ♔g6 25 ♘f4+ gf 26 ♕h5+ ♔f6 27 ♕h4+ ♔f5 28 ♕h5+), Belyavsky-Tal, 1981.

b) **14 c4** c5 (it would be interesting to try 14 ... ♘xe5 15 ♗xe5 ♘g4, or 15 de ♕c7!?) 15 d5 ♘xe5 (15 ... ed 16 ♘f5!) 16 ♗xe5 ♘g4 17 ♗xg7!? ♔xg7 (17 ... ♘xf2 18 ♕f3 ♘xh1 19 ♗xf8 ♗g5+ 20 ♔b1 ♘xg3 is unclear) 18 ♕e2 ♗g5+ (18 ... ♘f6 would be answered by 19 de ♕c7 20 ♘f5+ ♔h7 21 ♕c2) 19 ♔b1 ♘f6 20 de ♕c8 21 e7 ♖e8 22 ♖d6! ♕g4 23 ♕e5 ♔g8 24 ♖e1! (24 ♖xf6 ♗xf6 25 ♕xf6 ♕e6 would be to Black's liking) 24 ... ♘d7 25 ♖xd7! ♕xd7 26 ♘f5 f6 27 ♕d5+! ♕xd5 28 cd ♗f4 29 g3 ♗c7 30 ♔c2 b5 31 ♘xh6+ ♔h7 32 ♘f5 ♖g8 33

d6 &a5 34 ♖e6 ♖g5 35 ♖xf6
♖xh5 36 d7 ♖h2 37 ♘e3 1-0,
Karpov-Hübner, Tilburg 1982.
An exceedingly beautiful win by
the World Champion, although
not everything in it is convincing.
c) **14 ♘xd7 ♕xd7 15 &e5 ♖ad8**
(15 ... ♘g4!?) 16 ♕e2 ♕d5 17 ♔b1
♖d7? (17 ... b5) 18 c4 ♕a5 19 f4 b5
20 c5 ♖d5 21 f5 ♘d7 22 &f4 ♕d8
23 fe, and White won, Timman-
Hübner, Tilburg 1982.

These three games played 'at
top level' clearly point to the
dangers lurking round the black
king in this variation, but also to
the fact that the search for the best
continuations (for both sides) is
not yet finished.

B2

11 ... ♕a5+

A move showing that Black
admits his 'mistake' (10 ... e6) and
wants to return, after 12 &d2, to
traditional positions with his
queen on c7.

12 c3 *(82)*

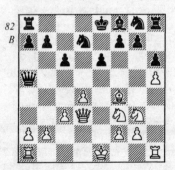

This is played on 'principle', but
reveals that White will castle short
(bringing about queenside castling
is more involved), despite the
weakening of his kingside. A
similar plan is considered in
Chapter 7, Variation B.

12 ... ♘gf6

13 a4

Intending to play 14 b4, driving
away the black queen (and so
removing the threat to the h-pawn),
and then to castle.

Another possibility is 13 ♕e2
&e7 14 ♘e5, likewise ensuring
kingside castling. A game Kapengut-
Shakarov, 1981, continued: 14 ...
0-0 15 a3 c5 16 dc ♘xe5? (16 ...
♕xc5) 17 b4 ♕a4 18 &xe5 ♘d7
&d4?! (after 19 0-0 Black's
position isn't worth the pawn) 19
19 ... e5 20 &e3 (20 ♘f5 ed 21
♘xe7+ ♔h8 22 cd ♖ae8 23 d5
♘xc5, or 23 0-0 ♘f6, is unclear)
20 ... f5 21 ♕c4+ ♔h8 22 ♘xf5
♖xf5 23 ♕e6 ♕c2 24 0-0 ♘f6 25
♕xe7 ♕e4, with good play for
Black.

13 ... c5

After 13 ... &e7, White carries
out his idea – 14 b4 ♕d8 15 0-0 –
but how to assess it objectively is
by no means obvious.

A game Panchenko-Bronstein,
Moscow Open Ch 1981, went 13 ...
♘d5!? 14 &d2 ♕c7 15 ♔f1 a5 16
♕e2 &e7 17 ♘e5 ♘xe5 18 ♕xe5
♕xe5 19 de ♘b6 20 &f4 f5 21 ef gf

22 ♔e2 ♔f7 23 ♖hd1 f5 24 ♗e3
♘d5 25 ♗d4 ♖hd8 26 c4 ♘f6 27
♗e5 ♘g4 28 ♗c7 ♖dc8 29 ♗f4 e5
30 ♗d2 ♔e6, and Bronstein
outplayed his opponent.

14 0-0 ♗e7

Gaprindashvili-Nikolac, Wijk
aan Zee saw 14 ... ♖c8?! 15 ♖fe1
c4 16 ♕c2 ♗e7 (do we infer that
Nikolac had first been planning
to take the h-pawn? Black's
position would then quickly have
become difficult: 16 ... ♘xh5 17
♘xh5 ♕xh5 18 ♕e4) 17 ♘e5 0-0
18 ♘f5 ♖fe8? *(83)*

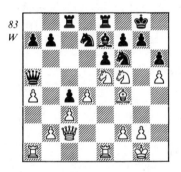

(18 ... ♕d8) 19 ♘xg7! ♔xg7 20
♗xh6+! ♔xh6 21 ♘xf7+ ♔xh5 22
g4+! ♔h4 23 f3 ♘xg4 24 ♖e4 1-0.

15 ♖fe1 0-0 *(84)*

After 15 ... cd 16 b4 ♕a6 17 b5
♕a5 18 ♘xd4, White's pieces
become very active. One more
indiscretion – 18 ... ♖c8? – and
Black was crushed in Vitolins-
Antom, USSR 1978: 19 ♖xe6!
♕xc3 20 ♖xe7+ ♔xe7 21 ♕d1
♖hd8 22 ♗d6+! ♔xd6 23 ♘df5+

♔c5 24 ♕d6+ ♔c4 25 ♘e3+ ♕xe3
26 fe etc.

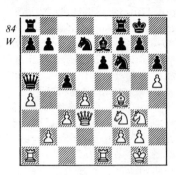

Black has finished his development, and the fate of the white
h-pawn becomes a major issue.
Vitolins-Kivlan, Latvian Ch 1978,
continued: 16 ♘f5 ♖fe8 17
♘xh6+ (Vitolins isn't happy with
17 ♘xe7+, because after that the
pawn on h5 would not be easy to
defend) 17 ... gh 18 ♘e5 ♘xe5 19
de ♘h7 20 ♗xh6 ♗f8 21 ♗f4 ♔h8
22 ♖e4 ♕c7 23 ♖ae1 ♗e7 24 ♗h6
♖g8 25 ♕f3 ♗g5 26 ♗xg5 ♖xg5
27 g4 ♖d8, and Black has a
winning position.

An improvement is 16 ♘e5, for
instance 16 ... ♘xe5 17 de ♘d5 18
♗d2 ♖fd8 19 ♘e4 ♘f6 etc, and
White's chances may be no worse.

To draw conclusions from the
material examined in this chapter,
we may say that the variations
10 ... e6 11 ♗f4 ♘gf6 and 11 ...
♕a5+ 12 c3 are undoubtedly
interesting and lead to sharp

situations; yet in the first case Black forfeits the stability of his position, while in the second case White does so.

Summary

11 b3					=
11 ♗d2	♘gf6	12 0-0-0	c5		±
			♕b6		±
			♗e7	13 ♖he1	∞
				13 ♕e2	∞
				13 ♘e4	♕b6 ±
					a5 ±
					0-0 =
					♘xe4 =
11 ♗f4	♘gf6	12 0-0-0	♗e7	13 ♘e4	=/∞
				13 ♔b1	=/∞
				13 c4	o
				13 ♘e5	a5 ±
					♘xe5 ±
					0-0 ±/∞
	♕a5+	12 c3	♘gf6	13 ♕e2	=
				13 a4	♘d5 ∞
					c5 =
		(12 ♗d2 ♕c7 – cf. 10 ... ♕c7)			

7   10 ... ♛c7

1	e4	c6
2	d4	d5
3	♘c3	de
4	♘xe4	♗f5
5	♘g3	♗g6
6	♘f3	♘d7
7	h4	h6
8	h5	♗h7
9	♗d3	♗xd3
10	♛xd3	♛c7 (85)

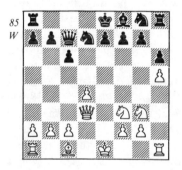

The customary continuation here is 11 ♗d2 e6 12 0-0-0, but now and again other lines have happened to become popular and displace it. Such lines are 11 ♖h4, 11 0-0 and 11 ♗d2 e6 12 ♛e2, or 12 c4. Their common factor is their obvious artificiality. The rook sortie (Variation A) makes ♗f4 possible, but the position of

the rook itself, on h4, leaves something to be desired . . . Kingside castling with the h-pawn far advanced (Variation B) sharpens the struggle, but the white king's defences are open to threats. The same can be said of White's commencement of warlike operations with his king still in the centre (Variation C).

It would only be just if all these tries allowed Black good counterplay.

From Diagram 85, White has:
A 11 ♖h4
B 11 0-0
C 11 ♗d2

A

11   ♖h4 (86)

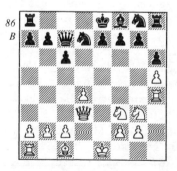

By way of explaining 8 h4,

Gligorić once wrote: 'White wants to bring his king's rook into play on the fourth rank and fight for the f4 square.' Nowadays White associates 8 h5 with quite other plans, but 11 ♖h4 does still occur occasionally.

11 ... e6

Or 11 ... ♘gf6 12 ♗f4 ♕a5+ 13 ♗d2 (13 ♔f1!? e6 14 ♘e5) 13 ... ♕b5 14 ♕xb5 cb 15 a4 ba 16 ♖xa4 e6 17 b3 ♗e7 18 ♔e2 a6 19 ♖h1, and the players agreed a draw, Sax-Hort, 1979.

12 ♗f4 ♕a5+

White's successes in the alternative variation 12 ... ♗d6 13 ♗xd6 ♕xd6 14 ♘e4 are illustrated by the following games:

a) **14 ... ♕b4+** 15 ♕c3 (if 15 c3, then 15 ... ♕xb2 is dangerous because of 16 ♘d6+ and 17 ♖b1, so Black would have to withdraw his queen to e7. Also after 15 ♕c3, Botvinnik considers it was not too late for 15 ... ♕e7) 15 ... ♕xc3+ 16 bc ♔e7 17 ♘c5! ♘gf6 ('if 17 ... b6, then 18 ♘xd7 ♔xd7 19 ♘e5+, winning a pawn; or 17 ... ♘xc5 dc, and again one of Black's pawns will fall' – Botvinnik) 18 ♘xb7 ♖hc8 19 ♘e5 (19 ♘c5!?) 19 ... c5 20 ♘a5 ♖c7 21 0-0-0 ♖ac8 22 ♘xd7 ♘xd7 23 d5! ed 24 ♖xd5, with the initiative as well as a slight material plus, Spassky-Botvinnik, Leiden 1970.

b) **14 ... ♕e7** *(87)*

15 ♕a3! ('the sort of move Tolush would suggest' – Botvinnik. In Keres-Bagirov, 1959, White obtained the better position after 15 0-0-0 ♘gf6 16 ♘xf6+ ♘xf6 17 ♘e5 0-0-0 18 ♕g3, but in a game against Gligorić in the Candidates' Tournament of that year, Petrosian strengthened Black's defence: 16 ... gf! 17 ♕d2?! ♘b6 18 ♕a5 ♕d6! 19 ♖d3 ♕d5 20 ♕a3 ♘c4 21 ♕b4 ♘d6 22 b3 a5 23 ♕d2 a4 24 c4 ab!, with advantage to Black. Another game Spassky-Botvinnik, 1970, went 16 ♘ed2 0-0-0 17 ♘c4 ♔b8 18 g3 ♘b6 19 ♕e2 ♘bd5, with a draw) 15 ... ♕xa3 16 ba ♗e7 17 ♖b1 (probably more exact than 17 ♘c5 ♘xc5 18 dc a5 19 ♖b1, when Seirawan in one of his games played 19 ... ♖a7 and succeeded in defending after 20 ♘e5 ♘f6 21 ♖d4 ♖c8 22 a4 ♖c7 23 ♖bd1 ♖a6); and now:

b1) **17 ... b6** 18 ♘e5 ♘xe5 19 de f5 20 ♘g3 ♖d8 21 ♖a4 ♖d7 22 ♖d1 ♖xd1+ 23 ♔xd1 a5 24 ♖d4 c5 25

♖d2 ♔f7 26 ♖d8, with a clear advantage, Belyavsky-Pomar, Las Palmas 1974.

b2) **17 ... ♖b8** 18 ♘c5 ♘xc5 19 dc *(88)*

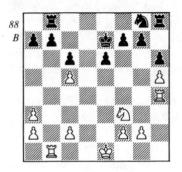

The same type of position (with a white pawn on c3 instead of a3) would have arisen in Spassky-Botvinnik – see (a) above – if Black had played 17 ... ♘xc5.

White's pawn structure, though ugly, allows him to exert strong pressure against b7 (♖b4). Does the position favour White, then?

At one time it was generally thought that the answer to this question was given by a game Bellon-Pomar, Olot 1975: 19 ... a5 20 ♘e5 (20 ♖a4 ♘f6 21 ♖xa5 ♘d7 is good for Black despite the pawn minus) 20 ... ♘f6 21 ♖d4 ♖hc8 22 ♖b3 ♖c7 23 g4 ♖d8 24 ♖xb7 ♖xd4 25 ♘xc6+ ♔d7 26 ♘xd4 ♖xb7 27 c6+ ♔c7 28 cb ♘xg4, with chances for both sides.

But the next encounter between the same opponents, Bellon-Pomar, Orense 1976, brought victory to White: 22 g4! (instead of ♖b3) 22 ... ♖c7 23 f3 ♖d8? 24 ♖xb7. The same blow as before, but this time White's pawn on g4 is defended.

Has Grandmaster Pomar since succeeded in proving that the position is drawn nonetheless? It would of course be interesting to find out – yet we have always felt that wasting his energy over such a tedious exercise was not worth Black's while. The ineffectuality of 11 ♖h4 can be brought out if Black refrains from 12 ... ♗d6. White will have to waste time moving his rook to a more suitable square, and the tempo is just what Black needs.

13 ♗d2 ♕b6

13 ... ♕c7 is also playable (provided Black has no objection to an immediate draw with 14 ♗f4). A game Kitces-Tavadian (1977) proceeded: 14 0-0-0 0-0-0 15 ♔b1 ♘gf6 16 ♗f4 ♗d6 17 ♗xd6 ♕xd6 18 c4?! c5 19 ♕a3 a6 20 ♖d2 ♕c7 21 ♕e3 cd 22 ♖hxd4 ♘b8! 23 ♘e4?! ♘xe4 24 ♕xe4 ♘c6 25 ♖4d3 ♖xd3 26 ♖xd3 ♖d8 (after all the rooks are exchanged it emerges that White's pawns are hard to defend, for example 27 ♖xd8+ ♕xd8 28 ♔c2 ♕a5) 27 a3 ♖xd3 28 ♕xd3 ♕f4 29 ♕h7 ♕g4! with a won game for Black.

14 0-0-0 ♗e7

A debatable point – is driving the rook away necessary?

15 ♖hh1

In Mukhamedzhanov-Vdovin (1979), White played 15 ♖f4 (15 ♖g4? ♘gf6) 15 ... ♘gf6 16 ♘e5, and . . . managed to draw after 16 ... ♖d8 17 ♛e2 c5 18 dc ♛xc5 19 ♘xd7 ♖xd7 20 ♖c4 ♛d5 21 ♗c3 ♛xd1+ 22 ♛xd1 ♖xd1+ 23 ♔xd1 ♔d7.

15 ... ♘gf6 *(89)*

89
W

Gilezetdinov-Shakarov, corres 1976, now continued: 16 c4 (16 ♖he1 appears best, aiming to meet 16 ... 0-0 or 16 ... 0-0-0 with 17 ♘f5. Black can choose between 16 ... c5 and 16 ... ♖d8) 16 ... ♛a6 17 ♔b1 ♗d6 (exploiting White's unpreparedness for 18 ♘e4) 18 ♘e2 ♘g4 19 ♗e1 0-0-0 (five years earlier, this position had been seen in a game Tatai-Larsen, though the players had taken three moves fewer to reach it: 10 ... e6 11 ♗d2 ♛b6 12 0-0-0 ♘gf6 13 c4 ♛a6! 14 ♔b1 ♗d6 15 ♘e2 ♘g4 16 ♗e1

0-0-0. After 17 ♘d2 c5?! 18 ♘e4 ♗c7 19 f3 f5?! 20 ♘d2 ♘gf6 21 ♛c2 ♔b8 22 ♗f2 ♗b6 23 ♘b3 cd 24 ♘exd4 Black was left in a dubious position, but 17 ... ♘gf6! followed by ... e5 or ... c5 would have given him a good game) 20 ♛c2 c5 21 ♖d3 (White's violent attempt to seize the initiative quickly produces the opposite result) 21 ... cd 22 c5 ♗e7 (not 22 ... ♘xc5? 23 ♖xd4) 23 ♘exd4 (23 ♖a3? fails to 23 ... d3 24 ♛c3 d2, or 24 ♖xd3 ♘xc5 25 ♖xd8+ ♔xd8) 23 ... ♘de5 24 ♖c3?! (he had to exchange queens with 24 ♖a3 ♛c4 25 ♛xc4) 24 ... ♘xf3 25 ♘xf3 ♗f6, and White's position is in disarray.

We will give the finale of this game (by way of advertisement!): 26 ♖b3 (26 ♖a3 ♛b5 27 ♖xa7? ♖d1+) 26 ... ♖d5 27 ♖b4? ♖hd8 28 a3 (or 28 ♗c3 ♘xf2! 29 ♛xf2 ♖d1+ 30 ♖xd1 ♖xd1+ 31 ♔c2 ♛d3+ 32 ♔b3 ♗xc3) 28 ... ♖d1+ 29 ♔a2 ♘xf2! 30 ♛xf2 ♖a1+! with a mating attack.

We hope to have convinced the reader that by avoiding the exchanging line 12 ... ♗d6?! Black obtains a fully satisfactory game.
B

11 0-0 *(90)*

An optimistic decision, bringing sharpness into the position in keeping with the tastes of A.Vitolins – the only master who

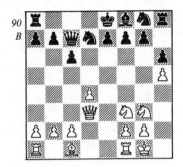

90
B

employs this variation regularly (or used to?).

In our view, the advanced pawn on h5 means, above all, an opportunity for Black in positions where the players castle on the same side. In practice, however, Black has preferred to castle queenside without delay.

11   ...   e6
12   c4

Alternatively:

a) Even Vitolins failed to shine in a game where Black castled kingside: **12 ♕e2 ♘gf6 13 ♘e5 ♗d6 14 ♖e1 0-0** (91).

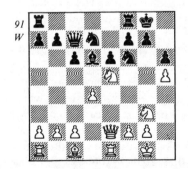

91
W

15 c4 ♖ad8 16 ♗f4 c5 17 dc ♕xc5 18 ♘d3 ♕c7 19 ♗xd6 ♕xd6 20 ♖ad1 a5 21 b3 ♘c5 22 ♘e5 ♕b6 23 ♕e3 ♕b4, Vitolins-Kivlan, 1980. With ... a4 in view, Black's position is the more promising; in fact, Vitolins sacrificed his h-pawn here with 24 ♘e2, to alter the unfavourable course the game was taking.

b) **12 ♖e1 ♘gf6 13 ♘e5** (92) is hardly any stronger

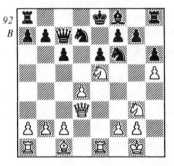

92
B

– although, in Schneider-Lauterbach, 1958, Black was crushed after 13 ... ♗e7? 14 ♘xf7! ♔xf7 15 ♕g6+ ♔g8 (if 15 ... ♔f8, then of course 16 ♖xe6 with ♘f5 to follow) 16 ♘f5! ef 17 ♖xe7 ♖h7 18 ♗xh6 ♘xh5 19 ♕f7+ ♔h8 20 ♖e8+. Instead 13 ... ♘xe5 14 de ♘d7 was good enough, while 13 ... ♗d6 14 ♘f5 0-0 (14 ... ♘xh5 15 ♘g6!) 15 ♘xh6+! gh 16 ♗xh6 ♘xe5 17 de ♗xe5 is problematic.

12   ...   ♘gf6! *(94)*

The alternative is 12 ... 0-0-0 *(93)*.

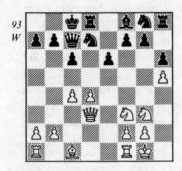

93
W

And now, from Diagram 93:
a) Vitolins-Mikhalchishin, 1978, continued **13 d5 ♘c5 14 ♕d4 ed 15 ♗f4 dc!** 16 ♕xc4 (after 16. ♗xc7 ♖xd4 17 ♘xd4 ♚xc7 Black's chances may even be better) 16 ... ♗d6 17 ♗xd6 ♕xd6 18 b4?! ♘e6 19 b5 ♘e7, and after beating off the assaults, Black won. The same outcome can be envisaged after 18 ♖ad1 ♕xd1 19 ♖xd1 ♖xd1+ 20 ♚h2 ♖d5, but in the case of 18 ♕xf7 the result is harder to predict.
b) Vitolins-Okhotnik, Onyepropetrovsk Otborochnii 1980, went **13 b4 ♗xb4 14 ♖b1 ♗d6 15 ♘e4 ♘gf6 16 ♘xd6+ ♕xd6 17 ♕b3 b6 18 a4 c5 19 a5 cd 20 ab ab 21 ♗a3 ♘c5 22 ♕xb6 ♕xb6 23 ♖xb6 ♘a4 24 ♖a6 ♘c3 25 ♖a7 ♖he8 26 ♖a1 ♖d7 27 ♖a6 e5 28 ♗d6 ♖xd6 29 ♖xd6 ♚c7 30 c5 ♘ce4 31 ♖a7+ ♚b8 32 ♖da6 ♘xc5 33 ♖a5 ♘cd7 34 ♖a8+ ♚c7 35 ♖xe8 ♘xe8 36 ♘xe5**, and Vitolins achieved the win.

Closely associating Black's failure with his decision to castle queenside would be wrong. We suggest 13 ... ♘gf6 as worth trying (14 b5 c5, or 14 c5 ♖g8 with the idea of ... g6), while even after 13 ... ♗xb4 not everything is clear.

However, the most precise move is 12 ... ♘gf6!, which doesn't commit the king for the moment.

94
W

On 13 ♖e1, the reply 13 ... 0-0-0 looks better than it did on move 12.

In a correspondence game Kneller-Kikust, 1981, Black met 13 ♖e1 with 13 ... ♗b4, aiming for kingside castling. There followed: 14 ♖e2 (quite good, since it threatens both 15 d5 and 15 c5) 14 ... ♖d8! 15 d5? (an ill-considered decision. 15 ♕b3 a5 16 a3 was more logical, prompting the bishop to go to d6 or e7, where the knight on g3 can reach it. But then, we would still prefer the black side after 16 ... ♗d6 17 ♘f5 0-0 18 ♘xd6 ♕xd6) 15 ... 0-0 16 de

♘e5 17 ef+ ♖xf7 18 ♕b3 ♘xf3+ 19 ♕xf3 ♖d1+ 20 ♘f1 ♕d8 21 g3 ♗c5, and the white position is hard to defend.

Let us frankly state that the plan of 11 0-0 is devoid of strength. The pawn on h5 is misplaced, as Black can demonstrate with careful play.

C

11 ♗d2 e6

At this point, we consider:

C1 12 ♕e2
C2 12 c4

C1

12 ♕e2

In the 1960s, White's successes with the variation 12 0-0-0 ♘gf6 13 ♕e2 0-0-0 14 ♘e5 made Black want to refine his play. The idea of delaying development of the king's knight, and playing 12 ... 0-0-0 13 ♕e2 ♗d6, so as to prevent ♘e5 (compare Chapter 10, Variation A), seemed to represent such a refinement. White, in turn, took counter-measures, and started making the queen's move earlier. As a result, a new set of variations arose: 12 ♕e2 0-0-0 13 ♘e5, 12 ... ♗d6, and 12 ... ♘gf6 13 ♘e5.

12 ... ♘gf6

A tough sentence was passed on 12 ... 0-0-0 as early as 1966. A game Nikitin-Lazarev went: 13 ♘e5 *(95)*.

13 ... ♘b6 (or 13 ... ♘xe5 14 de ♘e7 15 0-0-0 c5 16 f4 ♘c6 17 c3,

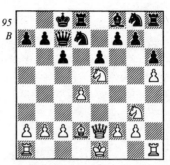

and Black's game holds few prospects; see analogous positions in Chapter 11, Variation A) 14 c3 ♘f6 15 0-0! ♗d6 (15 ... c5 16 b4!) 16 a4 ♖hf8 17 a5 ♘bd7 18 f4, and while Black remains passive, White prepares an attack on the queenside.

As to the manoeuvre 12 ... ♗d6 13 ♘e4 ♗f4, the following analysis by Boleslavsky purports to refute it. After 14 ♘e5 *(96)*, Black has (he says) an unpleasant choice:

a) **14 ...** ♘xe5 15 ♗xf4 ♘d3+ 16 ♕xd3 ♕xf4 17 g3 ♕c7 18 ♕a3.
b) **14 ...** ♗xe5 15 de ♘xe5 16 ♗b4 0-0-0 17 f4 c5 18 fe cb 19 0-0 ♕xe5 20 ♖xf7 ♕d4+! 21 ♘f2! ♘f6 22

♖d1 ♛b6 23 ♖xd8+ ♖xd8 24 ♖xg7 ♖d5 25 g4, and 'in view of the threats of 26 ♖g6 and 26 ♛f3, Black's position is difficult' (Boleslavsky).

c) **14 ...** ♗xd2+ 15 ♘xd2 ♘xe5 16 de 0-0-0 17 ♘c4 ♔b8 18 ♘d6 f6 19 f4.

Is all this incontestable? In the final position of (b), Black is not without chances: 25 ... ♖d4!? 26 ♛f3 (26 ♖g6 ♖f4) 26 ... e5! 27 ♛f5+ ♔d8 28 ♛xe5? ♖xg4+ 19 ♖xg4 ♛xf2+!

It seems to us that a simpler answer to 12 ... ♗d6 is 13 ♘f5 ♗f4 14 ♘e3 ♘gf6 15 g3; or 14 ♗xf4 ♛xf4 15 ♘e3 ♘gf6 16 0-0-0, transposing to a position from Chapter 10 (Variation A), which favours White.

13 ♖h4?! *(98)*

White has achieved his aim after 12 ... ♘gf6, and could simply castle here (for 13 0-0-0, see Chapters 11 and 12). But it is understandable that he should want to try out 13 ♘e5 *(97)*.

Tal-Kasparov, exhibition game, 1980, continued: 13 ... c5!? 14 ♘xd7 ♛xd7 15 dc ♗xc5 16 0-0-0 ♛a4 17 ♗c3! ♖c8 18 ♗xf6 gf 19 ♔b1 (19 ♘e4 ♗e3+! 20 fe ♛xe4) 19 ... ♗e7 20 ♖d3 (20 ♘e4 ♛c4!) 20 ... ♖g8 21 ♖hd1 f5! (all Black's pieces are well placed – except for his king, which Tal has resolved to get to grips with . . .) 22 ♘xf5? ef 23 ♖e1 ♛h4 24 ♖e3 ♖c7 25 ♛b5+ ♔f8 26 ♛e5 f4! 27 ♖e4 ♖c5! 28 ♛xe7+ ♛xe7 29 ♖xe7 ♖xg2 30 ♖xb7 ♖xf2 31 a4 f3 32 ♖e4 ♖f5 33 ♖b5 ♖xb5 34 ab ♖e2 35 ♖f4 f2 36 ♔a2 ♖xc2, and Black won.

Still, perhaps White will find a way to profit from Black's insecure king position. If so, Black should rely on 13 ... ♗d6 14 f4 0-0. Then 15 0-0-0 leads to a position examined in Chapter 4 (see 6 h4 h6 7 f4, as in the games Dückstein-Hort and Shamkovich-Dely), except that here White has played ♛e2 instead of Dückstein's 15 ♘e2 or Shamkovich's 15 ♛f3.

97
B

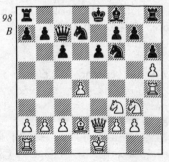

98
B

The move 13 ♖h4?! was played in a few games by Matulović:

a) **13 ... 0-0-0** 14 ♘e5 ♘xe5 15 de ♘d7 16 f4 ♘c5 17 0-0-0 ♗e7 18 ♖hh1 (compared with situations in Chapter 11, Variation A, Black has two extra tempi here!) 18 ... ♖d5 and now:

a1) **19 c4** ♘d3+ 20 ♔b1 ♖d7 21 ♗e3 ♖hd8 22 ♘e4 f6 23 ef gf, with chances for both sides, Matulović-Nikolic, Yugoslav Ch 1978.

a2) **19 ♗e3** ♖hd8 20 ♗xc5 ♗xc5 21 c4 ♖xd1+ 22 ♖xd1 f5! 23 ♘f1 ♕b6 24 ♖xd8+ ♕xd8 25 g3 ♕d4, and the advantage is on Black's side, Matulović-Nikolac, 1979.

b) **13 ... ♗e7** 14 0-0-0 ♘d5 (for 14 ... c5, see Chapter 10, Variation C) 15 ♖hh1 c5 16 dc ♘xc5 17 ♕b5+ ♕d7 18 ♕xd7+ ♘xd7 19 ♘f1 ♖c8 20 ♔b1 ♗c5 21 ♗e1 b5, and Black has the initiative.

C2

12   c4 (99)

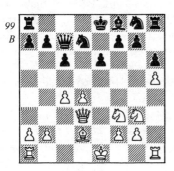

This continuation was especially popular in the first half of the 1970s. As in Variation C1, White is intent on gaining something by starting active operations one move earlier, instead of deciding on the position of his king.

12   ...   ♘gf6
13   ♕e2

One of the paths that were explored in investigations of the 12 c4 line was 13 c5, cramping Black and envisaging a queenside pawn advance *(100)*.

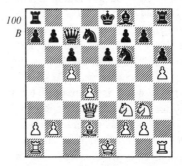

What is there to reassure Black here? The answer is, the d5 outpost for his pieces, the pawn on d4 to be pressurised, and various possibilities of breaking with ... b6, ... e5 or g6. On the whole this is quite enough for an optimistic appraisal of his chances:

a) The pawn break ... b6, combined with kingside castling, gave Black a good position in Romm-Porath, 1976: **13 ... b6** 14 b4 a5 (half measures – 14 ... bc 15 bc – are not very effective, as was shown in Vasyukov-Podgayets,

USSR Ch 1st L 1975: 15 ... ♗e7 16
0-0 0-0 17 ♖fb1 ♖fb8 18 ♖b3 ♘d5
19 ♖e1 ♖xb3 20 ab ♖b8 21 ♖a1
♖b5 22 ♖a4 a5 23 ♘e2 ♗f6 24
♕c2 e5 25 de ♗xe5 26 ♖c4 ♖b8
etc. Black's position is satisfactory,
but no more) 15 cb ♕xb6 16 ba
♕a6 17 ♕xa6 ♖xa6 18 ♘e5 ♗d6
19 ♘c4 ♗xg3 20 fg 0-0 21 ♔e2 c5
22 ♖h4 ♖c8 (Black creates
counterplay which compensates
for the white passed pawn on a5)
23 ♖c1 cd 24 ♖xd4 ♖ac6 25 ♔d1
e5 26 ♖h4 ♘d5 27 ♘d6 ♖xc1+ 28
♗xc1 ♖c6 29 ♘b5 ♖c5 30 a4 ♖c6
31 ♖e4 f5 32 ♖e2 ♖a6 33 ♗d2
♔f7, and by now Black has the
better chances.

b) **13 ... 0-0-0** is motivated by a
sceptical view of White's coming
attack on the queenside. And
indeed, the counterplay based on
pawn breaks in the centre or on
the kingside is powerful enough.
Play can proceed:

b1) **14 ♕a3** e5! 15 ♕xa7 ed 16 ♗a5
♖e8+ 17 ♔f1 ♗xc5 with advantage
to Black, Kayumov-Shakarov,
1976.

b2) **14 b4** ♖g8!? (not a bad plan,
but 14 ... e5 is more convincing) 15
a4 g6 16 ♔f1 gh 17 ♘xh5 ♖g4 18
g3? (White allows a forceful blow.
After 18 ♘xf6 ♘xf6 19 ♗xh6
♗xh6 20 ♖xh6 ♕f4, Black's
activity is worth the pawn) 18 ...
♘e5! 19 ♘xe5 ♖gxd4 20 ♕e3 ♖e4
21 ♕a3 ♘xh5 22 ♘f3 ♘f6 23

♗xh6 ♗xh6 24 ♖xh6 ♘d5 25 ♖b1
♘e3+! 26 ♔g1 ♘f5 27 ♖h3 ♖g8
28 ♔f1 ♕d8 29 ♕b3 ♕f6 30 b5
♘e3+ 31 ♔e2 ♘d5+ 32 ♔f1 ♖b4
0-1 Skulener-Tavadian, 1977.

b3) **14 ♕e2** *(101)* is directed
against ... e5.

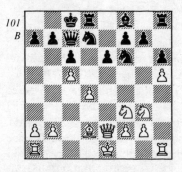

101
B

This position is often reached
by the move order 13 ♕e2 0-0-0 14
c5, but White cannot reach it at all
if Black is unwilling: 13 c5 b6 (see
Romm-Porath and Vasyukov-
Podgayets, above), or 13 ♕e2
♗d6! (which we analyse below).

Karpov-Hort, Portorož-Ljubljana
1975, continued: 14 ... ♖g8! (the
plan of .. e5 was successfully
countered in a number of games
by Ciocaltea. Ciocaltea-Sribar,
1976, went 14 ... e5 15 de ♖e8 16
0-0 ♗xc5 – *or 16 ... ♘xe5 17 ♗f4
♘fg4 18 ♖fe1 f6 19 ♘e4* – 17 b4
♗f8?! – *17 ... ♗b6!? 18 a4 ♘xe5* –
18 ♖fe1 ♘d5 19 b5, and Black's
king is in danger. Ciocaltea-
Valero, 1980, saw 14 ... ♘d5 15 b4
♖e8 16 ♔f1 e5 17 de ♘xe5 18 ♖e1

f6 19 ♖h4, and the threat of ♖e4 puts Black in a difficult situation) 15 b4 g6 16 ♖b1 gh 17 ♔f1 ♖g4 18 ♖b3 ♔b8 19 ♘xh5 ♘xh5 20 ♖xh5 ♘f6 21 ♖e5 ♗g7 22 b5 ♘d5 23 b6 ab 24 cb ♕d6 25 ♖e4 ♖xe4 26 ♕xe4 f5 27 ♕c2 ♗f6 28 ♕c4 ♖g8 29 ♕a4 h5, with chances for both sides.

13   ...   ♗d6!

On 13 ... 0-0-0, White is at a parting of the ways; should he start an offensive with 14 c5 (see 13 c5), establish a knight on e5, or make one more non-committal developing move (14 ♗c3)? The continuation 14 ♗c3 c5 15 0-0-0 leads to a position from Chapter 8, Variation A (12 0-0-0 ♘gf6 13 c4 0-0-0 14 ♗c3 c5 15 ♕e2), while on 14 ♘e5 *(102)* Black at once acquires a number of interesting possibilities:

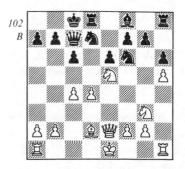

a) **14 ...** ♘xe5 15 de ♘d7 16 f4 ♘c5 17 0-0-0 ♘d3+ 18 ♔b1 ♘xb2! 19 ♔xb2 ♕b6+ 20 ♔c2 ♕a6 21 ♔b1 (avoiding the risk

entailed by 21 ♗c3, 21 ♖a1 or 21 ♖b1) 21 ... ♕b6+ 22 ♔c2 with a draw, Klovan-Andreyev, corres 1976.

b) **14 ...** ♘b6?! 15 c5 ♗xc5! (the only move which in some way justifies his last one. After 15 ... ♘bd5 16 0-0, Black has lost time and risks coming under attack) 16 dc ♖xd2 17 ♔xd2 ♕xe5 18 ♕xe5 (White loses after 18 cb? ♕xb2+ 19 ♔e3 ♕c3+ 20 ♕d3 ♘d5+, or 20 ♔f4 ♘d5+) 18 ... ♘c4+, with chances of a draw – an outcome that isn't worth it.

c) **14 ...** ♘b8!? 15 ♗c3 c5 16 0-0-0 ♘c6.

The choice between 13 ... 0-0-0 and 13 ... ♗d6 is a matter of taste. *We* choose 13 ... ♗d6!

14   ♘f5   0-0!?

Or:

a) In one of the first games with 13 ... ♗d6, only the minus side of this line was revealed. Karpov-Pomar, 1974, went **14 ... 0-0-0?!** 15 ♘xd6+ ♕xd6. Having exchanged a knight (indeed, such an un-appealing one as his knight on g3) for the black bishop, White obtained a clear advantage: 16 ♗a5 ♖de8 17 ♘e5 ♕e7 18 ♗c3 (18 f4!?) 18 ... ♖d8 19 f4 ♘xe5 20 fe ♘h7 21 0-0-0.

b) In a game Spassky-Karpov, match 1974, Black's position was again suspect: **14 ...** ♗f4 15 ♗xf4 ♕xf4 16 ♘e3 *(103)*

16 ... ♕c7?! 17 0-0-0 b5 18 cb cb+ 19 ♔b1 0-0 20 g4! with an attack.

Commenting on this game, Botvinnik wrote: '16 ... 0-0-0 would have been dangerous on account of 17 c5, threatening ♘c4-d6. Therefore, most likely, the correct decision was to break with 16 ... c5!, and if 17 ♘d5 ♘xd5 18 cd, then 18 ... 0-0 19 de ♖fe8.'

This was confirmed by a game Tal-Portisch, Bugojno 1978, which ended in a draw after 20 0-0 ♖xe6 21 ♕b5 ♕c7 etc.

But the evolution of this variation was to take a different course again. Black now allowed the knight on g3 to be exchanged for the bishop as in Karpov-Pomar, but castled on the kingside. This enabled him to exploit the resource ... b5 in order to seize the initiative.

15 ♘xd6   ♕xd6
16 0-0-0

As the following game shows, the counter-stroke ... b5 loses

none of its force through White's postponement of castling here. Nor is this surprising; in the present situation the white king is no more secure on the right flank or in the centre than it would be on the left flank.

Kapengut-Kasparov, Otborochnii 1978, went 16 ♗c3 b5! 17 cb cb 18 ♕xb5 ♘d5 19 ♘e5 ♘xe5 (19 ... ♘7f6 20 ♕e2 ♖fc8 was probably even better) 20 de ♘xc3 21 bc ♕c7 22 ♖h3?! (in our view White can more easily hold his shaky position after 22 0-0) 22 ... ♖fd8 23 ♕e2 ♖d5 (104)

24 f4 (Belyavsky-Bagirov, USSR Ch 1st L 1977, went 24 ♖e3 ♖xe5. An oversight? But Bagirov maintains that after 24 f4 which holds the extra pawn, White is worse off still! He's right – White's king now has nowhere to hide) 24 ... ♖ad8 25 ♖e3 ♕b6 (25 ... ♕e7! 26 g3 ♕b7, or 26 ♖h3 f6!, is also strong) 26 ♖c1 ♖b5 27 ♔f2 ♖b2 28 ♖c2 ♖b1 29 ♔g3 ♖bd1 30 ♖b2 ♕c5 31 ♕f3 a5 32 ♕e4 ♕a3 (32 ... a4!?) 33

♖c2 ♖h1 34 ♔g4 (34 ♕f3 ♕e7 35
♕g4 ♔h8, with ... ♖g8 to follow)
34 ... ♕c5 35 ♖h3 ♖hd1. Black
has handled the attack with
insufficient imagination, and although White's position is still
difficult, he managed to hold on.

16 ... b5

And now:

a) In a game Lukin-Gorshkov,
'Zenit' Ch 1975, there followed: **17
cb** cb **18 ♔b1 b4** (alternatively
18 ... ♖fc8 19 g4 ♕c6, or 19 ♘e5
♕c7) **19 ♘e5 ♘d5** *(105)*, and
Black's chances on the queenside
are no worse than White's on the
kingside:

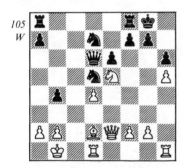

105
W

20 ♖h3 (the attack on the king with
pieces was not to materialise, but
nor does a pawn storm have much
chance of success: 20 g4 f6 21 ♘g6
♖fb8 22 ♔a1 a5 23 ♖he1 ♖a6 24
f4 b3 25 a3 ♘b4!) **20 ... f6 21 ♘c4
♕a6 22 ♖g3 ♔h8 23 ♖e1 ♖fe8 24
♖g4?! ♖ac8 25 b3 ♖c6 26 ♖e4 f5
27 ♖h4 ♖ec8 28 g4 ♘7b6**, and
Black is near to his goal (29 ♘xb6

♖c1+!).

b) The energetic **17 g4!** nearly
brought White a win in the game
Mnatsakanian-Bagirov, Kirovakan
1978: **17 ... bc 18 g5 hg 19 h6 g6 20
h7+ ♘xh7 21 ♘xg5 ♘xg5 22
♗xg5** *(106)*

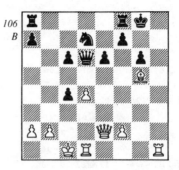

106
B

**22 ... f6? 23 ♕e4 ♔f7 24 ♖h7+
♔e8 25 ♗f4 ♕d5 26 ♕xg6+ ♔d8
27 ♕g7 ♔c8 28 ♖g1 ♖d8 29 ♕e7**
(with his last move Black prevented
29 ♕xf8+, but now 30 ♕xd8+! is
threatened) **29 ... e5! 30 de c3 31
b3? ♕f3! 32 ♗e3 ♕e2**, and by now
it is White who is on the brink of
defeat. However, there is no
ambiguity about the position after
23 ♕e4 – it is won for White. A
game Taran-Streltsov, corres 1980,
concluded: **27 ♖h5** (instead of
♕g7) **27 ... ♕f3 28 ♗d6 c3 29
♖dh1! cb+ 30 ♔b1 f5 31 ♕g7!
♕d3+ 32 ♔xb2 ♕d2+ 33 ♔b1 f4
34 ♖c5! ♕d3+ 35 ♔a1 1-0.**

In the position of Diagram 106,
Black missed a notable opportunity:
22 ... c3! Now White can't play

23 ♕e4? ♕b4 or 23 ♖d3? ♕d5, but after 23 ♕e5! cb+ 24 ♔b1 ♕xe5! 25 de f6 26 ♖xd7 fg 27 ♖hh7, the result of it all is perpetual check to the black king.

So we see that delaying castling and trying to utilise the tempo to seize the initiative promises no success for White, and merely gives Black the interesting choice between 14 ... 0-0 and 14 ... ♗f4; or between 13 ... ♗d6 and 13 ... 0-0-0.

Summary

11 ♖h4	e6	12 ♗f4	♗d6					±
			♕a5+					=
11 0-0	e6	12 ♕e2						=∓
		12 ♖e1						∞
		12 c4	0-0-0					±/∞
			♘gf6					=∓
11 ♗d2	e6	12 ♕e2	0-0-0					±
			♗d6					±
			♘gf6	13 ♘e5	c5			∞
					♗d6			=
				13 ♖h4				=
			(13 0-0-0 – cf. 12 0-0-0)					
		12 c4	♘gf6	13 c5	b6			=
					0-0-0	14 ♕a3		=∓
						14 b4		∓
						14 ♕e2		∞
				13 ♕e2	0-0-0	14 ♘e5		=
					(14 c5 – cf. 13 c5)			
					(14 ♗c3 c5 15 0-0-0			
					– cf. 12 0-0-0)			
					♗d6	14 ♘f5	0-0-0	±
							♗f4	=
							0-0	=

8 10 ... ♛c7 11 ♗d2 e6 12 0-0-0 ♞gf6

1	e4	c6
2	d4	d5
3	♞c3	de
4	♞xe4	♗f5
5	♞g3	♗g6
6	♞f3	♞d7
7	h4	h6
8	h5	♗h7
9	♗d3	♗xd3
10	♛xd3	♛c7
11	♗d2	e6
12	0-0-0	♞gf6 (107)

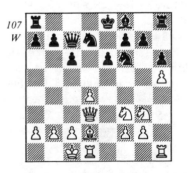

107
W

A key position for the whole Classical System, and one where there are various plans White can adopt in his fight for the advantage. From the mid-1960s, he chose the manoeuvre 13 ♛e2 followed by ♞e5. Today, 13 ♞e4 is more often seen.

But earlier, before the insertion of 8 h5 ♗h7 became popular, the plan of c4 and ♗c3 was considered the main line. Our analysis of this plan began in Chapter 5 (Variation B), and will be continued in the present chapter. Partly, the aim of this analysis will be to ascertain in what way the pawn placed on h5 affects positions similar to those examined in Chapter 5 – that is, 13 c4 0-0-0 or 13 ... b5 (Variation A), or 13 ♔b1 0-0-0 (Variation B1). However, we also study some new ideas here – for example, 13 ♔b1 c5 (Variation B2) – which would have featured in some of the lines in Chapter 5, but for the fact that 8 ♗d3 had departed from the scene by the time these new ideas came in.

From Diagram 107:

A 13 c4
B 13 ♔b1

A

	13	c4	b5 (112)

The alternatives are:

a) 13 ... 0-0-0 14 ♗c3, and now:

a1) 14 ... c5 (108).

108
W

Now **15 ♔b1** transposes into Variation B1, but has White anything more energetic? Let us see:

a11) **15 ♕e2** aims for ♘e5. This is hardly advisable, if only because 15 ... ♗d6 16 ♘e4 ♘xe4 17 ♕xe4 ♘f6 18 ♕e2 cd 19 ♘xd4 a6 leads to Chapter 9, Variation B, with the difference that here White has a tempo less (g3). Black can also play 15 ... cd 16 ♘xd4 a6, when a game Hulak-Bagirov (1976) continued: 17 ♘b3 (if 17 ♘f3, then 17 ... ♗d6 18 ♘e4 ♗e7! 19 ♘xf6 ♗xf6, with a draw in prospect) 17 ... ♗d6 18 ♘e4 (at this point the pawn sacrifice 18 ♗a5!? b6 19 ♗c3 is interesting; if 19 ... ♗xg3 20 fg ♕xg3, then 21 c5, with chances of penetrating to the black king) 18 ... ♘xe4 19 ♕xe4 ♘f6 20 ♕e2 ♕c6! 21 g3 ♗c7! (an ideal arrangement of the pieces!) 22 ♖xd8+ ♖xd8 23 ♖e1, and now Black could have secured the initiative with 23 ... ♕g2!

a12) Some writers give an ex-

clamation mark to **15 d5**, considering it the critical reply to 14 ... c5. But it isn't so simple. The retort 15 ... ♘b6 (109) threatens both the pawn on d5 and the one on c4 (on account of ... ♕f4+).

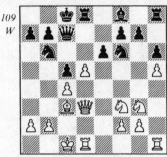

109
W

White is not likely to be pleased with either 16 ♗xf6 ♕f4+ (17 ♔b1 ♕xf6 18 ♘e4 ♕f5 19 d6 ♗xd6) or 16 ♔b1 ♘g4. Nor is there much future in 16 ♗e5 ♗d6 17 ♗xf6 gf 18 ♘e2.

a2) 14 ... ♗d6! starts a manoeuvre which exploits the position of the king on c1, and which we have seen before in Chapter 5. Further: 15 ♘e4 ♗f4+ 16 ♔c2 ♘e5! 17 ♘xe5 ♗xe5 (110).

110
W

If White plays 18 ♕e3 now, the mundane 18 ... ♘xe4 19 de (19 ♕xe4 ♗f6) 19 ... ♘xc3 20 ♕xc3 ♖xd1 21 ♖xd1 ♖d8 leads to a drawn position.

In a game Bronstein-Kotov, Amsterdam 1968, White continued with 18 ♘c5 ♗d6 19 ♘b3, preserving his minor pieces from exchange. After 19 ... ♕e7 20 a3 ♖d7?! 21 ♕e2 ♖e8 22 ♖he1 ♕f8?! 23 g4 ♖de7 24 ♕f3 ♘h7 25 ♘a5! f5 26 ♘xc6 bc 27 ♕xc6+ ♖c7 28 ♕a6+ ♔b8 29 c5 ♗f4 30 ♖xe6 ♖xe6 31 ♕xe6, Bronstein had chances of succeeding. However, the significance of this game should not be over-estimated. Transferring the knight from one flank square (g3) to another (b3) didn't strengthen White's position, and improving on Black's play is not difficult. A better move than 20 ... ♖d7 is 20 ... ♖he8, planning ... e5. Then, after 21 ♖de1, Black could choose between 21 ... ♖d7 (with a view to ... ♕d8, ... ♖de7, ... e5) and 21 ... ♘d7 (a sample variation being 22 g4 e5 23 de ♘xe5 24 ♗xe5 ♗xe5 25 ♕f5+ ♕d7 26 ♖xe5 ♖xe5 27 ♕xe5 ♕d3+ 28 ♔c1 ♕xb3).

b) There is also another way of utilising the king's position on c1 to force simplifications: **13 ... ♗d6** **14 ♘e4 ♗f4** *(111).*

But the bishop exchange weakens the black squares, and although in

111
W

a game Mnatsakanian-Shakarov (1981) Black did achieve a draw, this was not such a simple matter: 15 g3 (perhaps it was worth activating his rook with 15 ♖h4!? ♗xd2+ 16 ♘fxd2) 15 ... ♗xd2+ 16 ♘fxd2 0-0-0 17 ♕a3 ♘xe4 18 ♘xe4 ♔b8 19 f4 (another, probably better, method was 19 ♘d6!? ♘f6 20 c5 ♘e8 21 ♘c4; also, two moves earlier, White could have played 17 c5!? ♘xe4 18 ♘xe4 ♘f6 19 ♘d6+ ♔b8 20 ♕e2 ♘e8 21 ♘c4) 19 ... ♘f6 20 ♘c5 ♖he8 21 ♕e3 ♘d7 22 ♘xd7+ (after 23 ♘d3 f6, or 22 ... ♕a5, Black's position is solid; but the endgame that Mnatsakanian is heading for is simply drawn) 22 ... ♖xd7 23 ♕e5 ♕xe5 24 de ♖ed8 25 ♖xd7 ♖xd7 26 ♖h1 ♖d8! 27 ♖g4 ♖g8. The rook on g4 is no more than a symbol of activity. Another ten moves, and the players agreed to a draw.

The purpose of all three continuations – 13 ... 0-0-0 14 ♗c3

♗d6!, 13 ... ♗d6 and 13 ... b5!? – is to prove that White's move 13 c4 was over-hasty. But the difference between them is crucial. In the first two cases Black is counting on an easy draw, whereas 13 ... b5 fights for the point d5 and, ultimately, for the initiative.

112
W

14   c5

In Hanov-Shakarov, 1979, White played 14 ♞e5?!, hoping to exploit Black's delay in removing his king from the centre. There followed: 14 ... ♞xe5 15 de ♛xe5! (this involves some risk, but is stronger than 15 ... bc 16 ♛xc4 ♞d5 17 f4, with f5 to follow) 16 ♖he1 bc 17 ♛c2 ♛b5 18 a4 (18 ♞f5 looks attractive, but after 18 ... ♖d8 it isn't easy to find a continuation of the attack. The combination 19 ♞xg7+ ♗xg7 20 ♖xe6+ fe 21 ♛g6+ gives a draw after 21 ... ♔f8? 22 ♗b4+ ♛xb4 23 ♖xd8+ ♔e7 24 ♛xg7+ ♔xd8 25 ♛xf6+, but 21 ... ♔d7! is in Black's favour) 18 ... ♛b3?! (better 18 ... ♛b7, though even

then White's chances shouldn't be underrated; for example, 19 ♞f5 ♗e7? – *19 ... ♖d8* – 20 ♞xg7+ ♔f8 21 ♞xe6+ fe 22 ♛g6) 19 ♖xe6+ fe 20 ♛g6+ ♔e7 21 ♗c3 ♞d5! 22 ♞f5+!! (White loses with 22 ♗xg7 c3, or 22 ♖e1 ♔d8 23 ♗a5+ ♔c8 24 ♛xe6+ ♔b7 25 ♛d7+ ♔a6 26 ♛xc6+ ♞b6 27 ♗xb6 ♛xb6 28 ♛xa8 ♗a3!) 22 ... ef 23 ♖e1+ ♔d7 24 ♗a5! ♞e7 (perpetual check similarly results from 24 ... ♞b6 25 ♛f7+ ♔d6 26 ♖e6+ ♔c5 27 ♖e5+ ♞d5 28 ♖xd5+ cd 29 ♛c7+ ♔d4 30 ♛f4+) 25 ♛e6+ ♔e8 26 ♛xc6+ ♔f7 27 ♛e6+, with a draw.

Black is happy with 14 cb cb+ 15 ♔b1 ♛b7 or 15 ... ♗d6 (compare Chapter 5, Variation B1).

14 c5 concedes the d5 point just as 14 cb does, but at least it cramps Black. Also, there is reason to think that the black king will be easier to get at (on either wing) than the white king.

14   ...   ♗e7 *(113)*

113
W

The plan of 14 ... a5, 15 ... ♘d5 and then ... 0-0-0 (or ... ♚d8-c8-b7) deprives Black of the counter-chances based on queenside play against the white king or a break in the centre with ... e5.

In a game Shishov-Vdovin, Lokomotiv Ch Sochi 1980, Black succumbed to a pawn storm after castling on the kingside: 15 ♚b1 0-0 16 ♘e4 ♘d5 17 ♘c3 ♘xc3+ 18 ♛xc3 ♘f6 19 ♛c1 ♘d5 20 ♖de1 b4 21 g4 ♖ab8 22 ♚a1 b3 23 a3 a5 24 ♚b1 ♛c8 25 ♛c4 ♗d8 26 ♖hg1 ♛b7 27 ♘e5 f6 28 ♘g6 ♖e8 29 f4 ♛f7 30 ♛d3 ♘e7 31 g5 etc.

In this game, Vdovin showed what may await the white king. After ... b4 and ... ♖b8, the threat of ... ♘c3 hangs over it; if the king goes to a1, then the idea of ... b3 (aiming to answer a3 with ... ♘b4) comes into the picture. Yet Black lost ... Was Vdovin's whole conception faulty, or did he just show insufficient tactical flair?

As we have said, Black's other chance lies in the undermining move ... e5. For example, 16 ... e5 (instead of ... ♘d5) 17 ♘xe5 ♘xe5 18 de ♛xe5 19 ♘xf6+ ♗xf6 20 ♗c3 ♛xc5 21 ♗xf6 gf, or (to be more cautious) 19 ... ♛xf6 20 ♗c3 ♛f4.

An attempt by White to prevent this break with 16 ♖de1 is ineffective because of 16 ... ♘g4 17 ♛e2 (17 ♘e4 f5; 17 ♖e2 ♘xf2; or

17 ♘f5 ef 18 ♖xe7 ♘xc5) 17 ... ♖fe8.

On the whole, White has good reason to refrain from 13 c4 in favour of 13 ♚b1.

B

13 ♚b1

Now Black can choose between:

B1 13 ... 0-0-0
B2 13 ... c5

B1

13 ... 0-0-0
14 c4

14 ♛e2 in conjunction with ♚b1 looks like a loss of time, but is 'renowned' for bringing quick success to Kurajica in a game against Bagirov, Titovo Uzica 1978: 14 ... ♗d6 15 ♘e4 ♘xe4 (15 ... ♗f4!?) 16 ♛xe4 *(114)*

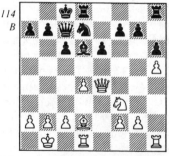

16 ... c5 17 dc ♘xc5 18 ♛c4!

Problems have unexpectedly arisen for Black. The threat is 19 ♗e3 and 20 ♖xd6; if the knight leaves c5, then ♛d4 follows, attacking the pawns on a7 and g7; nor does the bishop want to move from d6, on account of ♗f4

Bagirov played 18 ... ♖he8 19 ♗e3 ♗f8, and after 20 ♗f4 ♕c6 21 ♘e5 ♕xg2 (or 21 ... ♕c7 22 ♘d7! ♕c6 23 ♘xf8 ♖xf8 24 ♗e3 ♘d7 25 ♕xc6+ bc 2 ♗xa7 c5 27 ♖d3, with a won position) 22 b4 f6 23 ♘g6 ♕f3 24 ♖de1 b5 25 ♕xb5 ♕b7 26 ♕c4 a5 27 c3 ♕a6 28 ♖e4!, he lost a piece and the game.

The least of the evils was 18 ... ♖hg8, defending the g-pawn and preparing to meet 19 ♗e3 with 19 ... ♘a6.

A more general point is that when playing ... c5 before White's c4, Black has to be careful not to let White make effective use of the c4 square. This factor will crop up repeatedly in the sections which follow.

To come back to Kurajica-Bagirov, we would point out that in addition to 15 ... ♗f4 Black has another possibility, a move later: 16 ... ♘f6 17 ♕e2 ♖he8, with the idea of ... e5. White doesn't appear to have any convincing rejoinder: 18 ♘e5 c5 19 ♗c1 ♗f8 20 dc ♗xc5, or 18 c4 e5 19 c5 ♗f8 20 de ♘d7.

14 ... c5
15 ♕e2

Also 15 ♗c3. To what was said about the analogous 14 ♗c3 in Chapter 5 (B2), we will add another game: Spassky-Portisch, match 1980. On 15 ... cd 16 ♘xd4 a6 17 ♘b3, Portisch played 17 ...

♗e7, and after 18 ♗a5 b6 19 ♗c3 ♘c5 20 ♕f3 ♕b7 21 ♕xb7+ ♔xb7 22 ♘xc5+ bc 23 f3 ♖xd1+ 24 ♖xd1 ♔c6 25 ♖h1 ♘d7 26 ♔c2 ♖g8 27 ♘e2 ♗d6 28 a3 f5 29 b4, Black had the worse ending.

In Bagirov's view, Black should draw easily by either of two methods: 26 ... ♗f6 (instead of ... ♖g8) 27 ♗xf6 gf!, or 22 ... ♗xc5 (instead of ... bc) 23 ♗xf6 gf 24 ♘e4 f5! 25 ♘xc5+ bc, with counterplay on the open files.

15 ... ♗d6

The position after 15 ... cd 16 ♘xd4 a6 17 ♘b3! is unpleasant for Black; (again we refer you to Chapter 5), for in playing his queen to e2 White has more or less gained a tempo. (Instead of ♗c3-a5-c3, as in Spassky-Portisch, White will now play ♗a5-c3.) Is it all that important? To the variations 17 ... ♘c5 and 17 ... ♗d6 (compare Chapter 5), we will add one more: 17 ... ♗e7 (imitating Portisch) 18 ♗a5 b6 19 ♗c3 ♘c5, and now not 20 ♕f3, but 20 ♗e5, or 20 ♘xc5 ♗xc5 21 b4 ♗e7 22 c5, with the initiative.

16 ♘e4 ♘xe4
17 ♕xe4 ♘f6
18 ♕e2 (115)

What concerns us here is to see how the various possibilities for Black (examined in Chapter 5) are affected by the placing of White's h-pawn:

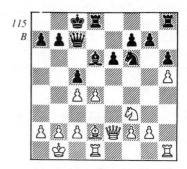

115
B

a) **18 ... ♕c6** 19 ♘e5 ♗xe5 20 de ♕e4+ 21 ♕xe4 ♘xe4 22 ♗e3. In Chapter 5 this endgame was dubious for Black, but here it looks acceptable, since the knight has been given the retreat square g5. Vasyukov-A.Zaitsev, 1969, continued 22 ... ♖xd1+ 23 ♖xd1 b6 24 ♖h1 f5 25 ef ♘xf6 26 ♖h4 e5, and Black drew without trouble.

b) In Kavalek-Karpov, 1979, the World Champion had the task of extinguishing White's powerful initiative: **18 ... ♖he8** 19 ♗c3 ♖e7 (if 19 ... ♘g4 here, then 20 dc ♗xc5 21 ♘d4 is adequate. Black doesn't have ... h5, and 21 ... ♕f4 loses to 22 g3) 20 ♘e5 cd 21 ♗xd4 ♗xe5 22 ♗xe5 ♕a5 (22 ... ♕c6!?) 23 ♖xd8+ ♔xd8 24 f3! ♖d7 25 g4 ♔e7?! (the ending after 25 ... ♕d2 26 ♖e1 is good for White on account of the pawn on h5, fixing the favourable situation on the king's wing. But the line Karpov goes in for is very risky) 26 ♖h2?!

(after 26 ♗c3 White would have good attacking chances) 26 ... ♘e8 27 a3 ♕a4! 28 ♖h1 ♕b3 29 ♗c3 ♘d6! (the position has become unclear; it still will be, when the draw is agreed) 30 ♖c1 ♘xc4 31 ♗b4+ ♘d6 32 ♖c3 ½-½.

c) We don't know of any games in which Black played *à la* Botvinnik: **18 ... cd** 19 ♘xd4 a6 20 ♗c3 ♖d7! etc. (Compare Chapter 5, Variation B2). In contrast to the 18 ... ♖he8 line, the position of the white pawn on h5 has in this case virtually no significance.

So queenside castling combined with 18 ... cd or 18 ... ♕c6 gives Black, if not equal play (in the full sense of the term), then at any rate a sound position.

B2

13   ...   c5 *(116)*

116
W

Instead of the usual queenside castling and the traditional play 'for equality', Black aims for a position where the players have castled on opposite wings and both have chances; this is the new way of handling the Caro-Kann (we have discussed it before). Admittedly, in practice this method of play has hardly ever been tried against 13 ♔b1, but the explanation is simple: the plan involving ♔b1 departed almost entirely from the scene at the same time as 8 ♝d3. (For instance, in the Kavalek-Karpov and Spassky-Portisch games from the previous section, the 13 ♔b1 line was reached almost accidentally; in the former game the move order was 13 ♛e2 c5 14 ♔b1 0-0-0?! 15 c4, and in the latter: 13 c4 0-0-0 14 ♝c3?! c5 15 ♔b1.)

In Chapter 10, we shall give games in which Black played 13 ... c5 as a reply to 13 ♛e2. Does 13 ♔b1 make the situation less favourable for this pawn break? Probably not.

How, in fact, is White to counter Black's immediate 13 ... c5 . . .? The reply 14 ♞e5 looks energetic, yet if Black avoids taking on e5 (14 ... ♞xe5 15 de ♛xe5?? 16 ♛b5+) and continues with 14 ... cd, White doesn't appear to have anything better than 15 ♞xd7 ♛xd7 16 ♝f4, equalising the pawns and the chances.

14 ♛e2

This solid and logical move presents Black with a choice:

a) **14 ... c4**, with the aim of securing d5 for a knight, inspires no particular confidence. After 15 ♞f5 0-0-0? 16 ♞e3 ♞b6 17 ♝a5 ♞fd5 18 ♞e5, Black is in trouble. Still, after 15 ... ♜c8! not everything is so clear.

b) The same position can also arise after **14 ... ♜c8** 15 ♞f5 c4, but in this line an interesting try is 15 ... cd 16 ♞3xd4 ♛c4 *(117)*.

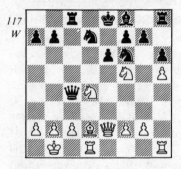

117
W

And now:

b1) In Meribanov-Shakarov, 1980, White exchanged queens and lost his chances of advantage: **17 ♛xc4** ♜xc4 18 ♜he1 ♔d8 19 b3 ♜c5 20 ♞g3 ♔c8 21 c4 a6 22 ♝b4 ♜e5 etc.

b2) Instead, a piece sacrifice promises a dangerous attack: **17 ♛f3!** ef 18 ♜he1+ ♔d8 19 ♛xb7, or 17 ... ♛d5 18 ♛xd5 (18 ♛g3?! ef 19 ♜he1+ ♞e4) 18 ... ♞xd5 19 ♞b5!? (19 ... ef 20 ♜he1+ ♔d8 21 ♝a5+ ♞c7 22 ♜d3 b6 23 ♞xa7).

c) A game Kupreichik-Castiglione, 1968, in which Black chose **14 ... cd** 15 ♞xd4 *(118)*, was won crushingly by White:

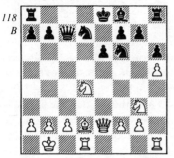

118
B

On 15 ... a6?, there followed

16 ♞xe6! fe 17 ♛xe6+ ♚d8 18 ♖he1 ♖c8 19 ♝c3 ♛c6 20 ♝xf6+ gf 21 ♖xd7+ ♛xd7 22 ♛b6+! ♛c7? 23 ♛xf6+ ♚d7 24 ♛e6+ and mates. In our view, 15 ... ♝c5 was adequate.
d) **14 ... ♝e7** is playable, postponing ... cd for a move or two.

Certainly 13 ... c5 solves Black's problem successfully and ensures him counterplay.

Summary

13 c4	0-0-0	14 ♝c3	c5	15 ♛e2		=
				15 d5		∞
			(15 ♚b1 – cf. 13 ♚b1)			
			♝d6			=
	♝d6					±
	b5	14 ♞e5				=
		14 cb				∓
		14 c5				∞
13 ♚b1	0-0-0	14 ♛e2				=
		14 c4	c5	15 ♝c3		=
				15 ♛e2	cd	±
					♝d6	=
	c5	14 ♞e5				=
		14 ♛e2	c4			±
			♖c8			±
			cd			−
			♝e7			=

9 13 ♘e4

1	e4	c6
2	d4	d5
3	♘c3	de
4	♘xe4	♗f5
5	♘g3	♗g6
6	♘f3	♘d7
7	h4	h6
8	h5	♗h7
9	♗d3	♗xd3
10	♕xd3	♕c7
11	♗d2	e6
12	0-0-0	♘gf6
13	♘e4 *(119)*	

119
B

Common sense in chess . . .
Before deciding which scheme to
adopt in his bid for the advantage
(c4 and ♗c3, or ♕e2 and ♘e5),
White improves the position of his
passive knight on g3. After 13 ...
0-0-0 14 g3, Black has to do

something about the threatened
15 ♗f4. Of several moves that
have been played, only two – 14 ...
♘c5 (A1) and 14 ... ♘xe4 (A2) –
have had a solid reputation, at
least until recently. In both cases,
by exchanging off the knight on
e4 Black acquires the possibility of
parrying ♗f4 with ... ♗d6. After
14 ... ♘c5 15 ♘xc5 ♗xc5, Black is
more actively placed than in the
14 ... ♘xe4 line; thanks to the
position of his bishop on c5 and
his knight on f6 (rather than d7),
the white d-pawn is under fire.
However, practice has shown that
his opponent's activity doesn't
bother White. The bishop on c5
will have to retreat 'of its own
accord'; also, in positions of this
type, Black's knight needs to be on
d7 for the moment, to guard the e5
point. In short, these days 14 ...
♘c5 cannot be called a solid
continuation.

The modern trend is represented
in this chapter by Variations B
and C – that is, 13 ... ♖d8 or
13 ... ♗e7, followed (of course!)
by kingside castling.

Black's choices, then, are:

A 13 ... 0-0-0
B 13 ... ♖d8
C 13 ... ♗e7

A

13   ...   0-0-0
14 g3

And now Black has:
A1 14 ... ♘c5
A2 14 ... ♘xe4
and also:

a) In Geller-Petrosian, 1967, the play took an unusual course: **14 ... ♘g4?!** 15 ♕e2 (15 ♗f4 ♕a5, with threats of ... ♕xa2 and ... f5) 15 ... ♘df6 16 ♗f4 ♕a5 17 ♘xf6! gf 18 ♘d2 f5? 19 ♔b1? ♕a6 20 c4 ♖g8 21 ♘b3, and Black 'merely' has the worse position. White could have won with 19 f3 ♘f6 20 ♘b3, threatening 21 ♕e5; hence 18 ... ♖g8 was essential (19 f3 e5 20 ♘b3 ♕a6).

b) **14 ... c5?** 15 ♗f4 c4, as in Tsheshkovsky-Kasparov, USSR Ch 1978, is also weak *(120)*.

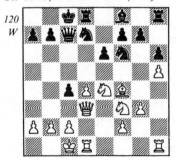

120
W

Black had assumed that 16 ♗xc7 cd 17 ♘xf6 ♔xc7 18 ♘xd7 dc 19 ♔xc2 ♔xd7 20 ♘e5+ ♔e8 21

d5 ♗d6 leads to a level ending, and that **16 ♕e2 ♕c6** 17 ♘xf6 gf 18 d5 ed 19 ♘d4 ♕a6 gives him counter-chances in a complex position.

Tsheshkovsky chose the latter variation, and obtained the better prospects after 20 ♔b1 ♗d6 21 ♕f3! ♗xf4 22 ♕xf4 ♘e5 23 ♕f5+ ♔b8 24 f4.

But we reject 14 ... c5 for another reason. It turns out that after 16 ♗xc7 cd, the unexpected 17 ♗xd8! ♘xe4 18 ♖h4! leaves White the exchange up.

A

14   ...   ♘c5
15 ♘xc5 ♗xc5 *(121)*

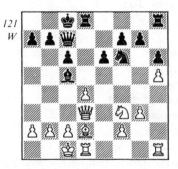

121
W

White's next few moves might seem obvious: 16 c4, 17 ♗c3, 18 ♕e2. In practice, strangely enough, he has tended to neglect this sound plan. For example:
a) **16 ♗f4 ♗d6** 17 ♗e5 ♗xe5 18 ♘xe5 c5 19 ♕c4 ♖d5 20 f4 ♘e4 with a good game for Black, Velikov-Podgayets, USSR Ch 1968.

b) Ljubojević-Karpov, Linares 1981, went: **16 ♕c4 ♗d6 17 ♕a4 ♔b8 18 ♘e5 ♘d5 19 f4 ♘b6 20 ♕b3 ♗xe5 21 de ♘d5 22 c4** (the World Champion considers it wasn't worth weakening the squares d3 and d4, and analyses 22 ♕f3, with the following results: 22 ... ♖d7 23 ♕g4 ♖hd8 24 ♕xg7 ♕b6 25 ♕g4 ♘e3 26 ♗xe3 ♕xe3+ 27 ♔b1 ♖xd1+ – 27 ... ♕xg3 28 ♖xd7 is in White's favour – 28 ♖xd1 ♖xd1+ 29 ♕xd1 ♔c8! with a drawn endgame) 22 ... ♘e7 23 ♗e3 c5 24 ♖xd8+ ♖xd8 25 ♖d1 ♖xd1+ 26 ♕xd1 b6 27 ♕d3?! g6! 28 hg fg 29 a3 a5 30 b3 h5 31 ♕e4 ♘f5 32 ♗f2 ♕d7, and the ending favours Black.

c) **16 ♕e2 ♗xd4 17 ♘xd4?** (17 ♗f4 e5 18 ♗xe5 ♗xe5 19 ♘xe5 promised White no advantage, but Tal's gambit is incorrect) 17 ... ♖d4 18 ♗f4 ♖xd1+ 19 ♕xd1 (or 19 ♖xd1 ♕a5) 19 ... e5 20 ♗e3 ♕a5, and White lacks both his pawn and the initiative, Tal-Chandler, Wijk aan Zee 1982.

d) A game Kapengut-Podgayets, USSR 1970, is interesting: **16 a3** (preparing for an early pawn attack on the queenside) 16 ... ♗d6 17 ♕e2 ♘d7 (17 ... c5 18 dc ♗xc5 19 ♗f4 ♗d6 20 ♗xd6 ♖xd6 21 ♖xd6 ♕xd6 22 ♘e5 ♕c7 23 ♖h4! ♔b8 24 ♖c4 ♕e7 25 ♖d4 with advantage – Boleslavsky) 18 c4 c5 (or 18 ... e5 19 de ♘xe5 20

♗c3, and again in Boleslavsky's opinion White stands better) 19 ♗c3 cd 20 ♘xd4 a6 21 ♘b3 ♖hg8 22 ♖d2 ♗e7 23 ♖hd1 ♘f6 24 ♘d4 ♖ge8 25 b4 ♗f8 26 ♔b2 ♖d7 27 ♘b3 ♖ed8 28 ♗d4 ♕c6! 29 ♗xf6 gf 30 ♖xd7 ♖xd7 31 ♘a5 ♕c7 32 ♖xd7 ♕xd7 33 c5 f5, and after conducting the defence well, Black has preserved hopes of drawing.

In this last example, did the reader notice how quickly Black renounced the 'advantages' which 14 ... ♘c5 has over 14 ... ♘xe4 (16 ... ♗d6, 17 ... ♘d7)? Essentially, White gained two free tempi; imagine 14 ... ♘xe4 15 ♕xe4 ♗d6, and then three moves for White at once: 16 a3, ♕e2, c4.

Boleslavsky has shown that the bishop retreat was pointless for Black; he recommends 16 ... ♖d7. Indeed, 17 c4 is then met by 17 ... ♗xd4 18 ♘xd4 e5, while after 17 ♗f4 ♗d6 18 ♘e5 ♖dd8 White has to reckon with ... ♘d5 (19 c4 c5).

In a recent game Christiansen-Chandler, Wijk aan Zee, White at last played the obvious-seeming move:

16 c4!

It's clear that 16 ... ♗xd4? doesn't now work: 17 ♘xd4 e5 18 ♕f5+, or 17 ... c5 18 ♘b5.

And in the game, Chandler had a rough time: 16 ... ♖he8 17 ♗c3 ♔b8 18 ♕e2 ♗f8 19 ♘e5 c5 20 dc ♗xc5 21 f4 ♘g8 22 ♔b1 f6 23 ♘g6

♕b6 24 ♖xd8+ ♖xd8 25 ♖d1
♖xd1+ 26 ♕xd1 ♔c8 27 ♕e2 ♔d7
28 g4 ♔e8 29 ♕e4 ♕d6 30 ♔c2
♕d7 31 a3 a5 32 f5 e5 33 ♘f4 a4 34
♘e6 ♗f8 35 ♗a5 ♘e7 36 ♗b4 ♔f7
37 ♕d3 ♕c8 38 ♕d8 1-0.

You get the impression that the
best answer to 16 c4 is 16 ... ♗d6,
asking White's permission to go
into Variation A22. But permission
may be refused, for example 17
♗c3 c5, and now not 18 ♕e2 cd 19
♘xd4 a6 (done it! – see A22), but
18 d5!

A2

14	...	♘xe4
15	♕xe4	

In recent years there has been
particularly intensive investigation
of this position. The search for the
best set-up for Black has taken
various directions. We shall examine:
A21 15 ... ♗e7
A22 15 ... ♘f6
and also:
a) **15 ... c5** *(122)*

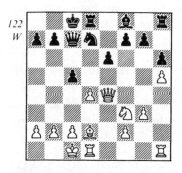

And now:

a1) A game Titz-Shakarov, corres
1979, was quickly drawn: 16 ♗f4
♗d6 17 ♗xd6 ♕xd6 18 ♘e5 ♘xe5
19 de ♕a6 20 a3 ♖xd1+ 21 ♖xd1
♖d8 etc. White rejected some
possibilities that were more
interesting, for example: 18 ♕g4
♕d5 19 c4!? ♘f6! 20 ♕f4 ♕e4, or
18 dc ♘xc5 19 ♕g4 ♕a6 20 ♔b1
♖xd1+ 21 ♖xd1 ♕e2 (the simple
21 ... ♖d8 22 ♘e5 leaves the
initiative with White) 22 ♕d4!
♘e4! (with 22 ... b6? 23 ♘e5, or
22 ... ♕xf3? 23 ♕xc5+ ♔b8 24
♕d6+ ♔c8 25 a3, Black is taking a
big risk) 23 ♘g1 ♕xh5 24 f3 ♘c5,
and White can regain his pawn
with equal chances.

This may seem all very well,
but if we know about Kurajica-
Bagirov (Chapter 8, Variation
B1), the following continuation
suggests itself:
a2) **16 dc!** If now 16 ... ♘xc5, then
17 ♕c4! and in view of the
threatened ♗f4 the position has
suddenly become unpleasant for
Black. the intermediate 16 ... ♘f6
transposes, after 17 ♕e2 ♗xc5 18
♖h4! *(123)*, into a no less
unpleasant position from Tal-
Hübner, Montreal 1979.

There can follow:
a21) **18 ... ♔b8?** This unfortunate
move was brilliantly refuted by
Tal: 19 ♗f4 ♗d6 20 ♖xd6 ♖xd6
21 ♘e5! ('though temporarily
blocking the key diagonal, White

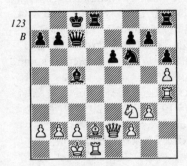

123
B

124
W

brings his knight into the fray with decisive effect. No satisfactory defence is to be found against the two threats of 22 ♘xf7 and 22 ♘c4. Thus, 21 ... ♘d5 fails against 22 ♘xf7 ♔xf7 23 ♖xf4 ♖f8 24 ♘xd6 ♖xf4 25 ♘b5 ♕c4 26 ♕e5+. Another hopeless line is 21 ... ♖hd8 22 ♘c4 ♘e8 23 ♘xd6 ♘xd6 24 ♖g4' – Tal) 21 ... ♔a8 22 ♘c4! ♘e8 23 ♖g4 ♕e7 24 ♘xd6 ♘xd6 25 ♖xg7, with a won position.

a22) However, even the better **18 ... ♕e7** doesn't solve the problem. According to Tal, after 19 ♖c4 ♔b8 20 ♘e5 ♖d5 White can choose between 21 ♘d3, and 21 ♗f4 ♗d6 22 ♖c6 with idea of ♖xd6.

Thus, the 'freeing' move 15 ... c5 dramatically enhances the activity of White's pieces. Black should postpone this break until after White's c4, as in the next examples.

b) **15 ... ♗d6** 16 c4 c5 *(124)*.

Play can continue:
b1) **17 ♔b1**, and now:
b11) **17 ... ♖he8** 18 ♗c3 ♘f6 19 ♕e2 ♖e7 20 ♘e5 leads to a position from Gheorghiu-Benko, Palma de Mallorca, 1968, which is favourable for White, although that game was drawn without much fight: 20 ... cd 21 ♗xd4 ♗xe5 22 ♗xe5 ♕c6 23 ♖xd8+ ♔xd8 24 ♖d1+ ♖d7 25 ♖xd7+ ♔xd7 26 ♗xf6 gf 27 b3 ♔e7 28 ♕e3 b6 29 ♔c2 ♕h1 30 ♕xh6 ♕f3 31 ♕d2 ♕xh5 32 b4 ♕f3 etc. White shouldn't have exchanged all the rooks; 24 ♖e1! ♖d7 25 g4 would have made life difficult for Black.

b12) In our view, Black has a good opportunity in **17 ... ♘f6!** 18 ♕c2 (for 18 ♕e2 cd 19 ♘xd4 ♗xg3! see Variation A22 below) 18 ... ♕c6 19 ♘e5 ♗xe5 20 de ♘g4.

b2) **17 ♗c3** is the most exact. Now 17 ... ♘f6 18 ♕e2 leads to A22, but Black may try 17 .... cd!? 18 ♕xd4

♗c5.

In the Gheorghiu-Benko game (see above), a different move order was employed: 15 ... ♗d6 16 ♔b1 ♖he8 17 c4 ♘f6 18 ♕e2 c5 19 ♗c3. This means that Benko didn't have the 'good opportunity' that we mentioned. He had another, though: 18 ... e5! (instead of ... c5) 19 c5 ♗f8 20 de ♘d7.

So it emerges that after 15 ... ♗d6 the play will generally transpose into Variation A22 (with 15 ... ♘f6), but some additional possibilities also crop up for Black (16 c4 c5 17 ♗e3 cd!?, and perhaps some other lines too – we can easily surmise that there should be positions where the knight on d7 is effective).

A21

15   ...   ♗e7 (125)

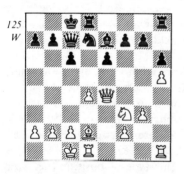

Without doubt a subtle move. The blow ♗f4 will be parried by ... ♗d6, while a good answer to 16 c4 c5 17 ♗c3 is 17 ... ♗f6. On 16 ♘e5, Black can choose either 16 ...

♘xe5 17 de ♖d5, or 16 ... f5 17 ♕e2 ♘xe5 18 de ♖d5.

16   ♔b1   ♖he8
17   ♕e2! (127)

Also 17 c4 c5 18 ♗f4 ♗d6, and now:

a) **19 ♘e5 (126)**

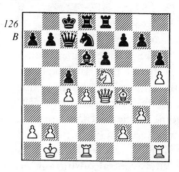

19 ... ♘xe5? 20 de ♗f8 (we are heading for the type of Caro-Kann ending that is normally desired by White. Black is tied down by the need to defend the pawns on f7 and g7; later, he will have to withstand a kingside pawn attack) 21 ♗e3 ♖xd1+ 22 ♖xd1 ♖d8 23 ♖xd8+ ♕xd8 24 ♔c2 ♕a5 25 a3 ♕a4+ 26 ♔c1 ♔c7?! (as Geller notes, 26 ... ♗e7! was more precise, aiming to answer 27 ♕g4 or 27 ♕f4 with 27 ... ♗g5. White could play 27 f4 ♔c7 28 g4, but Black would have saving chances due to the active position of his queen. Now the queen is forced to retreat) 27 ♕f4! ♕d7 28 b3 ♔d8 29 ♔c2 ♔e8 30 ♕e4 ♕c7 31 f4 ♗e7 32 g4

♗h4 33 f5 ♗g3 34 fe fe 35 ♕g6+
♔f8 36 ♕xe6 ♗xe5 (Black's
defence appears to have held, but
the white king now enters the
game with decisive effect) 37
♔d3! ♗g3 38 ♔e4 ♗h2 39 ♔f5
♗g3 40 ♗d2 ♗h2 41 ♗c3, and in
view of 41 ... ♕f7+ 42 ♕xf7+ ♔xf7
43 ♔e4 and 44 ♔d5, Black
resigned, Geller-Hort, Skopje 1968.

Geller's fine win contains a
significant flaw. In Diagram 126,
Black shouldn't have exchanged
knights. Nor was 19 ... f5? any
good in view of the combinative
stroke 20 ♘f7!, but 19 ... ♖e7!
basically refutes White's plan.
White's central position is shaky,
20 ... cd is threatened, and after
20 ♘xd7 ♖exd7 the initiative
passes to Black.

b) In a game against Vukić, Novi
Sad 1978, Geller varied with **19
♗xd6 ♕xd6 20 ♘e5.** Vukić was
evidently trying to win, and
therefore after 20 ... ♘xe5 21
♕xe5 he rejected an immediate
queen exchange in favour of 21 ...
cd 22 ♕xg7 e5 23 ♕xf7 ♖f8 24
♕g6 ♖xf2 25 ♕xd6 ♖xd6 26 ♖he1
♖b6 27 b3 ♖f5? (a serious
mistake) 28 g4 ♖g5 29 ♖e4 ♔d7
30 ♖de1! ♖e6 31 ♔c2 ♖e7 32 ♔d3
b6 33 b4 ♔d6 34 ♖f1, and the
endgame clearly favours White.
27 ... ♖a6 would have drawn
(28 a4 ♖f3).

17 ♕e2 is another discovery of

Geller's.

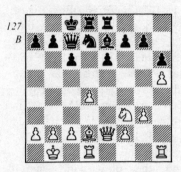

127
B

White doesn't now have to
reckon with ... ♘f6 (in reply to
♖he1) or ... f5 (in the case of ♘e5).
He is preparing 18 ♖he1. Although
his last two move (♔b1, ♕e2) look
like a loss of time, the freeing
advance ... c5 plays into his hands
as before: 17 ... c5? 18 ♗f4 ♗d6 19
♗xd6 ♕xd6 20 dc ♕xc5 21 ♖d3.

17 ...   ♗d6

17 ... ♗f8 is also possible, so as
to answer 18 ♖he1 with 18 ... ♘f6,
attacking both the h-pawn and the
d-pawn. If then 19 ♗f4, Black has
19 ... ♕b6. Although, after that,
20 ♘e5! appears to be to White's
advantage, a game Balashov-
Hübner, Wijk aan Zee 1982, took
a different course: 18 c4 c5
19 ♗c3 *(128)*.

This type of position (i.e. with
... ♖he8 and ... ♗f8 while the
knight is on d7) can also come
about (if Black wants it) after
15 ... ♗d6, or in Chapter 8,
Variation B1. It is therefore

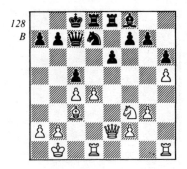

128
B

important to establish how reliable this position is for him. There was nothing attractive in Hübner's handling of it: 19 ... ♔b8 20 ♖he1 cd 21 ᗺxd4 a6 22 ᗺb3 ♔a8 23 ♕f3!, and Black was in difficulties. In our opinion, bringing the king to a8 was wrong. 19 ... a6 is correct, with a view to 20 ♖he1 cd 21 ᗺxd4 ᗺc5, or 21 ... ♗e7 with ... ♗f6 to follow.

    18 ♖he1 ♖e7

Or:

a) **18 ... e5** (like 17 ... c5 in Diagram 127) opens up interesting possibilities for White more than Black; two good lines are 19 c4 e4 20 ᗺh4 ᗺf6 21 ᗺf5 and 19 de ᗺxe5 20 ♗c3.

b) Geller-Kasparov, USSR Ch 1978, went: **18 ... ᗺf6 19 ᗺc5 c5 20 dc** (leads to the better ending. This is pleasant for White, but the 'risk' of drawing is great! After 20 ♗c1!? ♗f8 21 dc ♗xc5 we have a middlegame position, but then is it to White's advantage?) 20 ...

♗xe5 21 ♕xe5 ♕xe5 22 ♖xe5 ♖d4 23 ♔c1 ♖ed8 24 f3 ᗺd7 25 ♖ee1 (he should probably have kept the rooks on with 25 ♖e2 ᗺxc5 26 ♖de1) 25 ... ᗺxc5 26 ♗c3 (26 g4 was more precise) 26 ... ♖xd1+ 27 ♖xd1 ♖xd1+ 28 ♔xd1 f6 29 ♗b4 ᗺd7 30 ♔e2 (after 30 ♗e7! f5! 31 ♔e2 ᗺf6 32 ♗xf6 gf 33 ♔e3 e5 White cannot win, but now it is Black how gets ideas of victory) 30 ... ♔d8! Bringing his king to f7 and following with ... g6 gives Black a few chances, though not enough to win.

We shall now follow the game Kasparov-Vukić, European Team Ch, Skara 1980:

    19 c4 c5
    20 ♗c3 ᗺf6
    21 ᗺe5 *(129)*

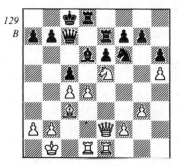

129
B

This sort of position is already known to the reader from the games Kavalek-Karpov (Chapter 8, Variation B1) and Gheorghiu-Benko (see above, 15 ... ♗d6). The difference is that Gheorghiu's rook was still on h1, while Kavalek hadn't played either ♖he1 or g3. It's clear that Vukić is in for a hard time.

21	...	**cd**
22	**♖xd4?!**	

22 ♗xd4 ♗xe5 23 ♗xe5 ♖xd1+ 24 ♖xd1 ♕c6 25 g4 ♖d7 26 ♖e1! was more accurate.

22	...	**♗xe5**
23	**♖xd8+**	**♕xd8**
24	**♗xe5**	**♖d7?!**

Vukić neglects the opportunity to cross his opponent's plans by 24 ... ♕a5! threatening ... ♘xh5. The game continued: 25 ♗c3 ♕b6 26 g4 ♕d6 27 f3 (27 g5 hg 28 h6 isn't very convincing in view of 28 ... ♕f4 29 hg ♖d8) 27 ... a6 28 a4! (a policy of confining and constricting. The endgame will be difficult for Black, but good prospects for him are not to be discerned in the middlegame either. If 28 ... ♕c6, then 29 b3, followed by ♔b2 and a5) 28 ... ♕d3+ 29 ♔c1 ♔c7 30 ♕xd3 ♖xd3 31 ♖f1 ♔c6 32 ♔c2 ♖d7 33 a5! ♘e8 34 ♖e1! ♖d6 35 f4 ♘f6? (one can understand Vukić's effort to prevent g5, after which a bishop sacrifice on g7 would be in the air; but . . .) 36 ♗xf6 gf 37 ♖d1! 1-0. In the pawn endgame White creates passed pawns on both wings.

A22

15	...	**♘f6**
16	**♕e2** *(130)*	

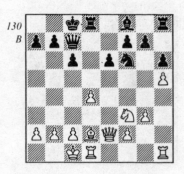

130
B

16	...	**♗d6**

Earlier, we noted that 'after 15 ... ♗d6 the play will generally transpose into Variation A22 (with 15 ... ♘f6), but some additional possibilities also crop up for Black'. It must be said that here again Black has alternative possibilities. They are, however, unfavourable for him:

a) For **16 ... c5** 17 dc! ♗xc5 18 ♖h4! see Tal-Hübner, above (15 ... c5).

b) **16 ... ♖d5**, and now:

b1) **17 ♗f4** led to a level position in Stein-Korchnoi, Sousse Z 1967: 17 ... ♗d6! (not 17 ... ♕a5 18 ♔b1 ♖xh5 19 ♘e5, or 18 ... ♘xh5 19 ♗d2 ♕a6 20 c4 ♘f6 21 ♘e5 ♖xd4 22 ♘xf7) 18 ♗xd6 (18 ♘e5 c5 is no better) 18 ... ♖xd6 19 ♘e5 ♖hd8 20 c3 c5.

b2) An effective refutation was carried out by Horvath against Vadasz (1980): **17 c4!** ♖xh5 18 ♗f4 ♕a5 (or 18 ... ♗d6 19 ♗xd6 ♕xd6 20 ♖xh5 ♘xh5 21 ♘e5) 19

♘e5 ♖xh1 20 ♖xh1 ♗d6 (20 ...
♕xa2? 21 ♘xf7 ♕a1+ 22 ♔c2
♕xa1 23 ♕xe6+ ♘d7 24 ♕e8
mate!) 21 ♘xf7 ♗xf4+ 22 gf ♕xa2
23 ♖h3 ♕a1+ 24 ♔c2 ♕a4+
25 ♖b3 with a won position.

So 16 ... ♗d6 must be considered
more precise!

17   c4

The nondescript waiting move
17 ♔b1 turns out to be a cunning
trap if Black does the same thing:
17 ... ♔b8? 18 c4 c5 19 dc ♕xc5 20
♗e3 ♕c7 21 ♖xd6! ♖xd6 22 c5.
The right course is 17 ... ♖he8!,
intending ... e5; and now neither
18 c4 e5 19 c5 ♗f8 20 de ♘d7, nor
18 ♘e5 c5 19 ♗c1 ♗f8 20 dc ♗xc5
promises White a plus.

17   ...   c5
18   ♗c3

But here 18 ♔b1 allows Black to
seize the initiative: 18 ... cd 19
♘xd4 (19 c5 d3!) 19 ... ♗xg3!
(131)

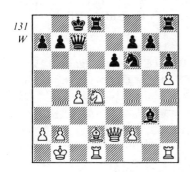

131
W

20 ♘xe6? ♖he8 21 fg (21 ♘xc7

was no better: 21 ... ♖xe2 22 fg
♖dxd2 23 ♖xd2 ♖xd2 24 ♘b5 a6
25 ♔c1 ♖d7 26 ♘c3 ♖d4 27 b3
♖g4, and White emerges a pawn
down) 21 ... ♖xe6 22 ♕f3 ♕c6!
(the tempting 22 ... ♖ed6? would
lead to a draw after 23 ♕f5+! ♕d7
24 ♕xd7+ ♖8xd7 25 ♔c2; for
example, 25 ... ♘e4 26 ♗f4 ♖xd1
27 ♖xd1 ♖xd1 28 ♔xd1 ♘f6 29
♗e5! ♘xh5 30 g4 ♘f6 31 ♗xf6 gf
32 ♔e2, or 25 ... ♖d3 26 ♗c3!
♖xg3 27 ♗xf6 gf 28 ♖hf1), and
White was forced to capitulate in
Perevyorzev-Shakarov, corres 1982,
on account of 23 ♕xc6+ ♖xc6 24
b3 ♘e4 or 24 ♖h4 ♖c5.

In the diagrammed position,
instead of 20 ♘xe6? White should
have played 20 ♘b5, although
after the obvious 20 ... ♕e5 the
chances are on Black's side.

18   ...   cd
19   ♘xd4

After 19 ♗xd4, Black's man-
oeuvres were successful in the
game Polovodin-Haritonov, 1980:
19 ... ♕a5! 20 ♔b1 ♗c7 21 c5
♕a4! 22 b3 ♕c6 23 ♘e5 ♗xe5 24
♗xe5, and now instead of 24 ...
♖hg8 a simpler line was 24 ...
♖xd1+ 25 ♖xd1 ♘xh5 26 ♕xh5
(or 26 ♖d6 ♕h1+ 27 ♖d1 ♕c6)
26 ... ♕e4+ 27 ♔a1 (but not 27
♔c1? g6 28 ♖d4 ♕e1+ 29 ♖d1
♕xf2!) 27 ... g6 28 ♖d4 ♕e1+ 29
♖d1 ♕e4, with a draw.

19   ...   a6 *(132)*

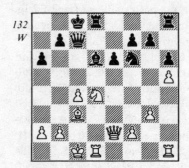

132
W

A critical position, of which the drawback, from Black's point of view, is that it merely leaves him with the prospect of fending off White's various tries for the advantage: 20 ♘f3, 20 ♘b3, 20 ♖d2 or 20 g4!? The last-mentioned move has not, to date, been seen in tournaments (although constructing the pawn chain f3/g4/h5 does strengthen White's position); the other three have produced these results:

a) **20 ♘f3 ♖d7** (20 ... ♕c6!?) 21 ♔b1 (21 ♘e5!?) 21 ... ♖hd8 22 a3 ♕c6 23 ♖h4 ♗c7 24 ♖xd7 ♖xd7 25 ♘e5 ♗xe5 26 ♕xe5 ♘e8 27 ♕e2 f6 28 ♖e4 e5 with no problems, Benko-Kagan, 1967.

b) **20 ♘b3 ♕c6** 21 ♖h4 (21 ♘a5 ♕c7) 21 ... ♗c7 22 ♘d4 ♕c5 23 b4 ♕g5+ 24 ♗d2 ♕e5 25 ♕xe5 ♗xe5 with chances for both sides in a complex endgame, Kudriashov-Haritonov, 1981.

c) **20 ♖d2 ♕c5** 21 ♔c2 ♗c7 22 g4 ♗a5!? 23 ♘b3 ♕c6 24 ♖xd8+

♖xd8 25 ♗xa5 ♕xh1 26 ♗xd8 ♔xd8 27 f3 ♕g1 28 ♕d2+ ♘d7, and a draw is to be expected, Cabrilo-Vadasz, 1981.

On the basis of what we have looked at, it is hard to draw categorical conclusions about the variation 13 ... 0-0-0 14 g3 ♘xe4. Advantage for White? Where is it? Fully equal play for Black? Perhaps not, Black *is* in the passive role here.

B

13 ... ♖d8 *(133)*

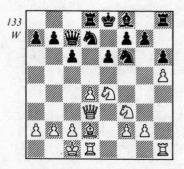

133
W

Here, as in Variation C, Black envisages kingside castling.

14 ♘xf6+ ♘xf6
15 ♘e5!

This is directed against 15 ... ♗d6 (16 ♕g3), or 15 ... c5 (16 ♕b5+; also 16 ♗f4 ♘d5 17 ♕b5+).

Karpov-Seirawan, Lucerne Ol 1982, continued instead: 15 ♕e2 c5 16 dc ♗xc5 (with Karpov's acquiescence, Seirawan has managed to gain a tempo over Variation C)

17 ♘e5 0-0 18 ♘d3 (there is risk in 18 f4 ♖d5 19 g4 ♖c8) 18 ... ♗e7 19 ♔b1 ♖c8 (19 ... ♖d4! is even better. This rook will have interesting possibilities on the 4th rank, while the other one will go to c8) 20 ♖c1 ♕c4 21 ♖he1 ♘d5 22 g4 a5 23 ♘e5 (an admission that Black's chances on the queenside are more substantial) 23 ... ♕xe2 24 ♖xe2 a4 25 a3 b5 26 ♘d3 ♖c4 27 f3 ♖fc8 28 c3 ♗d6, and Black has the more active position.

This game was played in round 3 of the Olympiad in Lucerne. At the same time as Karpov was up against difficulties, the Sweden-England match at a neighbouring table saw Wedberg, on the white side of this same variation, tear Grandmaster Stean's position apart! We are now following that game.

15   ...   a6

Intending 16 ... c5. A very important alternative is 15 ... ♗c5 16 ♕g3 (16 ♗e3 0-0) 16 ... ♗xd4 17 ♕xg7 *(134)*.

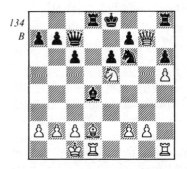

Black has a number of possibilities here, but they all seem to favour White:

a) **17 ... ♖g8** 18 ♕xf6 ♗xe5, and now not 19 ♕xh6?! ♖xd2!, but 19 ♕f3! with the better chances.

b) **17 ... ♖h7** 18 ♕xf6 ♕xe5 19 ♕xe5 ♗xe5 with a favourable endgame for White.

c) **17 ... ♕xe5** 18 ♕xh8+ ♔e7 19 ♕xd8+! (19 ♕xh6? ♗xb2+ 20 ♔b1 ♗a3) 19 ... ♔xd8 20 ♗e3 (20 c3!?) 20 ... c5 21 c3 ♘xh5 (after 21 ... ♕c7 22 cd cd+ 23 ♔b1 e5 24 ♗xh6, the pawn on h5 ought to decide the issue) 22 cd cd 23 ♗xd4 ♕f5, and Black's position, though not lost, is unpleasant.

16   ♗f4   ♗d6?

Black should of course have played 16 ... ♘d5 17 ♗g3 ♗d6, although after 18 c4 ♘f6 19 c5, or 18 ... ♘b4 19 ♕b3, things are again not easy for him.

17   ♕g3

Now Black has to abandon hope of castling and hence also of a settled life. There followed: 17 ... ♖g8 18 ♕f3 ♕a5 19 ♔b1 ♕d5 20 ♕h3 ♔e7 21 ♖he1, and White soon broke through to the black king.

Evidently 13 ... ♖d8, which holds up Black's kingside development, is a dubious idea.

C

13   ...   ♗e7 *(135)*

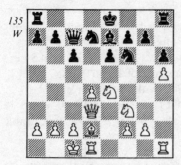

14 ♔b1

In a position where the players are castling on opposite wings, the manoeuvre to seize the d6 square by 14 g3 0-0 15 ♗f4 is pointless.

More likely, you would expect White to attempt the advance g4-g5 – but not to play 14 ♖dg1 before Black has castled! In that case Black could switch plans with 14 ... 0-0-0.

Matanović recommends 14 ♘xf6+!? ♘xf6 15 ♘e5 0-0 16 g4 ♖fd8 17 g5 hg 18 h6, or 14 ... ♗xf6 15 ♕e4! 0-0-0 16 ♗f4 ♕a5 17 ♔b1 ♖he8 18 ♗g3 as in Karpov-Seirawan, Linares 1983.

14	...	c5
15	♘xf6+	♘xf6
16	dc	0-0 *(136)*

In a game Hübner-Korchnoi, match 1980-1, Black played 16 ... ♗xc5. Exchanging queens by 17 ♕b5+ ♕c6 18 ♕xc6+ bc brings White no advantage (the pawns on f2 and h5 need defending), so Hübner preferred 17 ♕e2 0-0 18 ♘e5 ♖fd8 19 f4 ♖ac8 20 g4 with

sharp play. There followed: 20 ... ♗b6 (some annotators recommended 20 ... ♗d4!? 21 ♖c1 ♗xe5 22 fe ♘h7, with chances for both sides) 21 ♗c1 ♘d7 22 ♘xd7 (by now it was White they were advising: 21 ♘f3!? ♕c4 23 ♕g2) 22 ... ♖xd7 23 g5 ♖xd1 24 ♖xd1 ♕c4 25 ♖d3 hg 26 fg e5, and the position remains double-edged.

16 ... 0-0 seems more precise.

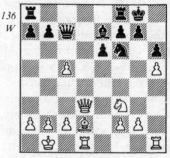

Geller-Christiansen, Moscow IZ 1982, continued: 17 g4 ♖fd8 18 ♕e2 ♕xc5 19 ♘e5 ♖ac8 20 ♗c1 ♕b4! (demonstrating what advantages Black gained through activating his queen. 21 g5 will be answered by 21 ... ♘e4) 21 a3. At this point, taking into account 21 ... ♕e4 22 ♕xe4 ♘xe4 23 ♗e3, the players agreed a draw.

New games and analyses in the near future will permit a truer assessment of the mutual chances in this interesting variation. It would seem that the only problem for Black is posed by 14 ♘xf6+.

Summary

13 ♘e4 0-0-0 14 g3	**♘g4**					±
	c5					±
	♘c5					±/±
	♘xe4 15 ♕xe4 c5					±
	♗d6 16 c4	**c5**	**17 ♔b1**			=
			17 ♗c3	**c5**		∞
			(17 ... ♘f6 –			
			cf. 15 ... ♘f6)			
		16 ♔b1				=
	♗e7 16 ♔b1	**♖he8 17 c4**				=
		17 ♕e2				±
	♘f6 16 ♕e2	**♖d5**				±
		(16 ... c5 – cf. 15 ... c5)				
		♗d6 17 ♔b1				=
		17 c4	**c5**			
		And now:				
		18 ♔b1				=/+
		18 ♗c3	**cd**	**19 ♗xd4**		=
				19 ♘xd4		±/=
13 ...	**♖d8 14 ♘xf6+ ♘xf6 15 ♕e2**					=
	15 ♘e5					±
13 ...	**♗e7 14 ♘xf6+**					∞
	14 ♔b1					=

10   13 ♕e2

1	e4	c6
2	d4	d5
3	♘c3	de
4	♘xe4	♗f5
5	♘g3	♗g6
6	♘f3	♘d7
7	h4	h6
8	h5	♗h7
9	♗d3	♗xd3
10	♕xd3	♕c7
11	♗d2	e6
12	0-0-0	♘gf6

The idea of 13 ♕e2 followed by
♘e5 had attention focused on it
after Spassky's win against Petrosian
in the 13th game of the 1966
World Championship Match (we
analyse this game in Chapter 11,
Variation A).

In the present chapter, we
examine continuations preventing
♘e5. Is 'preventing ♘e5' so
simple?

Well, 13 ♕e2 ♗d6 14 ♘f5 ♗f4
(Variation A) means either that
Black's king is unsettled by
15 ♘xg7+ ('White has three
pawns and an attack for the piece'
was the severe verdict passed not
so long ago . . .) or that his black
squares are weakened after 15

♗xf4 ♕xf4+ 16 ♘e3.

As for 13 ... c5 (Variation B),
which opens the position with
Black's king in the centre – this
too, at one time, was a step not
lightly taken! One particular
reason was that the books indicated
14 ♖h4 (see B2) as a very powerful
retort, threatening 15 ♗f4.

But nothing · stands still. If
today 13 ♕e2 is seen more rarely
than 14 ♘e4, an explanation is
that after trying out more or less
all conceivable replies to 13 ... c5,
White cannot say which one
promises him 'the better position'
or even 'a slight initiative'.

Two alternatives to 12 ... ♘gf6
are related to Variation A:
a) In a note to his duel with
Spassky (for this game see Variation
A in Chapter 11), Botvinnik wrote
that in the opening he 'did a
careless thing – playing ... ♘f6 too
early. Now Black will have
difficulties, since White is able to
establish his knight on e5.' What
method of development without
... ♘f6 did Botvinnik have in
mind? Naturally, **12 .. 0-0-0** 13
♕e2 ♗d6 *(137)*, as played in

Spassky-Barcza, Sochi 1966. Let's examine that game:

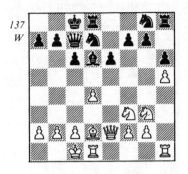

137
W

14 ♘e4 ♗e7?! **15 c4** ♘gf6 16 ♘c3 ♖he8 **17 g3** ♗f8 18 ♔b1 **♕a5?!** 19 ♘e5 ♘xe5 20 de ♘d7 21 ♘b5! ♕a6 22 ♘d6+ ♗xd6 23 ed ♘b6 24 b3 ♖xd6 25 ♗c3 ♕a3 (25 ... ♖xd1+ 26 ♖xd1 f6 is strongly answered by 27 ♕g4 ♖e7 28 ♗xf6) 26 ♗xg7 ♖xd1+ 27 ♖xd1 ♕c5 28 ♕f3! ♕f5+ 29 ♕xf5 ef 30 ♖h1 ♖e6 31 ♖h4 ♔d7 32 ♖f4, with a won position for White.

The significance of this game is diminished by some play (on both sides) that wasn't very convincing. In place of 18 ... ♕a5, a line to have been recommended is **18 ... e5!?** 19 de ♘xe5 20 ♗f4 ♖xd1+ 21 ♕xd1 (21 ♖xd1 ♘xf3) 21 ... ♘fd7.

Possibly on move 17 White should have played his knight to e5 at once, but if this doesn't give the desired advantage (**17 ♘e5** ♘xe5 18 de ♘d7 19 f4 f6? 20 ef ♗xf6 21 ♘e4 is in White's favour, but after 19 ... ♘c5 20 ♗e3 ♕a5

Black can reckon on drawing), he could try **15 g3** ♘gf6 16 ♔b1! (16 ♗f4 is ineffective because of 16 ... ♕a5, attacking the a-pawn). In view of the threatened 17 ♗f4, Black has nothing better than 16 ... ♘xe4 17 ♕xe4, transposing to an unfavourable position from Chapter 9 (A21).

13 ... ♗d6 ought to be combined with 14 ... ♗f4, exchanging off the black-squared bishops. A position of this type will be examined below (12 ... ♘gf6 13 ♕e2 ♗d6 14 ♘f5 ♗f4 15 ♗xf4 ♕xf4+ 16 ♘e3), but here the situation is more acceptable for Black; White's pieces aren't as effectively placed.

b) On the other hand, one other version of the same idea is clearly in White's favour: **12 ... ♗d6 13 ♘e4 ♗f4** (138)

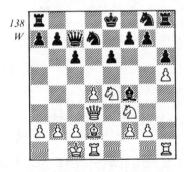

138
W

14 ♕a3! ♘gf6 15 ♖h4! ♘xe4 (or 15 .. ♗xd2+ 16 ♘fxd2 ♘xe4 17 ♘xe4) 16 ♗xf4 ♕d8 17 ♗e5! ♘ef6 18 ♘d2 (all White's moves deserve exclamation marks!) 18 ... b5 19

♕g3 ♖g8 20 ♗c7 ♕e7 21 ♗d6, with an overwhelming position; Timman-Ivanović, Nikšić 1978.

If White is intent on carrying out the plan of ♕e2 and ♘e5, and doesn't like the possibility of 12 ... 0-0-0 13 ♕e2 ♗d6 14 ♘e4 ♗f4, then he must make the queen move earlier – 12 ♕e2!, whereupon Black has nothing better than 12 ... ♘f6 (see Chapter 7, Variation C1).

13 ♕e2 *(139)*

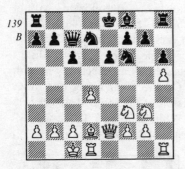

Here Black can choose between:
A 13 ... ♗d6
B 13 ... c5

A

13	...	♗d6
14	♘f5	♗f4
15	♗xf4!	

Alternatives:

a) The knight sacrifice 15 ♘xg7+ ♔f8 16 ♘xe6+ fe *(140)* robs the black king of its pawn cover, and at the same time gives White the full material equivalent: three pawns. Black might seem to be running a big risk, and yet you would not say so from looking at the games that have been played:

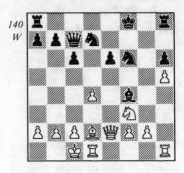

a1) Maltser-Bakharev, corres 1969, continued: **17 ♕xe6 ♖e8 18 ♕f5 ♗xd2+ 19 ♖xd2 ♖g8** (the king is solidly shielded by pieces which are also threatening to become active. What follows is not forced, but it is thematic) **20 ♖g1 ♖g4 21 ♘e5 ♘xe5 22 ♕xf6+ ♘f7 23 ♕f3 ♖ge4 24 g3 ♕a5 25 a3 ♕d5 26 ♖gd1 ♖d8**, and having failed to exploit the uncomfortable position of the black king, White already has trouble defending his extra pawns (27 c3 ♖xd4). 20 ♘h4!?, so as to occupy f5 with the knight after the queen's retreat, might be advocated in place of 20 ♖g1.

a2) In Shershnev-Bakharev, corres 1969, White didn't bother about getting enough pawns for his piece – he continued **17 ♘h4**. Though interesting, this move too is completely unclear in its consequences: 17 ... ♗xd2+ 18 ♖xd2

♔f7 19 ♘g6 ♖h7 20 ♖h3 ♖e8 21 f4 ♘f8 22 ♘e5+ ♔e7 23 g4 ♖g7 24 c4 ♔d8, and both sides can still have hopes of ultimate success.

So the old verdict 'White has three pawns and an attack for the piece' may have been over-simplifying.

b) The only published game in which White immediately withdrew with **15 ♘e3** was Buljovčić-Vukić, 1976. Indeed, the lack of followers for this move can be explained by the further course of events: 15 ... ♘e4 *(141)*

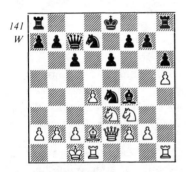

141
W

16 ♗e1 ♘df6 17 g3 ♗xe3+ 18 ♕xe3 0-0-0 19 g4? c5 20 ♖g1 ♖d5! 21 dc ♖xc5 22 c3 ♖a5! 23 ♔b1 ♖d8 24 ♖xd8+ ♕xd8 25 ♘d2 ♖e5! 26 ♔c2 ♕a5, and by now the activity of Black's pieces is hard to damp down.

Vukić's suggestion 19 ♘e5 c5 20 f4 cd 21 ♖xd4 ♖xd4 22 ♕xd4 ♔b8, 'with equality' (yes – after 23 ♗f2, gaining an important tempo!), is unconvincing because

of 22 ... b6!, when the initiative remains with Black.

We are also inclined to dispute another recommendation by Vukić: '16 ♗b4 a5 17 ♗e1 ±'. In our view, after either 17 ... 0-0 or 16 ... ♘df6 17 ♔b1 0-0-0, there are chances for both sides.

    15   **...**   **♕xf4+**
    16   **♘e3** *(142)*

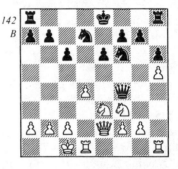

142
B

In this variation White has had considerable success! For example:
a) **16 ... b5?!** 17 ♖dg1 0-0-0?! (castling short is risky, but castling long doesn't fit in with ... b5) 18 c4 a6 19 ♔b1 ♔b7 20 ♖c1 ♖c8 21 a4! ba 22 c5! ♘d5 23 ♖c4, and Black's position is highly precarious, Ivanović-Vukić, Yugoslav Ch 1978.
b) **16 ... 0-0-0**, and now:
b1) **17 g3 ♕c7** 18 ♘c4 ♖he8 19 ♘fe5 ♘b6 20 ♘a3ʹ (White is planning c4-c5, with ♘c4 to follow) 20 ... ♔b8 21 c4 (21 f4, followed by g4-g5, is also strong) 21 ... ♘c8 22 ♖d3 ♖e7 23 c5 ♘d5 24 ♖hd1 f6 25 ♘g6 ♖ee8 26 ♘c4

♖d7 27 ♔b1 ♕d8 28 ♕e4 b5! 29 cb ab 30 ♖b3 ♖b7 31 ♘f4 ♘d6 32 ♘xd6 ♕xd6 33 ♘d3 ♖d8, and by now Black's position is safe, Mihaljčišin-Nikolac, 1978.

b2) **17 ♔b1** ♔b8 18 ♘c4 ♕c7 19 ♘fe5 ♘b6 20 ♘a5 ♖hf8 21 ♘b3 ♘fd7 22 ♘d3 ♖de8 23 f4 (total command of the black squares!) 23 ... ♘d5 24 g3 f5?! (Black is enticed by the prospect of activating at least one piece – he prepares to transfer a knight to e4. But it was better to continue *à la* Nikolac, with 24 ... f6) 25 c4 ♘5f6 26 ♖hg1 ♘g4 (26 ... ♘e4 27 g4) 27 ♘e5 ♘dxe5 28 de ♖d8 29 c5! ♖d5 30 ♖xd5 cd 31 ♖c1, and White won with an attack on the king, Magerramov-Vdovin, 1978.

Drawing conclusions from the material examined, we must say that Black's position is (a) resilient, in spite of the weak black squares, yet (b) so passive that playing it is not easy. Perhaps the course of the Mihaljčišin-Nikolac game (compare also Mnatsakanian-Shakarov in Chapter 8, Variation A) is most typical of this strategic set-up.

B

13 ... c5 *(143)*

This continuation combines three ideas: it prevents ♘e5, sets up the positional threat of ... c4 (securing d5 for a knight), and also prepares to open the c-file for active operations. The black king

plans to castle short.

White has these replies:

B1 14 ♘f5
B2 14 ♖h4
and also:

a) If White is seriously troubled by the possibility of ... c4, he can play **14 c4**. But the ease with which Black obtained a comfortable position in the following games speaks against this continuation. 14 ... cd 15 ♘xd4, and now:

a1) **15 ... ♗c5** 16 ♘b5 ♕c6 17 ♘f5 0-0 18 ♘xh6+?! (over-optimistic, but sooner or later White had to try to punish Black for castling short, whatever the means . . .) 18 ... gh 19 ♗xh6 ♖fd8 20 ♖h4 ♗f8 21 ♗xf8 ♘xf8 22 ♕e5 ♖xd1+ 23 ♔xd1 ♘8d7 24 ♕g3+ ♔f8 25 h6 ♔e7, and Black is justified in counting on a win, Velikov-Bagirov, Wroclaw 1976.

a2) **15 ... ♖c8** (the main defect of 14 c4 is that the c-pawn gives an additional stimulus to Black's queenside activity) 16 ♔b1 ♗c5 17

♗c3 0-0 18 ♖h4 a6 19 ♘b3 ♗e7 20 ♖hd4 ♘b6 21 ♗a5 ♕c6 22 ♖c1 ♘a4 23 f4 b6 24 ♗d2 ♖fe8 25 ♗e3 ♗d6 26 ♖dd1 e5 27 f5 ♖ed8 28 ♖c2 e4 29 ♘f1 ♗e5, and White soon resigned, Marjanović-Seirawan, Niš 1979.

b) **14 ♖he1**, and now:

b1) **14 ... c4** 15 ♘f5 (not 15 d5? ♘xd5 16 ♗xh6 ♘c3) 15 ... 0-0-0 16 ♘e3 ♘xh5 (if 16 ... ♘b6, then 17 ♗a5 is strong) 17 ♘xc4 (17 g3!?) 17 ... ♘f4, or 15 ... ♘d5 16 ♘e3 ♘xe3 17 ♗xe3 c3, leads to sharp positions not without dangers for Black.

b2) **14 ... cd** 15 ♘xd4 ♗c5 16 ♘b3 ♗b6 was played in Grünfeld-Stean, Biel 1981. With 17 ♗b4 White stopped his opponent from castling kingside, but in return Stean picked up a pawn: 17 ... ♕f4+ 18 ♕d2 ♕xf2. Then when Grünfeld prevented queenside castling too, by 19 ♕c3, Black ... increased his material advantage with 19 ... ♕f4+ 20 ♔b1 ♗f2 21 ♘e2 ♗xe1 22 ♕xe1 ♕g5 – and eventually pressed it home. An intriguing game!

c) **14 ♔b1** transposes into Chapter 8 (B2).

B1

14 ♘f5 *(144)*

The strength of this move is seen from the fact that it compels Black to castle queenside. In these circumstances, ... c5 may turn out

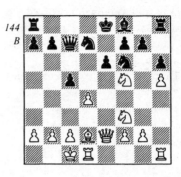

to have been premature. Also, White's knight is transferred to a more active post (though of course with loss of time).

14 ... 0-0-0

We said that 14 ♘f5 forced queenside castling. This is true unless one counts 14 ... ♖c8!?, with the idea of 15 ... cd 16 ♘3xd4 ♕c4! To avoid the queen exchange, the white pawn on a2 has to be defended; after 15 ♔b1 we reach a position already examined in Chapter 8 (B2), in which (as we recall) the critical line is 15 ... c4.

15 ♘e3 ♘b8!

Finding the right course for Black is not easy (15 ... ♗e7 16 ♘c4; 15 ... ♘e4 16 d5!?; 15 ... cd 16 ♘xd4 ♘e4 17 ♘b5). In the game Faibisovich-Okhotnik (1979), which we are following, we think that both sides essentially played in the best way.

16 ♖h4!

A familiar motif (see Tal-Hübner in Chapter 9, Variation

A2) – the rook heads for c4, to make Black regret his 'premature' 13 ... c5.

| 16 | ... | ♘c6 |

16 ... cd!? 17 ♘xd4 ♗c5 ought to be tried too.

17	♗c3!	♗e7
18	dc	♗xc5
19	♖c4!	♗xe3+
20	♕xe3	♖xd1+
21	♔xd1	♖d8+
22	♔c1	♘d5!

22 ... ♘xh5 23 ♘e5 is dangerous.

| 23 | ♕e1 | ♘xc3 |
| 24 | ♕xc3 | *(145)* |

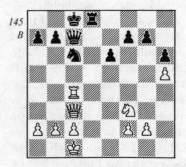

145
B

Up to here we are prepared to endorse all the moves by both sides, but the second phase of the game was not a success for Okhotnik: 24 ... ♕b6 25 b4! ♔b8? 26 ♘e5! ♕xf2 (the rook endgames after 26 ... ♘xe5 27 ♕xe5+ ♔a8 28 ♕c7 ♕xc7 29 ♖xc7 or 27 ... ♕d6 28 ♕xd6+ ♖xd6 29 ♖g4 are difficult for Black) 27 ♖xc6 bc? (rather than the dubious queen ending after 27 ... ♕f4+ 28 ♔b2 bc

29 ♘xc6+ ♔c7 30 ♘xd8+ ♔xd8 31 ♕c5, Okhotnik prefers a pawn ending which, alas, is hopeless!) 28 ♘xc6+ ♔c7 29 ♘xd8+ ♔xd8 30 ♕d2+! ♕xd2+ 31 ♔xd2 f5 32 c4 ♔c7 33 c5 ♔c6 34 ♔d3 ♔d5 35 g3 e5 36 ♔c3 a6 37 ♔d3, and the zugzwang seals Black's fate.

However, after 25 ... f6 26 ♖c5 ♔b8, or 26 ... ♖d5 (27 ♕e3 ♕xb4 28 ♕xe6+ ♖d7 29 ♖d5 ♕a3+ 30 ♔d1 ♕e7), Black would have a perfectly secure position, while 24 ... f6 was probably even more accurate (24 b4 ♖d5). In short, in the diagrammed position Black's chances are in no sense worse.

B2

| 14 | ♖h4 | *(146)* |

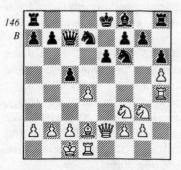

146
B

The threat is 15 ♗f4 ♕a5 16 d5; and Black also has to reckon with 15 dc followed by 16 ♖c4. If 14 ... c4, then 15 d5 is strong.

| 14 | ... | ♖c8 |

Or:

a) **14 ... 0-0-0** – is this as bad as it looks? At all events, the tempting 'refutation', 15 dc ♗xc5 16 ♖c4, can itself be refuted. After 16 ... ♘b6 17 ♗f4? ♖xd1+ White loses the exchange (18 ♕xd1 ♗e3+, or 18 ♔xd1 ♕d7+). The consequences of 16 ♗f4 ♕a5 17 ♔b1 ♘d5 are also unclear.

b) **14 ... ♗e7** (in one of the first games played with the 13 ... c5 line, this logical developing move gave Black a position with no problems – see (b1) below) 15 dc ♘xc5 *(147)*.

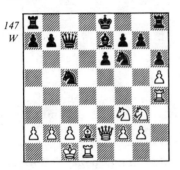

And now:

b1) **16 ♖d4** 0-0 17 ♔b1 ♖fd8 18 ♗f4 ♕b6 19 c4 ♖xd4 20 ♘xd4 ♖d8 21 ♘b5 a6 22 ♘c3 ♖xd1+ 23 ♕xd1 ♕c6 24 f3 b5 etc, Butnorius-Bagirov, 1975.

b2) An attempt to violate such harmony was made in L.Levin-Shakarov, corres 1982: **16 ♖c4!?** b5 17 ♖c3 ♕b7 (after 17 ... b4 18 ♕b5+, Black must sacrifice either a pawn with 18 ... ♘fd7 19 ♕xb4, or his castling rights with 18 ... ♔f8) 18 ♘d4 (on 18 ♘f5, Black

has an interesting choice between sacrificing a pawn with 18 ... 0-0 19 ♘xe7+ ♕xe7 20 ♕xb5, and winning the exchange with 18 ... ♘ce4 19 ♘xe7 ♘xc3 20 ♗xc3 ♔xe7 21 ♗b4+ ♔e8. It may well be better to take the exchange – White can hardly create serious threats against the black king) 18 ... ♘fe4! (18 ... a6? is very strongly answered by 19 ♘gf5!) 19 ♘xe4 ♘xe4 20 ♕f3! (20 ♖b3? doesn't work in view of 20 ... ♘xd2 21 ♖xb5 ♕xg2 22 ♖xd2 ♗g5) 20 ... ♖b8! (not 20 ... ♗b4? 21 ♖e3, or 20 ... ♗f6? 21 ♗f4!) 21 ♖b3 ♘xd2 22 ♔xd2 (forced, but perfectly safe, since avoiding the queen exchange is scarcely advisable for Black) 22 ... ♕xf3, and a couple of moves later a draw was agreed.

So even 14 ... ♗e7 neutralises 14 ♖h4 reliably enough, while 14 ... ♖c8 is basically an attempt to contend for the initiative.

15 ♗f4

Or:

a) **15 ♘f5**, and now:

a1) While **15 ... c4** (14 ... ♖c8 did not reinforce this 'threat') 16 d5 ♘xd5 17 ♗xh6 ♘c3 is to Black's liking, 16 ♘e3!, with d5 to follow, is highly unpleasant.

a2) The idea behind **14 ... ♖c8** was revealed in Mikhalchishin-Kasparov, Daugavpils Otborochnii 1978: 15 ... cd! 16 ♘3xd4 ♕c4! 17 ♕xc4

♖xc4. The players agreed a draw at this point, but the struggle was continued in another game – Gaprindashvili - Chiburdanidze, 1978 – which showed that Black even has the better chances owing to White's worries about the h5 pawn: 18 ♖e1 ♖c5! 19 ♘g3 ♝e7 20 ♘b3 ♖c8 21 ♝b4 ♝xb4 22 ♖xb4 ♖c7 23 ♘d4 a6 24 ♘df5 0-0 25 ♘e3 ♖fc8 26 ♖e2 b5 etc.

b) **15 ♔b1.** The point of guarding the a-pawn in this way is, for one thing, to avoid the main line given below (15 ♝f4 ♛a5 16 d5 ♛xa2); and secondly, to refuse a queen exchange in the case of 15 ... cd 16 ♘xd4 ♛c4. Black can nonetheless be happy with the latter variation, after 17 ♛f3 ♛d5. In a game Dadashadze-Shakarov, 1979, Black went in for 15 ... c4. The continuation was: 16 ♘f5 ♘d5 (16 ... c3 17 ♝xc3 ♘d5 is tempting, but after 18 ♝e1 ♘f4 19 ♛d2 ♘xg2 20 ♖g4 Black has difficulties due to his unsafe king position) 17 c3 ♛a5 (threatening 18 ... ♘xc3+; or, where appropriate, ... ♖c6-a6) 18 ♘e5 ♘xe5 19 ♛xe5 ♘xc3+ 20 ♝xc3 ♛xe5 21 de ef 22 ♖f4, with equal chances.

15	...	♛a5
16	d5	♛xa2
17	c4	

After 17 de ♛xe6 18 ♛b5 the position is unpleasant for Black, but the consequences of 17 ... fe

are unclear, for example: 18 ♛b5 ♝e7! 19 ♝d6 ♝xd6 20 ♖a4 (20 ♖xd6 a6!) 20 ... ♝f4+ 21 ♖xf4 a6!, or 18 ♛d3 ♘c6! 19 ♛g6+ ♔d8 20 ♘e5 ♛a1+ 21 ♔d2 ♖d6+ 22 ♘d3 ♛a5+ with counter-chances.

| 17 | ... | ♝e7! (148) |

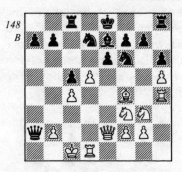

18 ♝d6!

This is stronger than 18 de fe 19 ♝d6, because of the immediate counter-attack 19 ... ♘c6! 20 ♘f5 ♖b6! But perhaps it pays White to drive a wedge into Black's position with 18 d6!?

| 18 | ... | ♝xd6 |
| 19 | de | 0-0 |

In Shakarov-Asrian, corres 1973, Black gave two preliminary checks – 19 ... ♛a1+ 20 ♔c2 ♛a4+ 21 ♔b1 – before playing 21 ... 0-0. The game continued: 22 ♖xd6 fe 23 ♛xe6+ ♔h8 24 ♘f5 ♖ce8 25 ♘e7 ♖xe7! 26 ♛xe7 ♖e8 27 ♖xd7! (but not 27 ♛f7? ♖e2) 27 ... ♖xe7 28 ♖xe7 ♛d1+ 29 ♔a2 ♛a4+, with a draw.

Instead of 22 ♖xd6, White may

play 22 ♘f5, and after 22 ... fe 23 ♕xe6+ ♔h8 24 ♕xd6 we reach a position that is examined below (see Kanani-Shakarov).

20 ♘f5

Also:

a) **20 ed** is weak on account of 20 ... ♕a1+ 21 ♔c2 ♕a4+ 22 ♔b1 ♕xd7 (or 21 ♔d2 ♕xb2+ 22 ♔e1 ♕xe2+ and 23 ... ♖c6).

b) **20 ♖xd6** transposes into Shakarov-Asrian (see above) after 20 ... fe 21 ♕xe6+ ♔h8 22 ♘f5 ♕a1+ 23 ♔c2 ♕a4+ 24 ♔b1 ♖ce8, but an attempt by Black to extract more from this variation is of interest: 22 ... ♖ce8 23 ♘e7 ♖xe7 24 ♕xe7 ♖e8 25 ♖xd7? ♖xe7 26 ♖xe7 ♕a1+ 27 ♔c2 ♕f1, with chances . . . However, White for his part could 'risk' 25 ♕f7! ♕a1+ 26 ♔c2 ♕a4+, and now not 27 ♔b1? ♖e2, nor even 27 ♔c1 ♕a1+ with a draw, but 27 ♔d2 ♕a5+ 28 ♔d3!?

20 ... fe
21 ♕xe6+ ♔h8
22 ♕xd6 *(149)*

We have already sufficiently analysed 22 ♖xd6, but 22 ♘xd6!? remains to be tried . . .

This sharp position was reached in a game Kanani-Shakarov,

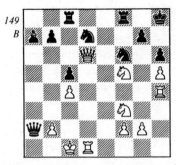

corres 1982. Accurately assessing the prospects for either side is not easy, but we feel the stronger player should win! Let's see how the struggle developed: 22 ... ♕a1+ (22 ... ♖c6? 23 ♕e7) 23 ♔c2 ♕a4+ 24 ♔b1 ♖ce8 25 ♘e3 ♖f7 26 ♖d3! ♖fe7! 27 ♖a3 ♕b4 28 ♖xa7 ♘b6 29 ♕d2 ♘e4 30 ♕xb4 cb 31 c5! ♘c8! 32 ♖a8 b3 33 ♘d5! ♘d2+! 34 ♔c1 ♖e2 35 ♘e3 ♘xf3 36 gf ♖d8 37 ♖h1 ♖xf2, and a few moves later a draw was agreed.

As we can see, 14 ... ♖c8 leads to positions that are interesting but perhaps rather dangerous for Black. The possibility that White may improve somewhere cannot be discounted (17 de!?; 18 d6!?; 22 ♘xd6!?). It is therefore important that Black has a solid method of play in 14 ... ♗e7.

Summary

12 ...	0-0-0	13 ♛e2	♗d6				=
			♗d6				±
		♘gf6	13 ♛e2	♗d6	14 ♘f5	♗f4	15 ♘xg7+	∞
							15 ♘e3	=
							15 ♗xf4	±
			c5	14 c4			=
				14 ♖he1			∞
				(14 ♔b1 – cf. 13 ♔b1)			
				14 ♘f5			=
				14 ♖h4	♗e7		=
					♖c8	15 ♘f5	=
						15 ♔b1	=
						15 ♗f4	∞

1	e4	c6
2	d4	d5
3	♘c3	de
4	♘xe4	♗f5
5	♘g3	♗g6
6	♘f3	♘d7
7	h4	h6
8	h5	♗h7
9	♗d3	♗xd3
10	♕xd3	♕c7
11	♗d2	e6
12	0-0-0	♘gf6
13	♕e2	0-0-0
14	♘e5 *(150)*	

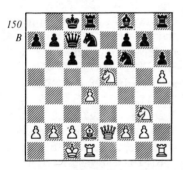

150
B

The idea of ♕e2 and ♘e5 had been applied to similar positions before the Spassky-Petrosian match; nor was Spassky the first to play 8 h5 ... Yet it was in the thirteenth game of the 1966 match for the World Championship that the position in the diagram first arose, becoming popular for a long time after.

Combining the old moves h4-h5 and ♘f3-e5 proved effective. The pawn-couple on e5 and h5 which is formed after 14 ... ♘xe5 15 de (Variation A) creates a special configuration on the kingside – one that favours White, since the pawns on f7 and g7 can be attacked by White's queen or rook, while the moves ... f6 or ... g6 produce weaknesses. In addition, White may obtain new assets by an advance of his own f-pawn and g-pawn, particularly in the ending (the reader has already seen this in the Geller-Hort game from Chapter 9, Variation A21).

If Black seeks counterplay based on undermining the knight's position on e5 by ... c5, he employs Variation B (below), or, more often, Variation C.

We consider:

A　14 ... ♘xe5

B　14 ... ♘b8

C　14 ... ♘b6

A

14	...	♘xe5
15	de	♘d7

Instead, 15 ... ♘d5 *(151)* 'looks dubious, but involves a cunning positional idea' (Botvinnik).

16 f4 (16 c4 ♘b4 17 ♗xb4 ♗xb4 18 f4 is weaker because of 18 ... f6 or 18 ... f5) 16 ... c5 ('forces events, for White cannot allow ... c4' – Botvinnik) 17 c4 ♘b4 18 ♗xb4 ('once a black pawn settles on b4, it will be hard for White to shelter his king comfortably. This is why Black will have counterplay in any endgame with queens on the board. Perhaps White should have preferred 18 ♔b1' – Botvinnik) 18 ... ♖xd1+ 19 ♖xd1 cb 20 ♘e4 ♗e7 21 ♘d6+ ♔b8, and now:

a) In Spassky-Botvinnik, USSR Team Ch 1966, White played 22 ♘xf7, whereupon 22 ... ♖f8 23 ♘d6 ♖xf4 24 g3 ♖f8 25 ♕g4 ♕d7 26 ♔b1 ♗g5 gave Black counterplay (27 ♘b5 ♖f1!).

b) In Boleslavsky's view, White

could have consolidated his advantage with 22 g3 *(152)*

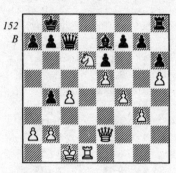

– and if 22 ... f6 (the move Botvinnik had in mind; on 22 ... ♖f8, Boleslavsky recommends 23 ♔b1 a6 24 ♕e4! with threats of 25 ♕xb7+ or 25 c5), then 23 ef! ♗xd6 24 fg ♖e8 25 ♕g4.

Boleslavsky's verdict appears mistaken. After 25 ... ♕xc4+ 26 ♔b1 ♕e4+ (but not 26 ... e5? because of 27 ♕d7 or 27 ♕g6 – or even 27 ♖xd6 ef 28 ♕xf4 ♖e1+ 29 ♖d1+ ♕xf4 30 g8♕+) 27 ♔a1 ♖g8 28 ♖xd6 ♖xg7 or 28 ... ♕c2, there are chances for both sides.

We agree, then, with Botvinnik: 18 ♔b1! (instead of ♗xb4). After 18 ... ♗e7 19 ♗c3, the black knight will retreat (at once or later) to c6; a position of this type is examined below (15 ... ♘d7 16 f4 c5 17 c4 ♘b8 etc).

16	f4	♗e7 *(153)*

Or:

a) Analysis shows that the plan of transferring the knight to d4 after

16 ... c5 17 c4 ♘b8 is ineffective: 18 ♗c3 ♗e7 (he can't keep the white knight out – 18 ... f5? 19 ef!) 19 ♘e4 ♘c6 20 ♕f2 (if 20 ♕g4, then 20 ... ♘d4) 20 ... ♕b6 (if 20 ... b6, then 21 ♘d6+! is strong) 21 ♔b1 (but at this point 21 ♘d6+ is unconvincing because of 21 ... ♗xd6 22 ed f6. Nor should White hurry with 21 ♕g3, in view of 21 ... ♕a6!) 21 ... ♖xd1+ (21 ... ♘d4? loses to 22 ♗xd4 cd 23 c5!, while on 21 ... ♔b8 White *does* play 22 ♕g3) 22 ♖xd1 ♖d8 23 ♖xd8+ (but not 23 ♘d6+? ♗xd6 24 ed ♘d4 25 ♗xd4 ♕xd6) 23 ... ♕xd8 24 ♔c2 b6 25 ♕d2, and the position is difficult for Black to hold. The exchange of queens gives an endgame which Parma won against Barcza in the 1970 European Championship at Kapfenberg.

b) E.Schiller advocates the original **16 ... ♖g8** 17 ♗c3 (17 ♘e4 f5) 17 ... f5 18 ♕c4 ♘c5. Now 19 ♘xf5? b5 20 ♘d6+ ♕xd6, or 19 b4 b5, or 19 ♗b4 ♖d5 should be welcome to

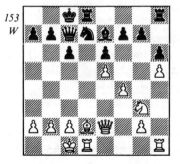

153
W

Black, but after 19 ♖xd8+ followed by ♖d1 and ♗b4, his position is suspect.

17 ♘e4

In our view, there is greater unpleasantness for Black in a more restrained strategy, directed towards exchanges and an endgame in which White has good chances owing (as ever) to those pawns on e5 and h5. Thus, 17 ♗e3 *(154)*.

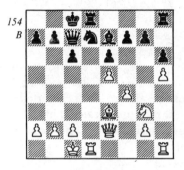

154
B

And now:

a) We call your attention to one vivid illustration of White's possibilities – a variant adapted from the game Zatulovskaia-Nünchert, 1968: **17 ... ♘c5** 18 ♗xc5 ♗xc5 19 ♘e4 ♗e7 20 g3 ♖xd1+ 21 ♖xd1 ♖d8 22 c4 c5 23 ♖xd8+ ♕xd8 24 ♕d2 ♕xd2+ 25 ♔xd2 ♔d7 26 g4 b6 27 g5 ♗f8 28 gh gh 29 ♘f2 ♗g7 30 ♘g4 ♗f8 31 ♔d3 ♔c6 32 a4 ♔d7 33 ♔e4 ♔c7 34 f5 ♔d7 35 f6 ♔c6 36 ♘f2 ♔c7 37 ♘d3 a5 38 ♘f4 ♔d7 39 ♔f3 ♔e8 40 ♔g4 ♔d7 41 ♘g6! ♔e8 42 ♔h4! – zugzwang.

b) Also in Suetin-Pachman, Titovo Uzice 1966, Black was unable to oppose anything to White's exchanging policy: **17 ...** ♕a5 **18** ♔b1 ♘c5 **19** c3 ♖xd1+ **20** ♖xd1 ♖d8 **21** ♖d4 ♖xd4 **22** ♗xd4 ♕d8 **23** ♕c2 a5 **24** ♘f1 ♕d5 **25** ♘e3 ♕e4 **26** ♗xc5 ♕xc2+ **27** ♔xc2 ♗xc5 (the endgame doesn't look hopeless for Black, but it quickly became so) **28** ♘c4 a4 **29** ♔d3 ♔d7 **30** g4 b5 **31** ♘d2 ♗g1 **32** ♔e4 c5? **33** b3 ab **34** ab ♔e7 **35** ♔f3! b4 **36** cb cb **37** ♔e4 ♗c5 **38** ♘f3 ♔d7 **39** ♘d4 g6 **40** ♔d3 etc.

Of course, we have been distorting the actual state of affairs – Black's position after **17** ♗e3 certainly isn't that desperate. That it is unpromising cannot, however, be denied.

17	...	♘c5
18	♘c3	f6!
19	ef	♗xf6

We are now at last examining the Spassky-Petrosian game that started it all.

Black has activated his pieces at the cost of weakening e6. But it turns out that Spassky is prepared to pay a bigger price for the initiative – he weakens his own king position!

20	♕c4	♕b6
21	b4! (155)	
21	...	♘a6

In Shabanov-Kuksov, RSFSR Spartakiad 1978, Black adopted

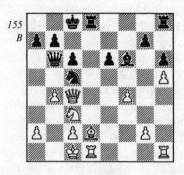

155
B

an old recommendation – **21 ...** ♕a6, which is based on the trap **22** ♕xc5? ♕a3+ **23** ♔b1 ♖xd2. The game went: **22** ♕xa6 ♘xa6 **23** ♘e4 ♖d4 **24** ♘xf6 gf **25** a3?! f5 **26** ♖de1 ♖d6 **27** ♗c3 ♖g8 **28** ♖e2 ♘c7 **29** ♗e5 ♖d7 **30** ♗xc7 ♔xc7 **31** ♖xe6 ♖xg2 **32** ♖d1, with a draw.

As Boleslavsky has rightly pointed out, White has the advantage after **25** c3 ♖e4 **26** g4 ♘c7 **27** g5.

22 ♘e4

22 ♕xe6+? ♔b8 heads straight for a loss.

22 ... ♘c7

22 ... ♖d5!? – Pachman.

23 ♖he1 ♖d4?!

A recommendation of Lilienthal's is very interesting: **23 ...** ♗e7!? **24** ♗c3 ♘d5 **25** ♗xg7 ♗xb4.

24	♕b3	♕b5
25	c3	♖xe4!
26	♖xe4	♕xh5
27	♕c4	♕f5
28	♕e2	h5 (156)

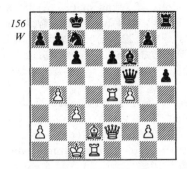

White's material plus is slight, and his king's position isn't very secure. Perhaps Black is not without chances, yet after 29 ♗e1 ♖e8 30 g3 a5 31 ba ♕xa5 32 ♕c2 ♕f5 33 ♖a4 g5 34 fg ♗xg5+ 35 ♔b2 ♕xc2+ 36 ♔xc2 e5 37 ♖e4, Spassky set about what has by now become an obvious advantage.

B

14   ...   ♘b8 *(157)*

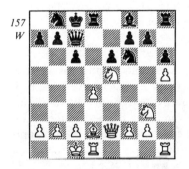

While avoiding the pin (♗a5) that is possible in the 14 ... ♘b6 line, Black plans, after 15 c3, to solve his problems by 15 ... c5 16 ♔b1 ♘c6 - when White has to

worry about his knight on e5 and his pawn on d4.

15   ♖h4!

Directed against 15 ... c5 (16 dc! followed by ♖c4).

15   ...   ♗d6

With this move Black renews the threat of ... c5, in the expectation that White will parry it with some such move as 16 ♖e1, or 16 c4 c5 17 ♗c3 *(158)*. In the latter case, the placing of the rook on h4 loses some of its point.

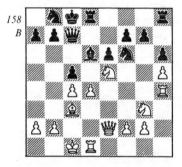

Let there be no mistake, though – White retains good chances, for example:

a) **17 ... cd** 18 ♖hxd4! (after 18 ♗xd4 ♘c6 19 ♘xc6 ♕xc6 Black has everything in order) 18 ... ♗xe5 (18 ... ♘c6? 19 ♖xd6) 19 ♖xd8+, and a tough struggle for the draw is in store for Black.

b) In a game Baikov-Tseitlin, 1973, Black chose **17 ... ♘c6?!** 18 ♘xc6 bc 19 ♘e4 ♗f4+ 20 ♗d2 ♗xd2+ 21 ♖xd2 ♘xe4 22 ♖xe4 cd 23 ♖exd4 ♖xd4 24 ♖xd4 ♖d8, and drew the endgame. White seems to have been aiming for that result too, otherwise he would have played 20 ♔c2 or 19 dc. Seeing that 18 ... ♕xc6 19 d5 is also in White's favour, it must be supposed that the idea of 14 ... ♘b8 followed by ... c5 and ... ♘c6 is faulty – for the reason that it consumes a great deal of time and hence comes up against strong counter-chances from White's well mobilised army.

There is one other continuation, suggested by Ivanović:

16 ♘c4! *(159)*

159
W

Accepting the sacrifice is dangerous (16 ... ♗xg3 17 fg ♕xg3 18 ♖f4), so in the game Ivanović-Vukić, Vukovar 1976, Black surrendered his bishop:

16 ... ♘bd7
17 ♘xd6+ ♕xd6

By now White's advantage is obvious, but we'll take a look at the further course of the struggle: 18 ♗f4 ♕b4 19 d5 (Ivanović has

visions of giving mate . . .) 19 ... cd? 20 ♖d3 ♘b6 21 ♖b3 ♕e7 (or 21 ... ♕f8 22 ♕e5) 22 ♘f5 ♕c5 23 ♖b5 ♕xb5 (or 23 ... ♕c4 24 ♗d6! ♕xe2 25 ♖c5+ ♔d7 26 ♖c7+ ♔e8 27 ♘xg7 mate!) 24 ♕xb5 ef 25 ♕c5+ ♔d7 26 ♕c7+ ♔e6 27 ♖h1 etc.

Black should have taken the pawn on d5 with his knight, and after 19 ... ♘xd5 20 ♗g5 ♘c3! 21 ♕d2 ♘xa2+ 22 ♔b1 ♘c3+ 23 ♔c1 he should play not 23 ... ♘a2+ with a draw, but 23 ... ♕a5! with a won position. Although Ivanović gives 20 ♘e4!? 'with compensation', this try is also illusory (20 ... e5 or 20 ... ♘7f6).

Instead of the incorrect 19 d5?, White should play 19 c4 – or something . . . Once Black's important bishop has been removed, White has, of course, clearly the better chances.

C

14 ... ♘b6

A continuation that has displaced both 14 ... ♘xe5 and 14 ... ♘b8 in tournament practice, and has given Black the best results. As in the 14 ... ♘b8 line, White cannot afford simply to guard his attacked d-pawn with 15 c3, since 15 ... c5 16 ♔b1 ♗d6! (not 16 ... ♔b8? 17 ♗f4 ♗d6 18 dc ♕xc5 19 ♘xf7) 17 f4 cd 18 cd ♔b8 (Boleslavsky) gives Black a very comfortable position.

These days, White nearly always replies 15 ♗a5. For this, see Chapter 12. But there was a time when the following move also had a good reputation:

15 ♖h4 *(160)*

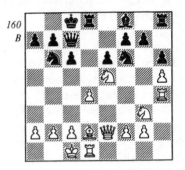

160
B

15 ... ♗d6!

In spite of the fact that the knight on b6 controls the c4 square, the plan of 15 ... c5 is, once again, risky. Soviet Master Ubilava has convincingly demonstrated this to his opponents: 16 ♗a5! *(161)*.

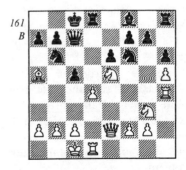

161
B

And now:

a) **16 ... ♗d6** 17 dc! ♗xe5 (or 17 ... ♗xc5 18 ♖xd8+ ♖xd8 19 ♖c4! – the entire operation for refuting 15 ... c5 turns on this idea) 18 ♖xd8+ ♖xd8 19 cb ♗f4+ 20 ♔b1 ab 21 ♗xb6 ♕xb6 22 ♖xf4, and Black is a pawn down with an unsafe king position, Ubilava-Peresipkin, USSR Cup 1974.

b) **16 ... cd** 17 ♖dxd4! ♗c5 18 ♖c4 ♖d5 19 ♘d3 ♔d7 (19 ... ♔b8 loses to 20 b4) 20 ♖c3 (but here 20 b4 is weaker, because of 20 ... ♗e3+ 21 fe ♕xg3 or 21 ♕xe3 ♘xc4 – the queen on c7 is captured without check!) 20 ... ♖c8 21 ♘e4 ♘xe4 22 ♕xe4 ♕b8 (or 22 ... ♕d6 23 ♕f3) 23 ♘xc5+ ♖dxc5 24 ♖xc5 ♖xc5 25 ♗c3, and the alarming position of Black's king settles the outcome, Ubilava-Fyodorov, 1977.

16 ♗a5

After 16 ♘f1, Black was outplayed in Gipslis-Suleimanov, 1978: 16 ... ♔b8?! 17 ♔b1 ♔a8?! 18 ♘h2 c5 19 dc ♗xc5 20 ♘hf3 ♕e7 21 c4 ♘bd7 22 ♗a5 ♗b6 23 ♗xb6 ♘xb6 24 ♖hd4 ♖xd4 25 ♘xd4 ♖d8 26 ♘b5 ♖xd1+ 27 ♕xd1 ♘fd7 28 ♘xd7 ♕xd7 29 ♕xd7 ♘xd7 30 ♘d6, and Black drew the knight ending with difficulty.

Quietly removing the king to a8 is unjustified; Black wanted to avoid some kind of vague dangers in the middlegame, but the distant position of his king told in the endgame.

The natural reaction to 16 ♘f1 is 16 ... c5 17 dc ♗xc5, when 18 ♗a5 is harmless in view of 18 ... ♖xd1+ 19 ♔xd1 ♖d8+, followed by ... ♖d5 or ... ♖d4.

16	...	♗xe5
17	de	♖xd1+
18	♔xd1	♘fd7
19	♖e4 *(162)*	

162
B

White neglects two opportunities to . . . lose the game. We are referring, in the first place, to a line recommended by several writers: 19 ♖g4 ♖g8 20 f4. Black's improvement consists in 19 ... ♘xe5! 20 ♖xg7 ♕d8+ and 21 ... ♕f6, when the rook is trapped.

The second possibility was found by Grandmaster Tseshkovsky in a game against Bagirov (1973): 19 f4? ♘xe5 (19 ... ♕d8 isn't bad either). The position, admittedly, turned out to be 'a draw': 20 ♔c1 ♘ed7 21 ♖g4 ♖g8 22 c4 ♕d6 23

♗c3 f5?! 24 ♖g6 ♕xf4+ 25 ♔b1 ♕xc4 26 ♕xc4 ♘xc4 27 ♖xe6 ♘f8?! 28 ♖e8+ ♔d7 29 ♖b8 ♔c7 30 ♖a8 g6 31 ♗b4 gh 32 ♘xf5 ♖xg2 33 b3 ♖f2 34 ♖xf8 ♖f1+ 35 ♔c2 ♖xf5 36 bc ♖xf8 37 ♗xf8 h4 38 ♗xh6 c5, and as the pawn on c4 gets exchanged off, White(!) cannot win.

19 ... ♕d8!

It was owing to this cunning move that the sting was considered to have been taken out of 15 ♖h4. Earlier, 19 ... ♖d8 20 ♔c1 ♘c5 had been played, but in a game Haag-Flesch, 1967, the position became difficult for Black after 21 ♖g4! (21 ♖e3 ♖d5 led to a level game in Holmov-Hort, Leningrad 1967) 21 ... ♖d5? (Flesch is striving for counterplay, but this loses by force. A more stubborn continuation was 21 ... ♖g8 22 ♗d2 ♕d8, when all is not yet lost!) 22 ♖xg7 ♘b3+ (or 22 ... ♖xe5 23 ♖g8+ ♔d7 24 ♕d2+ ♔e7 25 ♕xh6) 23 ab ♖xa5 24 c4 (or 24 ♖g8+ ♔d7 25 ♕d2+ ♘d5 26 c4) 24 ... ♖xe5 25 ♖g8+ ♔d7 26 ♕d2+ ♔e7 27 ♕xh6 etc.

After 19 ... ♕d8!, in a game Privorotsky-Makagonov (1969), White mechanically played 20 ♔c1 (20 ♕d2!?) 20 ... ♘c5 21 ♖g4, when the reply 21 ... ♕d5! *(163)* confronted him with an unpleasant problem.

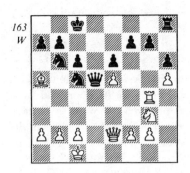

Privorotsky didn't have to solve it, though, because after 22 ♗xb6 ab the veteran master offered a draw.

Had he not done so, achieving this result would have been more difficult for White. For example, 23 b3 ♖d8 24 ♖xg7? ♕d4 25 ♔b1 ♘a4! (25 ... ♕c3 26 ♖g4 ♖d2 27 ♖c4) 26 ba ♕b4+ 27 ♔c1 ♕a3+ 28 ♔b1 ♖d4.

Summary

14 ...	♘xe5 15 de	♘d5				±
		♘d7 16 f4	c5			±
			♖g8			±
			♗e7 17 ♗e3			±
			17 ♘e4			±/∞
	♘b8 15 c3					=
	15 ♖h4	♗d6 16 c4				±
		16 ♘c4				±
	♘b6 15 c3					=
	15 ♖h4	c5				±
		♗d6 16 ♘f1				=
		16 ♗a5	♗xe5 17 de	♖xd1+		
				18 ♔xd1 ♘fd7		
					19 ♖e4 ♖d8	±
					♕d8	=

12 15 &a5

1	e4	c6
2	d4	d5
3	♘c3	de
4	♘xe4	♗f5
5	♘g3	♗g6
6	♘f3	♘d7
7	h4	h6
8	h5	♗h7
9	♗d3	♗xd3
10	♕xd3	♕c7
11	♗d2	e6
12	0-0-0	♘gf6
13	♕e2	0-0-0
14	♘e5	♘b6
15	♗a5 *(164)*	

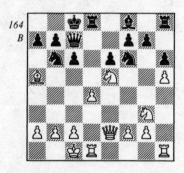

164
B

The pinning move with the bishop is White's chief weapon against 14 ... ♘b6, and, bearing in mind Variation C in Chapter 11, the only one worth using. Just now Black isn't threatened with anything, but he soon will be – when White follows with 16 c4.

Black's choice is between the standard pawn-break 15 ... c5 (Variation A), and 15 ... ♖d5 which sounds out the white bishop's intentions (Variation B). In the latter case, 16 b4 (see B1) compels Black to sacrifice the exchange. But the counterplay Black gets in return is so dangerous that in grandmaster practice 16 b4 is a remarkable event (we know of only one such case!).

There is a firmly established opinion that the exchange 16 ♗xb6 ab (see B2) guarantees White lasting pressure on Black's position. This widespread delusion is one that we aim to dispel.

From Diagram 164:

A 15 ... c5
B 15 ... ♖d5

A

    15 ...   **c5** *(165)*

This line has had a complicated history. Shortly after being devised it was discarded, since it was thought that Black has no good answer to . . .

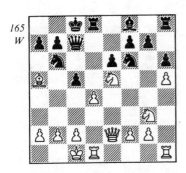

16 c4

White's idea is: 16 ... cd 17 ♔b1 ♗d6 18 c5!, and the new pin arising after 18 ... ♗xc5 19 ♖c1 is deadly. Nor are things altered much by 17 ... ♔b8 18 ♖c1, threatening 19 c5.

16 ... ♖xd4

It was always generally understood that 16 ... ♖xd4 was better than 16 ... cd, simply because one piece fewer will now be affected by the pin on the a5-d8 diagonal. But until recently Black never discovered a variation in which this was significant. For example, in an old game Haag-Golz, Zinnowitz 1966, Black lost in the familiar manner: 17 ♖xd4 cd 18 ♔b1 ♗d6 19 c5 etc.

However, in 1979, a new idea was suggested by Soviet Master Bikhovsky; for this, see the main variation below.

16 ... ♔b8 lead to a draw in Marić-Vukić, Kraljevo 1967: 17 dc ♗xc5 18 f4 ♗d4 19 ♘xf7 ♕xf7 20 ♖xd4 ♖xd4 21 ♕e5+ ♕c7 22 ♕xd4 ♕xc4+. But this made no great impression, since it was clear that after 17 ♔b1 (instead of dc) Black faces the same problems as before; if 17 ... cd, then 18 ♖c1, while after 17 ... ♗d6 18 dc ♗xc5 (18 ... ♗xe5 19 cb ab 20 ♗xb6) 19 f4, White has gained an important tempo (♔b1), and now 19 ... ♗d4 20 ♘xf7 is in his favour.

Later, in Runau-Mohadam, Hastings 1971-2, White was again successful with ♔b1, only he played it on move 19: 16 ... ♔b8 17 dc ♗xc5 18 f4 ♗d4 19 ♔b1! ♗xe5 20 fe ♘fd7 21 ♘e4! ♕xe5 22 ♗c3 ♕f5 (or 22 ... ♕c7 23 ♗xg7 ♖h7 24 ♗c3 ♘xc4 25 ♘f6) 23 ♖hf1 ♕h7 24 ♖xf7 ♘c5 25 ♖e1 ♖d7 (a lost ending likewise results from 25 ... ♘xe4 26 ♕xe4 ♖d1+ 27 ♔c2 ♖xe1 28 ♕xh7 etc) 26 ♖xd7 ♘bxd7 27 ♕c2 ♖f8 28 ♘xc5 ♕xc2+ 29 ♔xc2 ♖f2+ 30 ♔b1 ♘xc5 31 ♗d4 ♖f5 32 g4 ♖g5 33 ♖e5!, and a couple of moves later Black resigned.

17 ♖xd4

In A.Rodriguez-Armas, 1980, White sidestepped the controversy of the main line by playing a gambit of his own devising: 17 ♔b1!? ♖xd1+ (of course not 17 ... ♗d6 18 ♖xd4 cd – see Haag-Golz above) 18 ♖xd1 (166).

Although Black faces no direct threats, he has no convenient moves either. The point is, he has

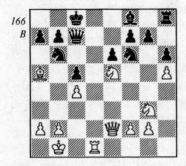

166
B

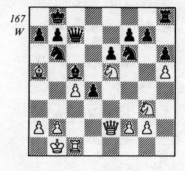

167
W

to guard d7 (18 ... ♘e8? 19 ♗xb6) and f7 (18 ... ♗d6? 19 ♘xf7 or 19 ♖xd6).

There followed: 18 ... ♖g8 19 f4 ♗d6! (otherwise he can't untangle) 20 ♘xf7 ♗xf4 21 ♕xe6+ ♔b8 22 ♘f5! ♖e8 23 ♕xe8+ ♘xe8 24 ♖d8+ ♕xd8 25 ♘xd8 ♘xc4 26 ♗c3 . With ♘e6 coming, White is assured of getting his pawn back, and has some chances in the endgame (which possibly is drawn, though).

17 ... cd
18 ♔b1 ♔b8
19 ♖c1 ♗c5! *(167)*

After 19 ... ♗d6 20 c5 ♗xe5 21 cb ♕d6 22 ba+ ♔xa7 23 ♗c7, Black loses his queen. He may happen to succeed in winning this position: 23 ... ♕xc7 24 ♖xc7 ♗xc7 25 ♕d3 ♖d8 26 ♔c2 ♗xg3 27 ♕xg3 d3+ 28 ♔d1 d2 29 ♕xg7? ♘e4 30 ♕xf7 ♖c8, Bogda-Santos, 1980. But trying to obtain it is definitely not worth while.

The point of Bikhovsky's 19 ... ♗c5! is that in the event of 20 b4 ♗d6 21 c5 ♗xe5 22 cb ♕d6 23 ba+ ♔xa7 24 ♗c7?, Black has the check 24 ... ♕xb4+. 24 ♖c5? is also bad: 24 ... ♗xg3 25 fg (25 ♗c7 ♕xc5, or 25 ♕c4 ♘e4!) 25 ... ♘d5 26 ♕c4 b6! 27 ♖c6 ♕e5. But perhaps after 24 ♘e4 ♘xe4 25 ♕xe4, Black doesn't win . . .

From the diagram, White has some other tries:
a) The first game with this line, Korsunsky-Bikhovsky, 1979, went: **20 a3 ♖c8 21 f4 ♘fd7 22 ♘d3 ♕d8?** 23 ♘e4 ♕f8 24 ♘exc5 ♘xc5 25 ♗b4 ♘bd7 26 ♘xc5 ♘xc5 27 ♕e5+ ♖c7 28 ♕xd4 b6 29 ♖d1, and White obtained a considerable advantage. Had Black played 22 ... ♕c6, a no less substantial plus would have been on *his* side.
b) A game Agapov-Shashin, 1982, developed in Black's favour: **20 f4 ♖c8 21 ♘e4 ♘xc4 22 ♕xc4 ♕e7 23 ♗xb6 ♗xb6 24 ♘d3 ♕f6,** and

White has no compensation for the pawn.

c) One more possibility is **20 ♘d3 ♕e7 21 b4 ♗d6 22 c5 ♗xg3 23 cb ♗d6 24 ba+ ♔xa7 25 ♕b2**, when you notice what a risk the black king is taking. However, after 24 ... ♔a8! the same can be said of the white king.

But if White fails to demonstrate an advantage in the 'Bikhovsky position' (i.e. after 19 ... ♗c5!), and if the ending in Rodriguez-Armas promises a draw, we would remind the reader that White has one other method: 16 ♖h4! (instead of c4). In this way he transposes to the highly favourable 'Ubilava position' that we analysed in Chapter 11 (Variation C).

B

15 ... ♖d5

Now White can choose between:

B1 16 b4
B2 16 ♗xb6

B1

16 b4 (168)

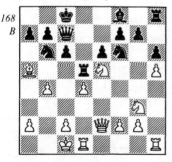

With c4 coming, White is winning the exchange. But at what cost? Black obtains a pawn and good prospects for hunting the white king.

16 ... ♖xa5

16 ... ♗d6!? also has its points, for example: 17 c4 ♗xe5 18 cd ♗xg3.

17 ba ♗a3+

Alternatively:

a) In Hermlin-Korchmar, 1969, the first game in which 16 b4 was tried, Black played 17 ... ♘bd5 here, and after 18 ♕c4 ♕xa5 19 ♖d3 ♗a3+ 20 ♔b1 ♖f8 21 ♕b3 (169)

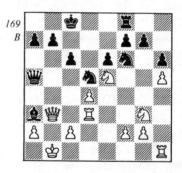

21 ... ♗e7?! 22 ♔a1 ♕c7?! 23 ♕a4 ♔b8 24 ♖b1, the roles were reversed and it was Black's king that was being hunted.

We think 17 ... ♘bd5 isn't so bad if followed up more astutely; in the diagrammed position we suggest 21 ... ♗b4! 22 a3 ♗e7, when the situation isn't entirely clear – in some lines the pawn on a3 may be left hanging, and there are possibilities of ... c5 and ... ♘f4 for White to worry about.

b) **17 ... ♘a4**, when White has:

b1) **18 ♕d3 ♘d5 19 ♘e2 ♕xa5 20 ♖h3** (20 ♘xf7 ♘ac3 21 ♘xc3 ♘xc3 22 ♘xh8 is dangerous because of 22 ... ♗b4!, cutting off the king's escape route – 23 ♔d2 ♘d5+ 24 ♔e2 ♘f4+. After 23 ♕c4 there doesn't appear to be a mate, but Black is guaranteed a draw with 23 ... ♘xa2+) 20 ... ♗b4 21 ♘c4 ♕a6 22 ♘b2 ♘ac3 23 ♘xc3 ♘xc3 24 ♕xa6 ba 25 ♖f1 (25 ♖dd3? ♘e2+ and 26 ... ♘f4) 25 ... ♘xa2+ 26 ♔b1 ♘c3+ 27 ♔a1 ♖d8 28 ♖d3 ♖d5 29 ♘d1 ♘xd1 30 ♖fxd1 ♖xh5, and Black is playing to win the ending, E.Zakharov-Vdovin, 1979.

b2) **18 ♖d3 ♘d5**, and now:

b21) **19 ♕f3 ♗e7!** 20 ♘e2 (if 20 ♕xf7?, then 20 ... ♘f4! 21 ♖b3 ♖f8 and wins) 20 ... ♗g5+ 21 ♔b1 ♕xa5 22 ♘xf7 ♖f8! *(170)*

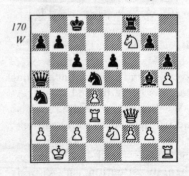

170 W

23 c4! (avoiding a sly trap; after

23 ♘d6+? ♔d7 24 ♕xf8 ♘dc3+! 25 ♖xc3 – not 25 ♘xc3? ♕b4+, and mates – 25 ... ♘xc3+ 26 ♘xc3 ♕b4+, Black ws not intending to give perpetual check; he can win with the forced continuation 27 ♔a1 ♕xc3+ 28 ♔b1 ♕b4+ 29 ♔a1 ♕xd4+ 30 c3 ♕xc3+ 31 ♔b1 ♕d3+ 32 ♔b2 ♗f6+ etc) 23 ... ♘dc3+ 24 ♖xc3 ♘xc3+ 25 ♘xc3 ♕b4+ 26 ♔c2 ♗f6 27 ♖b1 ♕e7 28 ♘e4 ♖xf7 29 c5 ♗e5 30 ♕g4, and a draw was agreed, Sorokin-Sichev, corres 1972.

b22) The little-known game Pegararo-Elstrand, 1969, is an example of quick retribution against the black king: **19 ♖b3!** *(171)*

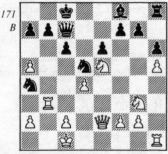

171 B

19 ... ♕xa5? 20 ♘xf7 ♘ac3? (astonishing carelessness!) 21 ♕xe6+ ♔c7 22 ♕e5+ ♔c8 23 ♕e8+ ♔c7 24 ♕d8 mate!

Instead of 19 ... ♕xa5? Black can try 19 ... ♘ac3 or 19 ... ♗e7, but frankly we don't like either 19 ... ♘ac3 20 ♕f3 ♕xa5 21 ♘c4, or 19 ... ♗e7 20 c4.

Did bringing the rook to b3 really alter the situation so much?

18	♔b1	♘a4
19	♖d3	

19 ♕f3 ♗b4 20 ♖d3 merely transposes, but 19 ♕e1 fails because of 19 ... ♘d5.

19	...	♗b4
20	♕f3	♕xa5
21	♘e2	♘d5!

After 21 ... ♖f8 22 ♖b3 ♘d5 23 ♘c4 ♕a6 24 ♕d3, White manages to consolidate, Byrne-Saidy, 1969.

22 ♕xf7! *(173)*

By continuing the struggle for the c3 point with 22 ♖h3?! *(172)*, White risks being routed.

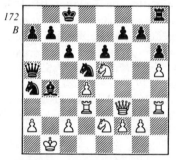

172
B

There can follow:

a) **22 ... f6** 23 ♘g6 ♖d8, and now:

a1) A game Schäpers-Tarnay, corres 1972, saw **24 ♘gf4**, when Black retorted with a striking combination: 24 ... ♘dc3+ 25 ♘xc3 ♗xc3 26 ♖xc3 ♕b4+! 27 ♔c1 ♖xd4 28 ♖d3 ♖xf4. But there was no need for it. The simple 24 ... ♕b5! would have left White in severe difficulties (25 ♖b3 ♘xf4).

a2) **24 ♖b3** appears stronger; sheltering his king, White prepares to drive Black's minor pieces back. This was played in Reid-Shakarov, corres 1977, and Black had to apply drastic measures: 24 ... c5! 25 c3 (or 25 c4 ♘db6 26 a3, when Black has the choice between 26 ... ♗e1 27 ♘gf4 e5 and 26 ... ♗xa3!? 27 ♖xa3 ♘xc4; in either case his attack looks irresistible) 25 ... c4 26 cb ♕b5 27 ♖b2 (after 27 ♖a3 ♕xb4+ 28 ♔c2 ♕b2+ 29 ♔d1 c3 30 ♘xc3! ♕xa3 31 ♘xd5 ♕xf3+? 32 ♖xf3 ed, Black's position is suspect – 33 ♘e7+. But 31 ... ♕xa2! gives him highly promising play for the piece. Another possibility for White is 27 ♖e3, which after 27 ... ♕xb4+ 28 ♔c2 ♕b2+ 29 ♔d1 ♕a1+ 30 ♔d2 ♕xa2+ 31 ♔e1 could lead to a draw – an unnatural result in such a position! Black really ought to think up something – how about 29 ... ♔b8!? threatening ... c3, and if 30 ♕e4, then 30 ... ♕a1+ 31 ♔d2 e5! etc) 27 ... ♘xb2 28 ♔xb2 ♕xb4+ 29 ♔c2 ♕a4+, and White can no longer hold out.

b) A method of play that was demonstrated in another correspondence game, Lisan-Margolite, 1975, appears even more convincing: **22 ... ♗e7** 23 ♕xf7 ♗e1+ 24 ♘c1 ♗g5 25 ♕xe6+ ♔c7 26 ♕d7+

♔b8 27 ♕d6+ ♔a8 28 ♕a3 ♗xc1
29 ♕xc1 ♘dc3+ 30 ♖xc3 ♘xc3+
31 ♔b2 ♘a4+ 32 ♔b1 ♕b4+ 33
♖b3 ♕xd4 (re-establishing the
material balance by force, Black
has retained a powerful initiative)
34 ♘d3 ♘c3+ 35 ♔a1 ♖e8 36 ♖b4
(if 36 ♕b2, then 36 ... ♖e1+!) 36 ...
♕d5 37 ♕a3 c5 38 ♖g4 ♘e4 39 f3
♘f2! 40 ♖a4 ♔b8 41 ♘c1 a6 42
♔b1 ♖e1 43 ♖a5 ♕d2 44 ♖xc5
♖xc1+ 0-1.

So the hazards in store for
White after 22 ♖h3 are evident.

True, the first edition of *ECO*
gives analysis to condemn 22
♕xf7 as well:

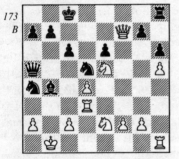

173
B

'22 ... ♘ac3+ 23 ♘xc3 ♗xc3 24
♕xe6+ ♔b8 25 ♖xc3 ♘xc3+ 26
♔b2 ♘d5 27 ♕d6+ ♔a8 28 ♕c5
♕d2 29 ♘d3 ♖e8 ∓.'

Yet virtually every move in this
line is an error. Above all, the
verdict on the final position is
wrong; White has an extra pawn,
and after 30 ♖e1 he goes over to
the attack too. But then, a move
earlier he could have won by 29

♘xc6! ♘b6 30 ♕b4! ♕xf2 31
♘xa7 etc.

Clearly, instead of 26 ... ♘d5?
Black should play 26 ... ♘a4+
(26 ... ♘b5!? is unclear, for
example 27 ♕c4 ♕a3+ 28 ♔b1
♖d8 29 ♖h3 ♕d6), and on 27
♔c1, either 27 ... ♘c3 or 27 ... ♕c3
28 ♕b3 ♕a1+ 29 ♕b1 ♕c3.

But before that, White can
improve with 26 ♔a1! (instead of
♔b2), intending to use the b-file
for attack. After this move, the
drawing line is truly mind-bending:
26 ... ♖d8 27 ♕b3 ♘b5 28 ♖b1
♖xd4! 29 c4 ♖d2 30 cb ♖xa2+ 31
♕xa2 ♕c3+, with perpetual check.

Finally (seeing that after 26
♔a1! Black has to show so much
ingenuity), a simpler line is 23 ...
♘xc3+ (instead of ... ♗xc3)
24 ♖xc3 (24 ♔c1? ♕xa2) 24 ...
♗xc3 25 ♕xe6+ ♔c7 (not 25 ...
♔b8? 26 ♕b3!) 26 ♕f7+ ♔c8, and
White has no reason to avoid
27 ♕e6+, repeating moves.

B2

16   ♗xb6   ab (174)

174
W

We promised to refute the notion that this is one variation of the Caro-Kann in which White has a durable advantage (however slight). Such an assessment has been called into question by some little-known games and analyses from recent years. Having demonstrated the solidity of his position in some lines, Black sought and found good counterplay in others.

17 c4

Evidently concluding that this move eases Black's problems (the d-pawn is, after all, being deprived of a defender, hence the knight's position on e5 becomes less secure), Grandmaster Romanishin continued with 17 f4 in a game against Bagirov (1978). There followed: 17 ... ♗d6 (the cautious recommend removing the rook first – 17 ... ♖d8) 18 ♔b1 ♖d8 (in Shamkovich-Grünfeld, 1980, Black was unsuccessful with 18 ... b5 19 ♘f1 b4 20 ♘e3 ♖b5 21 ♘3c4 ♖d8 22 ♖hf1 ♗f8 23 g4 etc) 19 c3 *(175)*

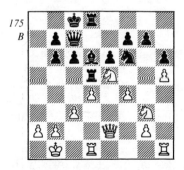

(observe that 19 c4 ♖a5 leads to a variation we shall examine later – since 19 ... ♗xe5, which looks attractive if answered by 20 cd ♗xf4 or 20 fe? ♖xd4, unmistakably favours White after 20 de! ♖xd1+ 21 ♖xd1) 19 ... ♔b8?! 20 ♘f1 ♗xe5 21 fe ♘h7 22 ♘e3 ♖5d7 23 ♘c4 ♘g5 24 ♖hf1. White's game is the more active, and although Bagirov cleverly created counterplay and drew after 24 ... c5 25 ♘d6 ♕c6 26 ♖f4 f6 27 ♖df1 cd 28 cd ♕d5 29 ♘b5 f5 30 ♘d6 ♖c7 31 g4 ♘h3 32 ♖4f3 ♘g5, Romanishin maintains he could have improved; as an example he suggests 31 ♖d1, with g4 to follow.

We believe that in the diagrammed position Black missed a good chance: 19 ... c5! The aim of this move is clear – to undermine the knight's position on e5, or, after ... cd, to give White an isolated pawn and consolidate the d5 square (for example, 20 ♖c1 ♔b8 21 ♖hd1 cd 22 cd ♕e7 23 ♘f1 ♗xe5 24 fe ♘e8). A very good answer to 20 ♘f1 is 20 ... cd 21 cd ♗c5! 22 ♘f3 ♕xf4 23 ♖c1 ♖xd4 24 ♘xd4 ♖xd4, or 23 ♖h4! ♕f5+ 24 ♔a1 ♘g4! 25 ♖c1 ♖xd4 26 ♘xd4 ♕g5! 27 ♕e1 ♖xd4 28 ♘e3 ♔b8 with chances for both sides.

17 ... ♖a5

Or 17 ... ♖d8 *(176)*, when practice has shown that Black's fortifications are secure.

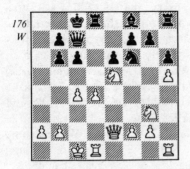

176
W

For example: 18 ♘e4 (it isn't only Black who should be concerned about security – 18 f4 ♗d6 19 ♕c2! c5 20 ♖he1 cd 21 ♖xd4 ♗xe5! 22 ♖xd8+ ♖xd8 23 fe ♘d7 24 ♕a4 ♚b8 25 ♕b5 f6, and White lost, Litvinov-Begun, 1978) 18 ... ♘xe4 (the careless 18 ... c5 proved costly to Black in Tatai-Pomar, 1968: 19 ♘c3! ♗d6 20 ♘b5 ♕e7 21 dc ♗xc5 22 ♘a7+! ♚c7 23 ♘xf7! was crushing) 19 ♕xe4 ♗d6, and now:

a) **20 ♘f3** *(177)*

177
B

20 ... ♗e7! (Black's play was unconvincing in Spassky-Pomar, 1968: 20 ... ♖he8 21 ♚b1 ♕e7 22

♖he1 ♕f6 23 g3 ♗c7 24 a3 ♕f5 25 ♕xf5 ef, with a tedious struggle for the draw) 21 ♖d3 ♗f6 22 ♚b1 (22 ♖hd1 ♖d5!?) 22 ... ♖d7 23 ♖hd1 ♖hd8. White's position is unpromising, whereas Black could be advised to try the plan of ... ♚b8 and ... b5!?

We even think that after 20 ... ♗e7! White does better to return his knight to e5 (21 ♘e5 ♗f6?! 22 f4), so that on 21 ... ♗d6 he can either agree a draw at once or . . . do so afterwards.

b) For some time, there was a debate about the ending arising after **20 f4 f5!** 21 ♕e2 ♗xe5 22 ♕xe5 ♕xe5 23 de *(178)*:

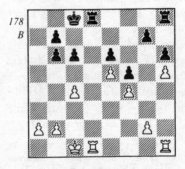

178
B

b1) The pawn endgame turned out to be hopeless for Black: **23 ... ♖hg8?** 24 ♖xd8+ ♖xd8 25 ♖d1 ♖xd1+? 26 ♚xd1 ♚d7 27 ♚c2 – White brings his king to b4 and breaks through with a4 and c5.

The dangers of certain types of rook endgames are shown by the

following variations: 25 ... ♖e8 26
♖d6 ♔c7 27 ♔c2 ♔c8 28 ♔c3 ♔c7
29 ♔b4 ♔c8 30 a4 (White handles
this rook ending like the pawn
ending we have spoken about)
30 ... ♔c7 31 b3 ♖e7 32 c5 bc+ 33
♔xc5 b6+ 34 ♔c4 ♖e8 35 b4 ♖e7
36 b5 c5 37 a5 etc; or 24 ... ♔xd8 25
♖d1+ ♔c7 (if 25 ... ♔e7, then
26 ♖d3, threatening ♖b3) 26 ♖d6
g5 27 g3! gf 28 gf ♖e8 (the position
after 28 ... ♖g4 29 ♖xe6 ♖xf4 30
♖xh6 ♖xc4+ 31 ♔d2 is also lost)
29 ♔c2 ♖e7 30 ♔b3, and play
proceeds on the same lines as
before, Martin-Pomar, 1977.

b2) The discussion was closed
once the right solution had been
found: **23 ... g5!** 24 hg (24 g3 ♖hg8
25 ♖hg1 ♖d7!) 24 ... ♖dg8 25 ♖d3
♖xg6 26 g3 ♖hg8 27 ♖h3 h5 28
♔c2 h4 29 gh ♖h6, with an
obvious draw.

Well, if 17 ... ♖d8 resolves all
the questions so simply, why play
17 ... ♖a5 ... ? After all, the rook
may end up out of play . . .
However, 17 ... ♖a5 may only be
denounced for 'crudity' if Black
has some answer to 17 f4 other
than 17 ... ♗d6 18 ♔b1 ♖d8. We
recall that 19 c4 then forces 19 ...
♖a5.

18 ♔b1 ♗d6
19 f4 ♖d8 *(179)*

We find it hard to believe that
19 ... ♕e7, followed by ... ♔c7 and
... ♖ha8, is a sound idea.

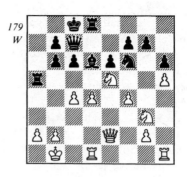

179
W

20 ♖d2

Recommended by Boleslavsky.
The alternatives are:
a) **20 ♘e4 ♘xe4 21 ♕xe4** *(180)*.

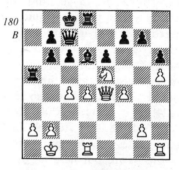

180
B

Boleslavsky considered that the
knight exchange eases Black's
task. There can follow:
a1) **21 ... ♔b8** 22 g3 b5 23 c5 ♗xe5
24 de? (24 fe) 24 ... ♖a4! 25 ♕e3
♖d5 26 b3? (26 ♖xd5) 26 ... ♕d7!
27 ♖xd5 ♕xd5 28 ♖c1 ♖d4, with
a won position for Black, Maeder-
Podgayets, 1969. (In a note to this
game, Boleslavsky wrote that, if
White had kept the knights on,
then after 20 ♖d2 b5 21 c5 ♗xe5

22 fe ♘d5 23 ♘e4 this knight would occupy the d6 strongpoint and ensure White the advantage. Later, we shall show that the matter is not so simple.)

a2) Malchikov-Morgulyov (1978) went: **21 ... f5!?** (after 21 ... f6 22 ♘d3 ♕d7 23 g3 White kept up the pressure for a long time in Bednarski-Smyslov, 1967. A doubtful alternative is 21 ... b5 22 c5 ♗xe5 23 fe – 23 de? ♖a4 – 23 ... ♖a4 24 b3 ♖a3 25 ♖h4, and Black's kingside pawns are threatened. If you gave Black the extra move ... f5 in this last variation, the verdict would be altered. That explains Morgulyov's 21st move) 22 ♕e2 b5 23 c5 ♗xe5 24 de ♖a4 25 ♖d6 (an entirely correct decision. Black threatened not only 25 ... ♖xf4, but also 25 ... ♖ad4!) 25 ... ♖xf4 26 ♖hd1 ♖xd6 27 ed ♕d7 28 ♖d3 ♖e4 29 ♖a3? (White does have compensation for the pawn, but here he overestimates his position, and what's more, allows a powerful stroke. In Mokatsian-Vdovin, corres 1979, a draw was agreed after 29 ♖e3 b6 30 ♖xe4 fe 31 b4 bc 32 bc ♕a7 33 ♕f2 ♕a3) 29 ... b6? (29 ... ♕xd6 wouldn't be at all bad here . . .) 30 ♕d2 b4 31 ♖a8+ (involves a trap, but Black sees through it. 31 ♕d3! ba 32 ♕a6+ ♔d8 33 ♕a8+ ♕c8 34 ♕a7 would have forced a draw by repetition!) 31 ... ♔b7 32 ♖f8 bc

33 ♖f7 ♕xf7 34 d7 ♖e2! (White had been looking forward to 34 ... ♖d4 35 ♕xd4 cd 36 d8♕+!) 35 ♕d3 ♕f6! 36 ♕xe2 ♕d4, and Black won.

b) **20 ♖d3** b5 (if 20 ... c5, a strong answer is 21 ♖hd1, with pressure on the d-file that is being opened. In Vogt-Bönsch, 1979, Black first regrouped with 20 ... ♕e7 21 ♖hd1 ♗c7, and only after 22 ♘e4 ♘xe4 23 ♕xe4 did he play 23 ... b5. The delay was of benefit to White, who broke through the front at once with 24 d5! f5 25 ♕e1 bc 26 d6 ♗xd6 27 ♘g6 etc) 21 c5 ♗xe5 22 fe ♘d5 *(181)*.

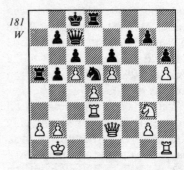

181
W

In Boleslavsky's view, the defect of 20 ♖d3 as opposed to 20 ♖d2 is that in this position White must lose time owing to the threats of ... ♘f4 and ... ♘b4. A game Malchikov-Shakarov, 1976, continued: 23 ♕d2 ♖a4 24 b3 ♖a3 25 ♘e4 b4 26 ♖f1 (on 26 ♖g3, the exchanging continuation 26 ... ♕a5? 27 ♘d6+ ♖xd6 28 ed ♘c3+

29 ♖xc3 bc 30 ♕c2 is clearly in White's favour. But a fascinating battle would develop after 26 ... f5! 27 ef ♘xf6 28 ♘d6+ ♖xd6 29 cd ♕xd6. White's salvation lies in counter-threats: 30 ♖xg7! ♘e4 31 ♕xh6 ♘c3+ 32 ♔c2 ♔b8! 33 ♖g8+ ♔a7 34 ♕f8! The queen exchange with which Black is threatened – 34 ... ♕xd4? 35 ♕a8+ ♔b6 36 ♕d8+ – compels him to go after perpetual check: 34 ... ♖xa2+ 35 ♔d3 ♖d2+! 36 ♔xd2 ♕xd4+ 37 ♔e1 ♕e3+ 38 ♔f1 ♕e2+ 39 ♔g1 ♕e1+ 40 ♔h2 – not 40 ♕f1? ♘e2+, and mates – 40 ... ♕h4+ etc) 26 ... ♔b8 27 ♖df3 ♖d7 28 ♖1f2 ♔a7 29 g4 ♕d8! 30 ♕c1 (the pawn could have been taken – 30 ♖xf7 ♖xf7 31 ♖xf7 ♕h4 32 ♕e2 ♕h1+ 33 ♔b2 – not 33 ♖f1? ♕xe4+ – 33 ... ♕g1 34 ♖f2 ♖a6, and neither the attacker nor the defender can make progress. Incidentally, if instead of 34 ♖f2 White chose the 'energetic' 34 ♕f2 ♕xg4 35 ♘d6?, he would lose to 35 ... ♖xa2+!) 30 ... ♕h4 31 ♕g1 ♘c3+ (there was no necessity to force events. 31 ... ♔a8 32 ♖xf7 ♖xf7 33 ♖xf7 ♕h3 was also acceptable) 32 ♘xc3 bc 33 ♖c2 ♖xd4 34 ♕xd4 ♕h1+ 35 ♖c1 ♕xf3 36 ♖xc3 ♕e2 37 ♖c2 ♕e1+ 38 ♖c1 ♕e2 39 ♖c2 ♕e1+ 40 ♔b2 ♕a5 41 ♔b1 ½-½.

> **20 ... b5**
> **21 c5 ♗xe5**

On 21 ... ♗f8, Boleslavsky considers that a good reply is 22 ♘e4 ♖a4 23 ♖hd1 ♘xe4 24 ♕xe4, when 24 ... ♗xc5 fails against 25 b3 ♖b4 26 ♕e3, threatening 27 dc or 27 a3.

> **22 fe**

As the Malchikov-Shakarov game has already shown, the possibility of ♘e4-d6 does not by itself determine our assessment of the position. Black has his counterchances: with ... ♖a4 and ... ♕a5 he can induce b3 (a3 is met by ... b4), after which White has to reckon with the threat of ... ♘c3.

Therefore the verdict depends on whose threats are more dangerous. The element of timing is important, isn't it? If White had played 20 ♖d3, he couldn't follow with 23 ♘e4, because of 23 ... ♘f4. On the other hand, there is also a snag to having the rook on d2, since it turns out that Black can exploit the undefended position of the knight on g3.

> **22 ... ♖a4!** *(182)*

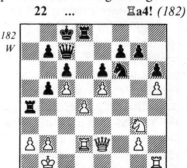

182
W

The thematic move, conveniently attacking the pawn on d4. Of course, both 23 ef? ♕xg3, and 23 ♖h4 ♘d5 24 ♘e4 ♕a5 25 b3 ♖a3 26 ♖g4? f5 27 ef gf, are no good for White. Instead:

a) In Korolyov-Vdovin, corres 1979, White played solidly: **23 ♖hd1** ♘d5 24 ♘e4 ♕a5 25 b3 ♖a3 26 ♕f3 f5 27 ef gf 28 g4. It's noticeable that White has to think in terms of security rather than advantage: 28 ... b4 29 ♕g3 f5 30 gf ef 31 ♕h3 ♔b8 32 ♕xf5 ♖e8 33 ♖c1 ♔a7 34 ♕g6 ♖e7 35 ♖f2 ♕a6 36 ♖d2 ♕a5 ½-½.

b) In E.Zakharov-Shakarov, corres 1978, White gave up the exchange with **23 ♖h3** ♘d5 24 ♘e4. This kind of sacrificial possibility has been 'in the air' – isn't the knight on d6 stronger than a rook? But you still have to give some thought to finding the best possible conditions for the sacrifice; here it is unconvincing: 24 ... ♘f4 25 ♕f2 ♘xh3 26 gh ♔b8 27 ♘d6 ♖f8 28 b3 ♖a6? (underestimating White's chances on the kingside; Black should have brought the rook into play via a8) 29 ♕g2! (Black had envisaged 29 ♕g3? f6 30 ♖g2 fe 31 ♕xe5 ♖f1+ 32 ♔b2 ♖xa2+!) 29 ... f6 30 ef gf 31 ♕g6 e5 32 ♖g2! (not 32 ♕xh6? ♖g8), and Black had to struggle for a draw.

c) **23 ♕f2**, which defends the pawn on d4 and the knight on g3, and

takes aim at the f7 pawn in advance, seems the most logical. What would happen after 23 ... ♘d5 24 ♘e4 has yet to be clarified, since in Marzell-Shakarov, corres 1977, Black was tempted into 23 ... ♘g4 24 ♕f4 *(183)*

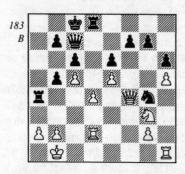

24 ... ♘xe5 25 b3 ♕a5!? (25 ... ♖b4 26 ♖hd1 is no less risky) **26 ba** ♕b4+ 27 ♔c1 (27 ♖b2? ♕xb2+) **27 ... ♕c3+?!** 28 ♔d1 ♘c4. After 29 ♖f1! e5 (29 ... ♘xd2? 30 ♘e2!) 30 ♕f5+ ♔b8 31 ♘e4 ♕b4, the position is quite complex although probably in White's favour. (However, White didn't succeed in stabilising the situation – the problem is his king! – and after a sharp fight the game ended in a draw: 32 ♔e2?! ♘xd2 33 ♕xe5+ ♔a7 34 ♘xd2 ♖xd4 35 ♕e3 ba 36 ♔e1 f5! 37 a3 ♕b2 etc).

Instead of 27 ... ♕c3+?!, there is more to worry White in **27 ... ♕c4+!** 28 ♔d1 ♘d3 28 ♕e3 (29 ♕xf7 ♕xd4 is worse) 29 ... ♖xd4 30 ab f5! 31 bc f4, with advantage to Black; or 30 ♘e2 ♕xa4+ 31 ♖c2 ♖d7, with the same verdict; or 30 ♔e2 ♘e5+ 31 ♔e1 ♕c1+ 32 ♔e2 ♕c4+, drawing.

We must add that White didn't have to take the rook at once; he could have played 26 ♖hd1 or 26 ♘e4. Analysis of these possibilities has given the following results: **26 ♖hd1 ♘c4!** 27 bc (27 ba ♕c3) 27 ... ♕c3 28 ♖b2 ♖b4, with a draw; or **26 ♘e4 ♘d3!** (putting pieces *en prise* is the main theme of this variation!) 27 ♕e3!? (27 ♖xd3 ♖xa2) 27 ... ♖axd4 28 ♘d6+ ♖4xd6 29 cd ♘b4 30 ♕c3! ♕a3 31 ♕xg7 ♘d5, and the outcome is obscure.

There is one more interesting course for Black. From Diagram 183 he can play **24 ... ♕xe5!?** 25 ♕xg4 ♖axd4 26 ♖xd4 ♖xd4 27 ♕f3 ♖d2 *(184)*, with good chances.

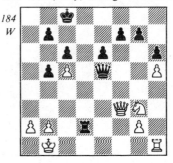

184
W

For example: 28 ♕a3 (if 28 ♕c3, then 28 ... ♕d5! is strong) 28 ... b4!? (or 28 ... f5!?, after which White would lose with 29 ♕a8+? ♔d7 30 ♕xb7+ ♔d8 31 ♕a8+ ♔e7 32 ♕a3 ♖xg2, and must therefore play 29 ♖c1) 29 ♕a8+ (29 ♕xb4? is bad on account of 29 ... ♖xg2 30 ♘e4 ♖xb2+!) 29 ... ♔c7 30 ♕a5+ ♔c8 (30 ... ♔b8 31 ♕xb4 ♖xg2 32 ♖d1) 31 ♕a8+ and draws.

We have come a long way in our analysis, but as a result we can say with assurance that in the complex and at times sharp struggle that results from 17 ... ♖a5, Black has substantial counter-chances.

* * *

Having concluded our investigation of the Classical Caro Kann, we will state that the modern way of handling it (13 c4 b5; 13 ♔b1 c5; 13 ♘e4 ♗e7; 13 ♕e2 c5; 10 ... e6) is characterised by Black's effort to create positions where the players have castled on opposite wings and both have their full share of the play. At the same time, the traditional method (13 ... 0 0 0) has retained its solid reputation.

Summary

15 ...	c5	16 c4	cd				±
			♔b8				±
			♖xd4 17 ♔b1				±
			17 ♖xd4				∞
			(16 ♖h4! – cf. 15 ♖h4)				
	♖d5	16 b4	♖xa5 17 ba	♘bd5			±/∞
				♘a4			±/∞
				♗a3+ 18 ♔b1	♘a4	19 ♖d3 ♗b4	

And now:

20 ♕f3	♕xa5 21 ♘e2	♖f8	±
		♘d5 22 ♖h3	∓
		22 ♕xf7	=

16 ♗xb6 ab	17 f4	♗d6	18 ♔b1	♖d8	19 c3	♔b8	±
						c5	∞
				(19 c4 –			
				cf. 17 c4)			
	17 c4	♖d8					=
		♖a5					∞/=

Index of Variations

1 e4 c6 2 d4 d5 3 ♘c3 de 4 ♘xe4 ♗f5